The Evolving Global Trade Architecture

For Vasanti,
who knows the fiction and non-fiction of my
life, as well as all that cannot be put in words.

The Evolving Global Trade Architecture

Dilip K. Das

Edward Elgar
Cheltenham, UK • Northampton, MA, USA

Published by
Edward Elgar Publishing Limited
Glensanda House
Montpellier Parade
Cheltenham
Glos GL50 1UA
UK

Edward Elgar Publishing, Inc.
William Pratt House
9 Dewey Court
Northampton
Massachusetts 01060
USA

A catalogue record for this book
is available from the British Library

Library of Congress Cataloging in Publication Data

Das, Dilip K., 1945–
    The evolving global trade architecture / Dilip K. Das.
        p. cm.
    1. Free trade. 2. International trade. 3. Foreign trade regulation. 4.
General Agreement on Tariffs and Trade (Organization) 5. World Trade
Organization. 6. Uruguay Round (1987–1994) 7. Globalization — Economic
aspects. 8. International economic relations. I. Title.
Policy sicences. 2. Policy sciences — Case studies. I. Title. II.
Series: New horizons in public policy.

    HF1713 D342 2007
    382'.92—dc22

                                                                2006034555

ISBN 978 1 84720 218 5 (cased)

Printed and bound in Great Britain by MPG Books Ltd, Bodmin, Cornwall

There is a tide in the affairs of men,
Which taken at the flood, leads on to fortune;
Omitted, all the voyage of their life
Is bound in shallows and in miseries.
On such a full sea are we now afloat;
And we must take the current when it serves,
Or lose our ventures.

William Shakespeare
(Julius Caesar, Act IV, Scene III)

Contents

Acronyms

ACP	Africa, Caribbean and Pacific
AD	anti-dumping
AGE	applied general equilibrium
AGOA	Africa Growth and Opportunity Act
AITIC	Agency for International Trade Information and Co-operation
ASEAN	Association of South East Asian Nations
ATC	Agreement on Textiles and Clothing
BPO	business-process outsourcing
BTA	bilateral trade agreement
CCG	Chairman's Consultative Group
CGE	computable general equilibrium
CTS	Council for Trade in Services
CTD	Committee on Trade and Development
CP	contracting party
DDA	Doha Development Agency
DFQF	duty-free quota-free
DGE	dynamic general equilibrium
DSM	Dispute Settlement Mechanism
EBA	Everything-But-Arms
EMEs	emerging-market economies
FAO	Food and Agriculture Organization
FTA	free trade agreement
GATS	General Agreement on Tariffs in Services
GATT	General Agreement on Tariffs and Trade
GSP	Generalized System of Preferences
GPG	global public good
GTAP	Global Trade Analysis Project
IF	integrated framework
IMF	International Monetary Fund

IMFC	International Monetary and Financial Committee
ITO	International Trade Organization
JITP	Joint Integrated Technical Assistance Program
LDCs	least developed countries
LMG	Like-Minded Group
MDG	Millennium Developmental Goal
MFN	most-favored-nation
MTN	multilateral trade negotiations
NAMA	non-agricultural market access
NGMA	Negotiating Group on Market Access
NGOs	non-governmental organizations
NIEs	newly industrialized economies
NTBs	non-tariff barriers
OLS	ordinary least square
PTA	preferential trade agreement
QRs	quantitative restrictions
RIAs	regional integration agreements
ROO	rules of origin
RTA	regional trade agreement
SAR	Special Administrative Region
SCM	safeguard and countervailing measures
SDT	special and differential treatment
SSM	special safeguard mechanism
SVEs	small and vulnerable economies
TBTs	technical barriers to trade
TFP	total factor productivity
TPA	trade promotion authority
TRIMS	Trade Related Investment Measures
TRIPS	Trade Related Intellectual Property Rights
TRQ	tariff rate quota
TRTA	trade related technical assistance
UNCTAD	United Nations Conference on Trade and Development
URAA	Uruguay Round Agreement on Agriculture
WTO	World Trade Organization

About the author

Professor Dilip K. Das has been associated with several prestigious business schools around the globe, including the European Institute of Business Administration (INSEAD), Fontainebleau, France; the ESSEC, Paris; the Graduate School of Business, University of Sydney; the Australian National University, Canberra and the Webster University, Geneva. He also was Professor and Area Chairman at the Indian Institute of Management, Lucknow, India, and EXIM Bank Distinguished Chair Professor in the International Management Institute, New Delhi. The areas of his expertise include international finance and banking, international trade and WTO-related issues, international business and strategy and Asian economy, including the Chinese and Japanese economies. His most recent interest is globalization and global business environment.

Professor Das has worked as a consultant for several international organizations, such as the USAID, the World Bank, and the World Commission on Development and Environment in Geneva. He organized 13 large international conferences over ten years. He is presently a Toronto-based consultant to international organizations.

He has an immense appetite for researching. He has written extensively and published widely. He is an author of 26 books, which include four edited volumes. He edited *The International Finance Reader,* which was published by Routledge, London and New York, in 2003. The last two books he authored were entitled *Financial Globalization and the Emerging Market Economies,* Routledge, London and New York, 2004, and *The Doha Round of Multilateral Trade Negotiations: Arduous Issues and Strategic Responses,* Palgrave Macmillan Ltd, London UK, 2005. He has contributed over 70 articles to professional journals of international repute and 75 of his papers have appeared in prestigious research and working paper series. Twenty-two of them have also been posted on the well-regarded web sites of business schools and universities.

He was educated at St John's College, Agra, India, where he took his BA and MA (Economics) degrees. He went on to study at the Institut Universitaire de Hautes Études Internationales, the University of Geneva, Switzerland, where he did his MPhil and PhD in international economics. He is fluent in French.

Acknowledgments

I take this opportunity to thank my son, Siddharth, for providing prompt and efficient research assistance and three anonymous referees for providing detailed comments on the manuscript. They were as helpful as they were constructive. Citations from the works of A. Narlikar and J.S. Odell have been made after seeking their permission. I am grateful to Alan Sturmer, Tara Gorvine and Bob Pickens of Edward Elgar Publishing for handling the publication of this book in an exceedingly efficient manner. I have been in the business of researching, writing and publishing for over three decades now. Their level of efficiency is an absolutely rare commodity in the publishing industry. To nurture excellence in any area of human endeavor, credit should be given where it is deserved. One needs neither a sword nor a gun to kill excellence in any society. Ignore it and it will wilt away.

Dilip K. Das
Toronto
July 2006

Preface

If one casts a cursory look at the six decades of history of the multilateral trade regime, or the General Agreement on Tariffs and Trade/World Trade Organization (GATT/WTO) system, one is certain to see that while it has progressively evolved, its evolution has been anything but easy and smooth. As a great deal of scholarly writing is available on the genesis and initial, or the GATT, period of the multilateral trade regime, this phase has been treated briefly in this book. While it does not fail to establish linkages with the past – particularly the systemic evolution during the Uruguay Round – the essential focus of this book is the present, or the WTO, phase of evolution of the multilateral trade regime. One of the many important conclusions of this book is that of the two phases, the latter has turned out to be the more arduous, intricate and complex phase of evolution.

The GATT/WTO system was repeatedly pushed to the brink of utter and ignominious disasters. Yet the participating economies continued to be resilient and instead of abandoning it they persevered. Consequently the fabric of multilateral trade regime is stronger, its foundation deeper and its framework wider now than it was a generation ago. Unlike the GATT era, its membership is close to universal today. One glance at the recent history also indicates that evolution of the multilateral trade regime was far from even and steady. Two germane characteristics worth focusing on in this regard are: the unbalanced development of the multilateral trade regime over the preceding six decades and its evolution in fits and starts.

By means of various rounds of multilateral trade negotiations (MTNs), the multilateral trade regime has constantly adjusted itself to the new realities of the global economy. In the on-going Doha Round of MTNs it is once again endeavoring to fine-tune its alignment as well as correct its systemic tilt. With transformations and evolution in the global economy, dynamics of country groups and negotiations in the multilateral trade regime have constantly changed and evolved. In its short life span, the WTO has amply demonstrated that the multilateral trade regime has been undergoing a transformation in terms of both substance and process. That said, judging by the progress, or lack thereof, in the Doha Round, one can reiterate that evolution has not been kind to the multilateral trade regime. Yet, notwithstanding the contretemps and disappointments, the WTO members and country groups are engrossed in finding ways to keep the MTNs on course.

Myriad small and large changes have occurred in the global economy over the preceding quarter century. Shifting contours of the global economy, the advent of new economic players on the global stage, the continuing global economic and financial integration, major advances in technology, all underscore that we are on the cusp of momentous changes in the global economic system. In consonance with them, the global trade architecture has also been in a state of flux. It has been discernibly evolving in accordance with the changing global *mise-en-scène*. The Doha Round of MTNs, like its predecessors, is not only an integral part of the evolving global trade architecture but also an instrument of ushering in to it essential modifications, enhancements and upgrading.

One significant change underway in the global economy has been the steady shift in balance of global economic power. Although it did not occur in a theatrical manner overnight, it was a gradual and steady process. It had, and is sure to have in future, a sizeable impact over multilateral trade as well as influence the evolution of multilateral trade regime. The surfacing of new groups of economies, christened the emerging-market economies (EMEs), is an economic event of global significance. The lax monetary policies in the mature industrial economies, particularly over the 2000–5 period, *inter alia* helped the EMEs to come into their own. In 2005, the EMEs produced slightly more than half of world output measured at the purchasing power parity (PPP) exchange rate. They also accounted for more than half of the increase in the global GDP in current-dollar terms. This is the largest realignment in global economic strength since the emergence of the United States as an economic powerhouse over a century ago. Some of the EMEs have also come forward as large traders. Several Asian economies, particularly China, epitomize this trend. Following the same streak, more EMEs can reasonably be expected to emerge in the foreseeable future. Slow but steady and methodical integration of the EMEs into the global economy, particularly Brazil, China and India, has given the biggest boost to the global supply since the industrial revolution.

Similarly, integration of global labor markets has had far-reaching consequences for the global economy and multilateral trade. Expanding trade in services in the form of outsourcing in the industrial economies, particularly business-process outsourcing (BPO), is one of the novel global trends that is affecting the domestic and global economies. Low-wage labor producing manufactured goods in the EMEs and exporting them globally has cut the cost of goods and kept the rate of inflation under tight control. The impact of rapidly expanding trade in commercial and professional services is the same. In the mature industrial economies, the threat that jobs could move offshore has helped hold down domestic wages. Although expanding demand from

EMEs – particularly Brazil, China and India – has fueled the surge in oil and commodity prices, the newcomers' effect on balance has been to restrain inflation in the industrial economies.

Since the early 2000s, the persistence of macroeconomic imbalances has emerged as another characteristic feature of the contemporary global economy. They were driven by macroeconomic causes in several economies, including some of the largest ones. To a degree, they have led to a climate of uncertainty and apprehension in the global economy. Strategic realignment in values of major currencies has been underway since the early 2000s, along with a shift and repositioning in the individual economic strengths of the large countries. These developments are of material importance to the world of trade. The member economies of the WTO also need to facilitate, adjust to and support these on-going transformations in the global economy.

The WTO, which is equated with liberalization of trade, is one of the three critically important supranational institutions of the global economic governance. It is at the center of the present global economic integration phenomenon. Its institutional role in the continuing transformations of the global economy is a necessary, albeit not a sufficient, condition. It contributes meaningfully to the smooth functioning of the global economy and enhances the synergetic forces in it. Evolution and modifications in the multilateral trade regime is vitally important so that it grows more equitable and relevant for healthy, if not vigorous, trade expansion and growth in the twenty-first century. To that end, successful culmination of the Doha Round of MTNs is an indispensable objective. It will indubitably make an invaluable and far-reaching contribution to the evolving multilateral trade regime, a global public good (GPG) of progressively increasing significance in the contemporary global economy.

Since its post-War birth, the multilateral trade regime has developed, or evolved, almost ceaselessly. The GATT was amended and supplemented progressively, with the passage of time. While the Kennedy Round (1964–7) of MTNs, and more so the Tokyo Round (1973–9), helped in consequential institutional development, it was the Uruguay Round (1986–94) that should be credited with bringing about the largest systemic transformation in the multilateral trade regime in an effective manner. It was the most ambitious and comprehensive round of MTNs, which enhanced the systemic relevance of the GATT to the closing decades of the twentieth century. Although neither rapidly nor efficiently, the Doha Round is presently attempting to achieve the same objective, that is make the WTO more relevant to the demands of changing global economy of the twenty-first century.

As the GATT/WTO regime grew, *pari passu* it became significantly more intricate and complex. The WTO is a much larger organization in scope, reach and effectiveness than its predecessor the GATT, which was not even an organization. As the multilateral trade regime evolved, simple and compelling basic principles, like promoting non-discrimination through the most-favored-nation (MFN) clause, that lay at the foundation of the GATT, have been repeatedly compromised. Numerous deviations and exceptions to these basic principles have evolved over the years. As the evolving multilateral trade regime adjusts to the ever-changing realities of the global economy, this trend seems likely to continue. For all appearances, the Doha Round seems set to make more such compromises. The possibility of plurilateral agreements in trade in services is one such case in point.

Since its launch in 2001, the Doha Round has suffered from a multitude of contretemps and setbacks, emanating from serious dissensions in opinions and positions among the WTO member countries, and groups thereof. These disagreements repeatedly purveyed negative reports of disappointments and failures. The achievements of six years of negotiations have been quite insubstantial, to say the least. Progress in this round of MTNs has been conspicuous by its absence, making the Doha Round an antithesis of the earlier GATT rounds of MTNs. Further evolution in the multilateral trade regime is in the throes of mercantilist mindset of the negotiators. That is not to deny the presence of multilateral and domestic economic factors as well as the changing contours of the global economy that have decisively contributed to the stagnation in the MTNs. For historical reasons, many deep seated disagreements in the MTNs tended to take a North–South axis. Under this set of circumstances, who should be squarely blamed for deficient advancement and frequent under achievements in the MTNs? Accusations of a lack of political energy and commitment among the governments of the member sovereign countries have been made frequently. It is open to question whether they are just and fair, or were impetuously made injudicious and disingenuous allegations. Could there be a more complex set of factors contributing to stagnation?

One causal factor comes to the fore most frequently. The mercantilist mind-set among the negotiating delegations is often named as the principal obstruction, or one of the outsized stumbling blocks, in the on-going MTNs. To be sure, there is an imperious need for the negotiating delegations to abandon it for a successful culmination of the Doha Round. Adam Smith excoriated the age old doctrine of mercantilism. It has no place in today's globalizing world economy. Member countries of the WTO need to take a liberal, pragmatic and open-minded approach and earnestly seek trade liberalization under the MFN principle of the GATT/WTO system. There are meaningful welfare gains to be derived by achieving the benevolent goal of establishing a free-trade regime in the global economy, or something as close to it as feasible. The free-trade doctrine propounded by the classical economists of yore is a source of enormous economic synergy. Its welfare implications continue to be robust. Free trade, or even freer trade, is more than likely to lead the global economy and the members of the multilateral trade regime to a win-win set of circumstances. Several economies, including developing ones, testify to this probability. The high-performing economies of East and Southeast Asia are a hopeful showcase.

As regards the question how the multilateral trade system should evolve in the near future, a pragmatic answer is that it needs to go on changing, growing and recreating itself endlessly. In the process, it needs to go on legitimizing itself as well as its institutional structure in such a way that it continues to liberalize trade and favorably influence the economic and financial globalization process, resulting in a decisive welfare impact for the member economies of the WTO. To what degree and effectiveness the WTO will underpin, first, the expansion of multilateral trade in goods and services, and second, the on-going globalization phenomenon will be the litmus test of its institutional efficacy and relevance to the contemporary global economy.

Although growth rate of multilateral trade in goods and services is still robust, its recent performance was a trifle dispiriting. In dollar value terms the growth rate has decelerated since 2003. The value of world merchandise exports rose by 13 percent in 2005, compared to 21 percent in 2004, but it exceeded the $10 trillion mark for the first time. The value of world exports of commercial services increased by 11 percent in 2005, compared to 19 percent in 2004. Its dollar value was $2.4 trillion in 2005. Together multilateral trade in goods and services amounted to $12.62 trillion in 2005. Notwithstanding the deceleration, multilateral trade is an enormously significant variable for the global economy, both quantitatively and qualitatively. It decisively influences the global growth and that in individual member economies of the WTO. Equally decisively it can potentially underpin poverty alleviation endeavors in the developing member economies. It can be a compelling instrument of achieving the first Millennium Development Goal (MDG) of halving the income poverty by 2015.

The essential focus of this book is the evolution of the multilateral trade regime in an ever-changing global economic environment, particularly during the WTO era. As this cannot be done without paying a lot of attention to the various rounds of MTNs, particularly the on-going Doha Round, this book also examines the progress, or lack thereof, made during the Doha Round. As alluded to earlier, it is an instrument of upgrading and modifying the WTO system. Comparable accounts for the GATT period were attempted in the past by noted scholars. An outstanding feature of this book is that it is written in a comprehensive and authoritative manner and covers large areas of the multilateral trade regime. In taking a contemporary view of the various Ministerial Conferences and their achievements, this book offers the latest knowledge related to relevant themes on the multilateral trade regime. The selection and rejection of the thematic strands for coverage in this book has been done exceedingly carefully.

The style of writing is neither overly technical nor highly model-oriented. This book essentially employs narrative analysis and avoids utilizing empirical analytical tools provided by econometric analysis (time-series analysis, cross-section and panel data analysis) or applied general equilibrium analysis. Excessive emphasis on technicalities, equations and econometric modeling discourages many potential readers. These characteristics narrow down the market to a small expert readership. The book is easy to access for the target readership because of its descriptive analysis style, which stops short of mathematical formulations and econometric modeling. Many students and other readers who have good analytical minds and sound knowledge of economic principles feel lost in mathematical formulations. This writing style makes the book accessible to a much larger number of readers.

It is written in a reference book style, as scholarly books are written. As noted above, students and other readers find the latest knowledge and concepts on several important themes on the multilateral trading system, in a manner in which they can appreciate and absorb them as well as use them as input in their decision making. Students, particularly those from business schools, who may hold global economy and multilateral trade related jobs after completing their studies, would find this knowledge extremely relevant, usable and helpful.

In a succinct manner, this tightly written volume covers a great deal of ground and imparts a great deal of knowledge on the economics of international trade. The number of academic institutions, including business schools, offering courses related to international trade is already significant and growing. The target readership of the book is master's level students in economics, international trade, international political economy and international relations as well as MBA students. Ambitious senior level undergraduates as well as policy mandarins and researchers can also benefit from the book. A background of initial microeconomics, macroeconomics, and economics of international trade should be sufficient to comprehend this book because definitions and explanations of terminology and advance concepts used in the text are provided in the notes to each chapter.

As regards the structure of this book, Chapter 1 prepares the background by dwelling on the initial phase of development of multilateral trade regime and the delayed active association of the developing economies with it. It also deals with the imperative issue of trade-growth nexus and the role of multilateral trade in achieving the first MDG of poverty alleviation. The on-going Doha Round has been named the development round; Chapter 2 provides the rationale for organizing such a round. The focus of Chapter 3 is the special treatment of the developing economies in the multilateral trade regime. This issue has become controversial and has become more significant since the 1980s. The Fifth Ministerial Conference in Cancún collapsed completely, and this provided the first glimpses of a possible failure of the Doha Round. The divergences in negotiating positions and difficulties of the Cancún Ministerial Conference are the subject of Chapter 4. The developing economies began playing a proactive role in the multilateral trade regime in the 1980s, which transformed its landscape. Chapter 5 provides a detailed analysis of this transformation. For various reasons, it was known that the Hong Kong Ministerial Conference would not be able to achieve a lot, although it succeeded in eschewing a complete fiasco. The hows and whys of it have been examined in Chapter 6. Success still eluded the Doha Round after the Hong Kong Ministerial. The evolutionary process of the multilateral trade regime has continued to be a difficult one. Chapter 7 delves into these difficulties.

Dilip K. Das
Toronto
July 2006

1. Development, developing economies and the multilateral trade regime

> One of the most important achievements of the last ten years has been the enhanced integration of developing countries into the WTO system. Never before have so many been such active participants in the global trading system and the development focus of the Doha Round is an appropriate reflection of this. ... The development dimension can no longer be an after thought or an add-on, a sort of pisco you add to the main dishes of market opening. Exceptions and derogations have their place, but they can too easily lock developing countries into the status quo and put a ceiling on their future possibilities.
>
> (Pascal Lamy, 2006a)

INTRODUCTION

Notwithstanding recent improvements, the global economy is far from free of the scourge of poverty. A disconcerting level of it obstinately persists around us. During the post-War period, the global community has demonstrated repeated and sincere commitment to growth and poverty alleviation. Economists and trade analysts have dwelt upon the possibility of a theoretical link between trade expansion and economic growth for over two decades. The present stock of knowledge suggests that adoption of the strategy of export-led growth benefits economies and that the external sector can be a dynamic growth engine. It has benefited a good number of Asian economies. The People's Republic of China (hereinafter China) is the latest beneficiary of this growth strategy. This chapter argues that, like the Millennium Development Goals (MDGs) of the United Nations (UN), the global community needs to adopt the policy objectives of economic growth and poverty alleviation by means of an ambitious program of multilateral trade policy reforms in which both the developing and industrial countries participate.

To this end, we examine whether multilateral trade liberalization can provide an impetus to global trade and thereby underpin growth and poverty alleviation endeavors of the global community. In so doing, we also delve into the evolution of the contemporary multilateral trade regime and its impact on the member economies as well as on the global economy. Two germane long-term characteristics worth focusing on in this regard are: first, the unbalanced

1

and uneven development in the multilateral trade regime over the preceding six decades, and second, it did not evolve smoothly at an even pace but in fits and starts. With the passage of time, the multilateral trade regime has matured and become more intricate and complex.

The developing economies took a belated interest in the multilateral trade and the system of regulations governing it. Therefore, development relevance of the multilateral trade regime did not begin to emerge until the mid-1980s. Several deep-seated transformations took place in the global economy and the multilateral trade regime realigned itself to them. The global economic scenario, and with that global trade, underwent marked transformations. Assuming change was essential for the multilateral trading system; failing to do so would have relegated it to irrelevance and dysfunctionality.

This chapter begins with the global community's commitment to economic growth and poverty alleviation in the following section, while the third section re-examines the much-debated trade-growth nexus and the conventional wisdom regarding it. An inspiring stock of empirical and theoretical knowledge exists on this important policy issue. The contemporary multilateral trade regime and its evolution from the General Agreement on Tariffs and Trade (GATT) to the World Trade Organization (WTO) are the subjects of the fourth and fifth sections. The question whether multilateral trade discipline improves macroeconomic performance and therefore leads to poverty amelioration is addressed in the sixth section. The persistent evolution of the multilateral trade regime, followed by the rationale of its unbalanced evolution, is the subject of the seventh and eighth sections. The issue of belated development relevance of the multilateral trade regime is dealt with at length in the ninth section. Transformations in the global economic scenario and *pari passu* changes in multilateral trade are the focus of the tenth section. In the following section, a detailed analysis of the plausible poverty alleviation that the Doha Round can bring about is addressed. The final section provides a summary and concludes.

GLOBAL COMMITMENT TO ECONOMIC GROWTH

The commitment and dedication of the global community to the goals of economic growth and poverty alleviation is an age-old one. These policy objectives have been at the center of policy debates in every national, regional and international development organization and non-governmental organizations. Over the last half century, several UN commissions were committed to the promotion of growth and development. Two of the notable commissions were headed by Lester B. Pearson and Raúl Prebisch. Both developing and industrial economies were part of these commitments to global economic development. The final outcomes of many of these Commissions were creations of worthy development institutions like the Food and Agriculture Organization (FAO) and the United Nations Conference on Trade and Development (UNCTAD). A recent endeavor of this kind was the enthusiastic accord of the global community on the MDGs, which represented a calibrated and expanded vision of global development and poverty alleviation. Halving of global income-poverty by 2015 is the first of the eight MDGs, precisely articulated by the United Nations General assembly. While these developmental targets were first set out in international conferences and summits held in the 1990s, they were eventually adopted as the MDGs by the UN General Assembly in September 2000.

Soon after espousing the MDGs, the global community further expressed its unqualified support for these universally agreed development and poverty alleviation objectives during 2002 in the United Nations Conference on Financing for Development, held in Monterrey, Mexico, and in the World Summit on Sustainable Development, held in Johannesburg, South Africa.[1] At these global conferences, the developing economies accepted responsibility for their own development by strengthening governance, providing the investment required to sustain private sector-led growth and making optimal utilization of domestic resources to strengthen growth and development. On their part, the industrial economies committed themselves to supporting the developing economies that adopted credible and transparent growth strategies by increasing development assistance as well as reinforcing establishment of a more development-oriented multilateral trade regime, represented by the WTO. The World Summit expressly committed to harnessing globalization for sustainable development and economic uplift of the global community, so that *inter alia* the first MDG of halving income-poverty by 2015 may be achieved. These global initiatives are sure to play a major role in restructuring the international trade and development agenda in the foreseeable future. The plans of action that have been profiled in these global initiatives are, and will be, the principal reference points for governments, civil society, supranational institutions and the global business community in designing the multilateral trade regime and development strategies of the contemporary period.

Moral Imperative and Developmental Rationale

The global community appreciates the moral imperative and development rationale of achieving the MDGs, particularly the first one. One proof of this is the frequent references to this objective that one comes across in the policy papers of the national governments and regional and international institutions of global economic governance. The global economic recovery that started in

2003 continued unabated. A favorable global growth environment has helped sustain global poverty alleviation endeavors over the 2001–5 period. This upswing of the global business cycle brought major improvement in the living standard and employment situation of millions of poor in the developing economies. Buoyant trade volume expansion, low interest rates and strong growth performance in the industrial economies helped the developing economies grow at a brisk rate. The low- and middle-income developing economies grew at an average rate of under 5 percent in 2005, which was well above their historic rates (WB, 2006). Macroeconomic indicators in these country groups were markedly superior in 2005 than they were over the decade of the 1990s, albeit the gains were uneven. Much of the improvement was focused in East and South Asia and in Eastern Europe and Central Asia. During 2000–5, GDP growth rates in the middle-income economies was higher and less volatile than those in the low-income ones. They also displayed greater resilient to external shocks. To be sure, there is a great deal of room for improvement.

Like the MDGs, the global community needs to adopt the policy objectives of economic growth and poverty alleviation by means of an ambitious program of trade policy reforms. To be sure, such a reform program will need to have an ambitious vision of coordinated multilateral action and necessarily encompass significant tariff slashing on the most-favored-nation (MFN)[2] basis on labor-intensive products, which are of interest to the exporting firms from the developing economies, as well as thorough reforms of trade in agriculture. This comprehensive reform program could cover all the sovereign member countries of the WTO, both developing and industrial economies. Such a reform program has immense potential to become a source of welfare gains to the developing economies, and the absolute poor in it.

MACROECONOMIC POLICY AND THE TRADE–GROWTH NEXUS

Owing to its immense policy implications, this nexus has been paid a great deal of attention by researchers. Numerous cross-country and panel regressions found evidence of 'outwardness', or 'outer-orientation' or 'openness' being strongly linked to faster economic growth. This relationship held irrespective of the fact whether openness is measured in terms of a country's trade policies, that is, by the level of tariff and the non-tariff barriers (NTBs), or as a policy outcome, that is, the ratio of exports plus imports to GDP.

This subject is not without its contentious aspects. While there are sound empirical and theoretical reasons supporting a move to a more liberalized trade regime, there are equally sound theoretical arguments that support protection from international competition for some domestic industrial sectors, at least in the initial stages of industrialization. Economic theory does not reject infant industry protection. The large body of empirical literature, based on comparable methodological approaches, which largely entail exploring cross-country evidence at the macroeconomic level, came up with conclusions that were far from uniform. Numerous multi-country case studies were conducted in the past, which also utilized similar analytical frameworks.[3] They also came up with results that were not harmonious. These empirical and statistical studies subsequently became the target of criticism for their methodological weaknesses.

Evaluating the Nexus

Intense evaluation by the economics profession of the trade–growth nexus brought them to the inference that that in a liberal multilateral trade regime, countries that trade more grow faster. This is a simple but meaningful policy statement, which is testified by the experiences of successful economies. While opening up to trade does not guarantee faster growth, all the economies that took off successfully over the preceding quarter century without exception included trade or an external sector in their reform program. Plentiful examples are available to demonstrate unmistakably that protectionist measures cause distortions that work their way through the economy in a most unplanned and undesirable manner and have a high welfare cost.

Liberalized multilateral trade regime and domestic policies are positively correlated with growth. While this was the leitmotif of numerous empirical studies conducted over a long period, there was no certainty regarding the direction of causality. In addition, this empirical evidence of a relationship was not without its controversies. There were fundamental problems that permeated them, casting a shadow of doubt over the validity of their estimates. For instance, endogeneity bias and omitted variables were among the two most serious problems with the set of studies. Due to these statistical flaws, the Ordinary Least Squares (OLS) regression technique commonly used in the early empirical studies tended to yield biased estimates of the coefficient of interest, that is, of the impact of openness on the GDP growth. Also, mere examination of correlation coefficients could not identify the direction of causation between trade and growth.

Frankel and Romer (1999) suggested a remedy to address some of the methodological weaknesses. Their innovation was to take a size-weighted distance measure between countries. Dollar and Kraay (2002) reconstructed this instrument for their sample economies and found that there is a highly significant positive effect of trade expansion on the per capita income of a developing economy. This methodological improvement not only confirmed the results of Frankel and Romer (1999) but also yielded a larger coefficient than OLS regression analyses of past studies. Making an inter-temporal distinction, Dollar and Kraay (2002) also inferred that trade expansion plays a larger role in the short-run on growth than does institutional development, which has a greater effect in the longer run.

Theoretical Improvements in Research

The improvements in the theory of edogenous growth which took place in the latter half of the1980s and the early 1990s made a decisive contribution to this debate.[4] The new growth theory was partially based on the relationship between trade and growth. Improvements in theory and the availability of more comprehensive data made it possible to launch more sophisticated cross-country economic analyses relating various measures of openness to the growth rate of GDP and total factor productivity (TFP). These studies also found a strong positive relationship between outward-looking policies and growth. Cross-country evidence at macroeconomic level was once again positive.[5] Some of these studies further improved the methodology by using measures of trade intensity instead of measures of trade policy as the relevant variable determining GDP growth. This measure captured more than just the influence of policy-induced trade barriers like tariffs and non-tariff barriers (NTBs). Like the earlier empirical studies, this subset of studies also found more open developing economies growing at a faster GDP growth rate. Like the earlier studies, this group of researchers also did not go unchallenged. Rodriguez and Rodrik (2001) not only questioned their results and the robustness of their results but also regarded the 'search for such a relationship futile'.

In a comprehensive research project, Dollar and Kraay (2004) examined the effect of liberalization, trade expansion and globalization on growth, inequality and poverty. Over half the developing country population presently lives in globalizing economies that have seen large increases in trade and significant declines in policy-induced trade barriers, both at the domestic and multilateral levels. These developing economies are catching up with the industrial countries, while the rest of the developing world is falling farther behind. Second, they examined the effects of trade and globalization on the poor. The increase in growth rates leads on average to proportionate increases in incomes of the poor. The evidence from individual cases and cross-country analysis supports the view that promotion of trade and globalization leads to faster growth and poverty reduction in the poor countries.

Policy Preference for Outward-Orientation Despite Disagreements

Following the post-war performance of the Japanese economy, the four East

Asian dragon economies (Hong Kong, the Republic of Korea, Singapore and Taiwan) and subsequently Southeast Asian economies (Indonesia, Malaysia, the Philippines and Thailand) turned to the traded goods sector in order to function as an engine of growth. Adopting outward orientation helped these economies achieve stellar economic performances, which turned Asia into the most dynamic region of the global economy (Das, 2005a). The hopeful showcase of the Asian economies has been analysed endlessly. From the Asian scenario, lessons were sought for the other developing economies. Thinking in the academe and policy-making institutions, like the Bretton Woods twins and the WTO, markedly shifted in favor of outer-orientation of growth strategy and a liberal global trade regime.

Disagreements among the researchers apart, a number of cross-country studies have supported the trade–growth nexus. It is increasingly believed in the policy-making community that the protectionist environment promotes and perpetuates inefficient industries in developing economies. Also, protectionist policies were usually combined with inflexible industrial regulations and over-valued exchange rates. South Asian and Latin American developing economies testify to these facts. Trade does not stimulate growth in developing economies with excessive regulations (Bolaky and Freund, 2004). While the strategy of inward-oriented or import-substituting industrialization (ISI) can stimulate domestic production, it suffers from obvious and severe anti-export, anti-labor and anti-agriculture biases. Consequently, developing economies that adopted this growth strategy were deterred from specializing in accordance with their perceived comparative advantage.

Both the static and dynamic effects of trade expansion on the domestic economy are well known. The static effects work through efficiency in resource allocation in the domestic economy, while the dynamic ones work by transporting growth-enhancing factors like technological advances and knowledge. The dynamic effects are divided into the following five categories, namely: spillover effects; scale-economies effects; competition-generated effects; imitation effects; and an increased variety of intermediation (Acemoglu and Zilibotti, 2001). Little wonder that efficiency gains are directly correlated with liberalization of trade policy in the developing economies and a liberalizing multilateral trading environment and that TFP gains are regarded as one of the standard outcomes of trade expansion (Bernard and Jensen, 1999).

CONTEMPORARY MULTILATERAL TRADE REGIME

Created in 1995 under the aegis of the Uruguay Round (1986–94) by 123 participating countries, the WTO is the multilateral institution that essentially deals with the formulation, modification and implementation of rules of trade between nations.[6] Its success in this task depends upon frequent negotiations among national governments. These negotiations set down the system of trade laws as well as determine how trade conflicts between members should be resolved. They have successfully created the related regulatory structure, which is based on numerous agreements and decisions. The WTO rules and agreements are binding and commitments are enforceable. This gives the WTO its value. These rules and agreements create a framework of legally binding rights and obligations for all the member countries. The global regulatory structure of trade thus produced is based on negotiation scholarship of the member countries, which underrepresented the experience and needs of developing economies.

The genesis of the GATT – predecessor of the WTO – goes back to the aborted International Trade Organization (ITO) in 1947. It was a trade treaty that was significantly less ambitious than the original vision of the ITO. The multilateral trade regime, or the so-called GATT/WTO system, forms the legal foundation of contemporary commerce. Two of its fundamental principles are: (a) most-favored-nation (MFN) treatment, that is, non-discrimination between exporters; and (b) national treatment, that is, treating imports and domestic supplies equally inside the national markets.

A member-driven system, its ultimate objective is to establish a rule-based multilateral trading system, which has little element of unpredictability. As one trade analyst observed, the GATT/WTO system is as much about protectionism as it is about free trade. 'Global economic rules are not written by Platonic rulers, or their present-day pretenders, academic economists. If WTO agreements were truly about "free trade", as their opponents like to point out, a single sentence would suffice ("there shall be free trade")'(Rodrik, 2002). The GATT played an imperious role in multilateral trade liberalization and expansion since its inception in 1948. Although it is the governments of the member countries that seem the *prima facie* participants and beneficiaries from this system of trade laws, the bona fide stakeholders and ultimate beneficiaries of the multilateral trade regime are the businesses and consumers in the member countries. The ultimate measure of success of an efficiently functioning multilateral trade regime is the benefits derived by the consumers in the trading economies that are part of the GATT/WTO system.

Ministerial Conferences

The Ministerial Conference of the GATT/WTO system is the apex decision-making body of the multilateral trading system. These Ministerial Conferences are the thread that runs through the history of the trading system, beginning with the ill-fated Havana Conference of 1947, which drafted the

Charter for an International Trade Organization (ITO), which was stillborn.[7] Negotiations on the ITO draft were long and difficult; the 56 participating countries had differing, often conflicting, views on it.

Since the failed GATT Ministerial Conference of 1982, several Ministerial Conferences came repeatedly close to a catastrophic end, yet the contemporary multilateral trade regime 'is stronger, deeper and wider now than a generation ago' (Wolfe, 2004). Since the birth of the WTO, the Ministerial Conferences have become a biennial event, which is the most important event for the WTO regime and the world of multilateral trade.[8] It is through these conferences that the multilateral rule-making system in trade evolves and advances.[9]

Joys and Woes are Woven Fine

As alluded to above, the Ministerial Conferences have had a troubled past. Following the ignominious collapse of the Third Ministerial Conference of the WTO in Seattle in 1999, the Fourth Ministerial Conference in Doha, Qatar, was successfully held in 2001. The approach to this Ministerial Conference was more representative and inclusive than that of any previous GATT or WTO Ministerial Conferences. In Doha it was decided to launch the on-going Doha Round of multilateral trade negotiations (MTNs).[10] Advancing the agenda of growth and poverty alleviation within the framework of multilateral trade regime, or the General Agreement on Tariffs and Trade/World Trade Organization (GATT/WTO) system, and within the mandate of the Doha Round of MTNs, is in the commercial and development interest of both developing and industrial economies. Its moral imperative has been noted on pp. 3–4. Failure of the Doha Round will indeed risk the near-term prospects for growth in the developing economies, particularly in the middle- and low-income ones, in the process impairing the global income–poverty reduction endeavors. Conversely, a successful conclusion of the Doha Round would bolster growth and income–poverty alleviation endeavors. Its successful culmination would also provide a reliable engine of trade-led growth for the global economy, which has recently (2000–6) enjoyed a period of buoyant growth.

While it was launched in a harmonious manner following the Doha Ministerial Conference, we shall see in the following chapters that since its launch the Doha Round of MTNs progressed neither briskly nor smoothly. There were roadblocks galore, with negotiations on trade in agriculture being the largest of them all. The major trading powers missed the strategic deadline of 30 April 2006, for putting in order an agreement on core modalities on farm and industrial goods. The term modality in the WTO parlance implies precise numerical formula, targets and timetable for implementation of tariff and subsidy reduction rates. First, the comprehensive failure of the Cancún Ministerial Conference, followed by lack of any substantive realization in the Hong Kong Ministerial Conference, subsequently missing the 30 April deadline by the major trading economies in the MTNs and the disarray in the mini-Ministerial in July 2006 engendered rational and sincere skepticism regarding a successful conclusion of the Doha Round. In various chapters of this volume we shall analyse these developments, their rationale and how they are helping or hindering the evolution of the multilateral trade regime.

FROM THE GATT TO THE WTO

The edifice of the WTO was created on the foundation of the GATT, relatively a much smaller organization in terms of coverage of trade rules and membership. The WTO qualitatively evolved from the GATT and is a much larger organization. Membership obligation of the WTO entails accepting the whole package of obligations, or none at all. It is known as the 'Single Undertaking', an invention of the Uruguay Round. The Dispute Settlement Mechanism (DSM) under the WTO is stronger and its regulatory reach goes beyond the traditional border measures. Members can no longer ignore the adverse ruling from the WTO dispute panels. Unlike the GATT, trade in commercial services, intellectual property rights, sanitary and phytosanitary barriers to trade, and technical barriers to trade come within the ambit of the WTO. However, in its rule-making process and day-to-day functioning the WTO preserved the comportment and approach of its predecessor. It also retained the member-driven character of the GATT era. Similarly, consensus still rules the decision-making process, which is arrived at by informal diplomacy. The WTO Secretariat, like that of the GATT, still plays a minimal role. Consequently, member sovereign states find themselves bound to an elaborate, intrusive, legally binding and expanding set of disciplines, which they often contest.

Uniqueness of the WTO

The Marrakesh Agreement of 1994, which was instrumental in the creation of the WTO as the apex supranational organization monitoring, supervising and refining the system of world trade, is 26000 pages of legal text of national commitments. The WTO is the only multilateral institution that has been recently created to oversee increased liberalization of multilateral trade and serve the interests of the interdependent and progressively integrating global community of nations. The 123 CPs that participated in the creation of this institution, agreed that while the text of the agreement may have imperfections, it was in their vital national interests to be a part of the emerging multilateral trading system. The WTO was its institutional personification.

The WTO is a unique institution in that it is the only forum in which trade negations take place on almost worldwide basis. Presently in this forum, 149 sovereign states and independent customs territories exchange trade-liberalization commitments. Its agreements cover some 95 percent of international trade in goods and services. The WTO negotiations result in binding international agreements that can be enforced by an effective quasi-judiciary. Creation of the adjudication process is widely regarded as one of the most significant achievements in the formation of the WTO. With such a large membership and coverage, the multilateral trade regime represented by the WTO is generally regarded as a *de facto* global trade regime. Another unique feature of the GATT/WTO system is that it brings its entire membership together to negotiate a common set of rules to govern international trade (pp. 13–15).

Can an improved climate for external trade and a multilateral trade regime, in agreement with the domestic trade policy structure of the WTO member countries, make any contribution to achieving the MDGs in general and poverty alleviation in particular? Does trade expansion accelerate economic growth in the developing economies? Due to its high policy relevance, the latter subject has been over-researched by economists during the preceding quarter century (pp. 4–5). A library full of research is available on this issue. The saving grace is that the large empirical literature that was produced around this theme has led both policy mandarins and neoclassical economists to generally accept the view that trade expansion, together with improvement in human capital, is a key driver of growth and poverty alleviation, although there is a question mark on causality.[11]

Expanding Institutional Popularity

That a large number of members of the global community of nations accepted the WTO and are committed to contractual requirements of its membership speaks of the trust placed in the WTO and its institutional relevance. In mid-2006, WTO's membership was 149, eloquently demonstrating what the global community thinks of its value as an institution. More than three-fourths of the present members and over 25 percent of the accession candidates are developing economies. By 2010, WTO membership is expected to touch or even cross 170, which is close to universal. It members include the hegemonic economic powers like the European Union and the United States, medium-sized industrial economies like Australia, Canada and Sweden, emerging economic super-powers like China, emerging-market economies like Brazil,

India and South Africa, a wide range of developing economies and the least-developed countries (LDCs).[12] Not only is the present membership of the WTO much larger than that of the GATT, but also its diversity in membership is far larger.

The WTO has been described as 'in large measure a negotiating machine'. It is designed to search for and turn out negotiated solutions to the challenges of global trade. To fulfill its mandate, the WTO conducts negotiations among its member countries and tries to reach negotiated multilateral consensuses. This is the essential decision-making process of the WTO. Its principle charge is to negotiate conditions of market access for its members as well as 'supportive trade rules that provide opportunities for its membership to take commercial advantage of the global economy' (WTO, 2005a). The trend in economic globalization has intensified over the past quarter century and multilateral trade is one of its principal channels. In the process of supervising multilateral trade, the WTO contributes immensely to global economic governance.

MULTILATERAL TRADE DISCIPLINE IMPROVING MACROECONOMIC PERFORMANCE

A multilateral system of common rules and a mutually agreed code of conduct among the WTO members can and does reduce uncertainties among trading partners by placing boundaries on the policies adopted by the sovereign member countries. Convincing empirical evidence is available that supports this hypothesis. An environment of reduced uncertainty in turn helps in promoting domestic investment because investors see lower risk in making investments. It has been commonly observed that the private sector shies away from investing if a rule-based trade discipline and commensurate domestic reforms are in doubt, because investors logically perceive it as a high-risk environment. Furthermore, the existence of a framework of multilateral agreements renders the domestic policy measure more credible. Such a framework also renders domestic policy reversal or backsliding impossible because to all appearances they are locked in with a multilateral agreement.

While growing accession portends to the increasing value placed in the membership of the institution, on their part the acceding countries benefit from improved growth and investment performance. During and after the Uruguay Round, the requirements for accession were made more demanding than in the past. Subramanian and Wei (2005) documented that at this time, and thereafter, the new members of the GATT and the WTO tended to be systematically more open than the old developing country members. The trade to GDP ratio was used by them as the measure of openness. The authors found that the new or post-Uruguay Round developing country members of the GATT/WTO system traded 30 percent more than the old developing country members. As an accession requirement, many developing countries had to undertake a set of policy changes that concerned not only trade-related issues but also other broader policy regimes, like market access, competition policy, price controls, investment policy, privatization plans, transparency requirements and the like.

Economies that were subject to more rigorous accession procedures had a higher increase in real GDP growth rate and investment/GDP ratio around the accession period and thereafter (Wacziarg and Welch, 2003). Economies that were required to make substantial policy commitments at the time of accession experienced bigger improvements in their economic performance than those that were not. Tang and Wei (2006) concluded that the beneficial effects of policy commitments seemed more pronounced in countries with poor governance. They also concluded that binding policy changes enforced by a credible third party like the WTO tended to serve as a substitute for improvement in governance, eventually resulting in spurring economic development.

PERSISTENT EVOLUTIONARY ENDEAVORS

Trade barriers have a high welfare cost and the multilateral trade regime has been endeavoring to bring them down in a steady and methodological manner. Since its inception in 1948, the multilateral trade regime has developed, or evolved, almost ceaselessly. The GATT has been amended and supplemented progressively, with the passage of time. Among the international fora, the GATT/WTO system is exclusive in that it brings its entire membership together to negotiate a common set of rules to govern international trade (pp. 10–11). These negotiations are conducted during 'rounds' of MTNs. So far eight rounds of MTNs have been held under the sponsorship of the GATT, while the on-going Doha Round is being conducted under the aegis of the WTO.

The following seven rounds of MTNs under the sponsorship of the GATT were overwhelmingly dominated by industrial economies: the Geneva Tariff Conference (1947), the Annecy Tariff Conference (1949), the Torquay Tariff Conference (1951), the Geneva Tariff Conference (1956), the Dillon Round (1960-61), the Kennedy Round (1964–7), and the Tokyo Round (1973–9). Despite being part of the system, the developing economies remained virtually inactive and non-participative. During these seven rounds their attention was focused on obtaining preferential access in the markets of industrial countries. Few took any interest in the essential business of MTNs.

Trade liberalization has succeeded in deepening and widening the multilateral trade regime with each round of MTNs. The deepening occurred through first binding participating nations to a particular tariff rate for a particular line of product, then increasing the number of products covered, and then further lowering the tariff rates to which participating nations were bound. The national tariff schedules of the participants of a round of MTNs list tariff rates on a product-by-product basis. Trade in goods and tariff reduction or elimination is only one dimension of the multilateral trading system. The first five rounds of MTNs under the aegis of the GATT focused exclusively on tariff reduction, and elimination. The MTNs evolved further after that point in time and their scope went on progressively expanding to include a number of other instruments and areas of trade liberalization.

Variation in Coverage of Different Rounds

The coverage of trade issues in the above-named MTNs varied substantially. Tariffs were the only issue covered during the first five rounds. As the tariff rates declined with progress in the rounds of MTNs, policy-makers became increasingly creative in imposing non-tariff barriers (NTBs) of an imaginative range. Therefore scope of the subsequent rounds was progressively enlarged. Their coverage had to be extended to include NTBs of different genres. Each subsequent round covered more issues and entered new territories than the preceding one, and was correctly described as the most comprehensive round of MTNs so far.

In this context, mention should be made of the Kennedy Round, which covered tariffs, anti-dumping, agriculture and subsidies and countervailing duties. The Tokyo Round covered all that was covered in the Kennedy Round and also included technical barriers to trade (TBT), public procurement, safeguard and the GATT articles. Being even more comprehensive, the Uruguay Round covered all the areas of the preceding two rounds, plus the rules of origin (ROO), pre-shipment inspection and textiles and apparel, GATT functions, WTO organizational issues, trade-related investment measures (TRIMS), trade-related intellectual property rights (TRIPS), and most importantly agriculture and services. Following the same mode, the Doha Round covered all the issues of the preceding three rounds, plus industrial tariffs, regional integration agreements (RIAs), trade and environment, capacity building and implementation issues were added. About the Singapore issues there remained some mystification. One group of participants thought that they were on the agenda, while the other thought they were not. This confusion continued until the Fifth Ministerial Conference in Cancún, Mexico.

Three Larger and More Significant GATT Rounds

The scope of the trade policy issues and the areas of rule-making also went on expanding progressively with each round of MTNs. In addition, institutional significance of the GATT *pari passu* expanded with the subsequent round. To this end, the last three rounds of MTNs under the sponsorship of the GATT made an extensive contribution. While the Kennedy Round of MTNs, and more so the Tokyo Round, helped in consequential institutional development both in terms of substance and process, it was the Uruguay Round that is credited with bringing about the largest systemic transformation and evolution in the multilateral trade regime in an effective manner.

The Uruguay Round is justly regarded as the high point in the transformation of the multilateral trade regime (see Chapter 2, pp. 36–8). It helped make the system relevant to the global economy of closing decades of the twentieth century. Although neither rapidly nor efficiently, the Doha Round is once again attempting to achieve the same, that is to make the WTO more relevant to the demands of changing global economy of the twenty-first century. Its slow, often painful and arduous, process of evolution is continuing.

UNBALANCED EVOLUTION OF THE MULTILATERAL TRADE REGIME

The international treaty creating the GATT in 1947 was signed by 23 countries, which became the founding members of the GATT. This group included 12 developed and 11 developing economies.[13] When the GATT treaty came into force in January 1948, these 23 contracting parties (CPs) accounted for 60 percent of the world trade. During this period the industrial economies were the core trading economies and the multilateral trade regime was essentially created by them and for them. Historically, the participation of the developing economies in the multilateral trading system was marginal, or *à la carte*. They did not make any commitments in the MTNs at all. Therefore, in the initial period the evolution of many of the GATT rules reflected the perceived interests of the industrial economies. They overwhelmingly dominated it until the beginning of the Uruguay Round of MTNs in 1986.[14]

The dominance of industrial economies continued during the first seven rounds of MTNs under the sponsorship of the GATT, which have been named on p. 13. The coverage of trade issues in these MTNs did not vary substantially. Their scope was narrow; tariffs were the only issue covered during the first five rounds. As the tariff rates declined with progress in the rounds of MTNs, policy makers became increasingly creative in imposing non-tariff barriers (NTBs). The scope of the subsequent rounds progressively enlarged. Their coverage had to be extended to include NTBs of different genres.

As the rounds progressed, each subsequent round covered more issues and entered more new territories than the preceding one, and was correctly described as the most comprehensive round of MTNs so far. For instance, the Kennedy Round covered tariffs, anti-dumping, agriculture and subsidies and countervailing duties. The Tokyo Round covered all that was covered in the Kennedy Round and also included TBT, public procurement, safeguard and the GATT articles. Being even more comprehensive, the Uruguay Round covered all the issue areas of the preceding two rounds, plus the ROO, pre-shipment inspection and textiles and apparel, GATT functions, WTO organizational issues, TRIMS, TRIPS, and most importantly services. It was the largest round of MTNs in terms of participation; it was launched with 86 CPs participating in it. When it culminated in 1994, this number was 123.[15]

Following the same mode, the Doha Round covered all the issues of the preceding three rounds, plus industrial tariffs, regional integration agreements (RIAs), trade and environment, capacity building and implementation issues were added (see Chapter 2). About the four Singapore issues there remained some mystification.[16] One group of participants thought that they were on the agenda, while the other thought they were not. This confusion continued until the Fifth Ministerial Conference in Cancún, Mexico. The coverage of the Doha Round is almost as wide as that of the Uruguay Round, it is covering several issues in greater depth.

It was not the naissance but the subsequent evolution of the multilateral trade regime that was oblique and prejudicial to the developing country interests. If the GATT system remained skewed toward the industrial economies, it was certainly not the intention of the founding fathers. That said, in the first seven rounds of MTNs, the negotiations were focused on the areas of trade interest of the industrial economies because they dominated the world trade scenario as well as the multilateral trading system, and were the only meaningful participants in the MTNs and other GATT activities. Principal areas in which developing economies had comparative advantage, like agriculture and low-technology products like textiles and apparel were not even included in the GATT discipline, and the developing economies remained complacent about it because trade had not become a significant part of their economic structures. None of them during the early GATT period were among the significant trading economies.

Although the developing country CPs attended the MTNs and other GATT meetings, they were more or less passive participants. Their comprehension and preparation for the MTNs was rather limited, and therefore they were reduced to virtual non-participants, who looked in from the sidelines. Little wonder that the products and areas of limited interest to the developing economies were not addressed by the multilateral trading system. However, due to the MFN principle of the multilateral trading system the developing country CPs were able to avail themselves of the benefits of the industrial country liberalization.[17] This is where their contribution to and benefit from the GATT system terminated.

The industrial country CPs accepted non-participation from the developing country CPs readily because it allowed them to ignore trade liberalization in what they considered 'sensitive' sectors for their domestic economies. Two sensitive sectors for them were agriculture, textiles and apparel. What was more important was the fact that the developing country markets during this period were so small, in both relative and absolute terms, that they held little attraction for majority of the exporting firms from the industrial economies. Also, for the industrial economies, the benefits of asking the developing country CPs to liberalize their small import markets were decisively much smaller than the cost of liberalizing their own markets in labor-intensive import sectors.

Growing Intricacy and Complexity

As it grew, the GATT/WTO regime became progressively more intricate and complex. It has been shown on pp. 10–12 that the WTO regime is much larger in scope than the GATT. With expansion in scope the multilateral trade regime went on becoming more intricate and complex. Furthermore, simple and compelling basic principles, like promoting non-discrimination through the MFN clause, that lay at the foundation of the GATT, have been repeatedly compromised. Numerous deviations and exceptions to these basic principles have evolved over the years, which complicated the multilateral trade regime. As the evolving multilateral trade regime adjusts to the ever-changing realities of the global economy, this trend seems likely to continue. To all appearances, the Doha Round seems set to make more such compromises.

As regards the fundamental question about how the multilateral trade system should evolve in the near future, it needs to go on changing, growing and recreating itself. In the process, it needs to go on legitimizing itself as well as its institutional structure in such a way that it continues to liberalize trade and favorably influence the economic and financial globalization process. Its final outcome would be enhanced welfare for the members of the WTO, and therefore for the global economy. To what degree and effectiveness the WTO will underpin, first, the expansion of multilateral trade in goods and services, and second, the on-going globalization phenomenon will be the litmus test of its institutional efficacy and relevance to the contemporary global economy.

DEVELOPMENT RELEVANCE OF THE MULTILATERAL TRADE REGIME

On p. 8 we discussed the ITO, which was conceptualized as the third supranational institution along with the Bretton Woods twins, namely, the International Monetary Fund (IMF) and the World Bank. These three supranational organizations were intended to be the three pillars of global economic governance. The third pillar, originally conceptualized in the mid-1940s, was not erected until quite recently. Creation of the WTO in 1995 completed the triad that was originally contemplated at the time of the Bretton Woods conference. The WTO now plays the pivotal role in the on-going economic globalization.

The definitions of the multilateral trade regime and the WTO clarifies that it was not intended to be, and is not, a development institution. Those who originally conceived the GATT/WTO system did not design it for promoting economic development. That being said, efforts to enhance the development relevance of the WTO have constantly been made. There are certain facets of its mandate that decisively influence developmental endeavors of countries consciously striving to climb the ladder of growth, development and industrialization. The two quintessential functions of the WTO regime are: (a) negotiating commitments for improving market access, and (b) establishing a rule-based trading system that leaves no element of unpredictability in multilateral trade, as noted on p. 8.

These are two critically important dimensions of the WTO and the developing economies can benefit from both of them in their developmental endeavors. First, as noted on pp. 4–6, a domestic policy stance of openness is associated with brisk growth and poverty alleviation. If the WTO ensures greater market access for the developing economies and the products in which they have comparative advantage, it provides a spur to their growth endeavors. The developing economies that have reformed and liberalized their domestic policies and put a compensatory policy structure in place did experience acceleration in their growth performance. Tariffs and NTBs work as a tax on development. This observation applies to both developing and industrial economies (Das, 2001).[18] Second, the majority of developing economies are relatively weaker players in the multilateral trading system. By conceiving, designing and establishing a rule-based multilateral trade regime the WTO protects the interests of developing economies, particularly the smaller traders that have little ability to influence the policies of the dominant players in the world trade arena.

Developing Country Status

Developing country status in the multilateral trade regime brings certain rights. Several GATT agreements in the past, and WTO agreements at present, provide developing countries with longer transition periods before they are required to fully implement the agreements. Also, low-income developing countries and LDCs can ask for and receive technical assistance. Developing economies can also benefit from the unilateral preferential trade schedules, like the Generalized System of Preferences (GSP). However, when an economy proclaims itself as developing, it does not imply that it will become a mandatory beneficiary of the unilateral preferential trade schedules of the industrial economies. It is the preference-granting industrial economy that decides which developing economies will benefit from the preferences.

From a certain perspective, the developing economies has been a disadvantaged group in the GATT/WTO system. As set out on pp. 13–17, the evolution of the multilateral trade regime was skewed and prejudicial to the developing country interests. Also, many early GATT rules reflected the practices that were being followed in the industrial economies. Heavily subsidized production and export of agriculture in the industrial economies, high tariff barriers and distortion in trade in agricultural and agro-industrial products was considered acceptable because it suited the interests of the industrial economies. The same logic applies to binding of trade in textiles and apparels in stringent quotas, an anathema according to the GATT rules.

This was not only true of the past practices but has also persisted until the present. Many recent laws adopted under the new WTO regime still reflect the interests and practices followed in the industrial economies. For instance, the WTO rules on the protection of intellectual property rights are the very same laws that are followed in the industrial economies. This implies that while the developing economies are obliged to create a new regulatory framework on intellectual property rights, the status quo continues in the industrial economies. No changes are required by the WTO in their intellectual property rights regulations.[19]

Cost of Non-Participation

Unquestionably the largest cost of not exploiting the external sector as an engine of growth and of non-participation in the multilateral trade regime was in terms of deterred GDP growth. In addition, as a result of non-participation, the negotiated outcomes of various rounds of MTNs did not improve the access of developing country export products into industrial country markets. The ultimate result was that while developing countries protected their own markets, they had to accept high trade barriers against their most competitive exports in the large industrial country markets. The developing economies found this strategic stance on international trade politically convenient. The economic cost seemed not to matter to them. Special protection regimes like the Multi-Fiber Arrangement (MFA) and a highly distorted multilateral trade regime in agriculture were the direct outcome of non-participation.

This strategic stance underwent a transformation. A small group of developing economies realized that the strategy of limited engagement in the multilateral trading system was not a productive or a pragmatic one. The East and Southeast Asian economies epitomized this trend (Das, 2005a). Subsequently, during the mid-1980s, an increasing number of developing economies, particularly the large and middle-income ones, began implementing far-reaching macroeconomic reform and restructuring programs in their domestic economies. Their principal objective was to increase and diversify their exports and with that their economic structures. This was regarded as an instrument for integrating into the global economy. The reforms began showing tangible results in several developing economies, which were *inter alia* visible in their rising export volumes. The old GATT era mindset of the policy mandarins was undergoing a transformation. Consequently, the Uruguay Round saw a radical change in the mindset of policy-makers in the developing economies.

During the late 1970s, a small group of Asian developing economies recorded rapid and sustained real GDP growth by pursuing an export-led growth strategy. This sub-group of developing economies pursued sound macroeconomic policies, including open trade and investment regimes, and benefited from the multilateral trading system and integrated into the global economy. This innovative sub-group soon became a source of labor-intensive and light manufacturing products. Soon it developed export capability in assembling medium-technology products. Their export and import volumes consistently grew to significant amounts and members of this country group began appearing on the league tables of the principal exporting economies prepared first by the GATT and later by the WTO. Their success was a demonstration to the community of developing nations that these small but dynamic economies could make their mark on the global trade and economic scenario. Their success provoked protectionism in the industrial economies and instruments, such as voluntary export restraints (VERs), orderly marketing arrangement (OMAs), and anti-dumping and countervailing duties were frequently applied to restrain their market access in the large industrial country markets.

During and after the Uruguay Round more developing economies became proactive participants in the MTNs. An increasing number of them were *pari passu* becoming more proactively involved in multilateral trade. With entry into force of the WTO in 1995, developing economies' participation in the multilateral trade regime picked up a marked momentum. Many of them reinforced their missions in Geneva. During the preparatory phase of the Third Ministerial Conference in Seattle in 1999, developing countries participated in a large number of pre-Ministerial Conference deliberations, voiced their concerns on different issues and presented formal proposals and position papers in a sizeable number. Their dormant and apathetic comportment in the multilateral trade arena became a mere memory. During this period of increasing participation, many small trading economies that were either passive in the past or not even part of the GATT/WTO system, were drawn to the multilateral trade regime (see Chapter 4). Despite resource constraints, they invested in training their trade officials and in this endeavor they were supported by several old and new international organizations. Consequently, every sovereign member state of the WTO was able to send its trade minister to the Ministerial Conferences held in Seattle, Doha, Cancún and Hong Kong SAR (Special Administrative Region).

Developing Economies as Traders of Significance

The 1990s saw further transformation – or progress – in this scenario. Developing economies recorded an average merchandise export growth rate which was one-third higher than that of the industrial economies. In the space of one decade, the average trade-to-GDP ratio for the developing economies soared from 29 percent to 43 percent (Ingco and Nash, 2004). The year 2004 saw a marked increase in the share of developing economies in the world trade to 31 percent, the highest ever. This was essentially due to increase in their share in the export of manufactures. In 2004, they accounted for 28 percent of world exports of manufactures. Considering the fact that this share was only 22 percent in 1995, this was a significant achievement.

While this group of developing economies has reasons to be optimistic about their future, the fact remains that only a small number of them have so far benefited from the expansion in trade volumes. Developing economies are known for a wide diversity in their performance. Contrary to the EMEs[20] noted in the preceding paragraph, the 50 LDCs are not significant in terms of trade volume, even collectively. They account for about 1 percent of total world trade. The share of sub-Saharan countries was 2 percent in 2005.

Thus viewed, over the last decade several developing economies have emerged as important trading economies. With the progressive involvement of the developing economies, a new objective was logically needed for the multilateral trade regime, namely, economic growth and development. It needs to be made part of multilateral thinking, deliberations and negotiations. The implications of the new WTO rules are to be carefully evaluated in the light of transformations in the setting of multilateral trade. They should be so designed that they proactively lead a member developing economy to the new growth target. Economic growth is indeed a difficult metaprocess, which *inter alia* requires active, and educated involvement of the developing economies in the multilateral trading system.

Successful Exporters of Manufactures

In the recent past, the developing economies have been more successful in exporting manufactured goods than agricultural products. This was partly due to the idiosyncrasies of the multilateral trade regime. During the two decades ending in 2001, multilateral trade growth in agriculture and manufacturing trade took place at similar paces. Table 1.1 shows that exports of agricultural products from developing economies rose in the 1990s, so did the growth rate of manufacturing products. However, these statistics conceal an important difference. During the period under consideration, developing countries' exports of agricultural products to other developing economies more than doubled, while those to industrial economies stagnated. Consequently, the share of developing countries' agricultural exports to other developing countries increased from 9.5 percent to 13.4 percent during the 1980–2001 period. Over the same period, their share of agricultural exports to industrial economies declined from 25.8 percent to 22.9 percent. Conversely, their share of manufactured goods exports to industrial economies soared from 12.7 percent in 1980–1 to 15.2 percent in 1990–1, and further to 21.1 percent in 2000–1.

This set of simple statistics portends to the fact that trade barriers have been more effective in stifling agricultural exports from the developing

Table 1.1: Export growth rates in constant (1995) dollars (in percent)

	World export growth rates		Developing countries export growth rates	
	1980–90	1990–2001	1980–90	1990–2001
Agriculture	4.5	3.6	3.5	4.8
Manufacturing	5.9	4.8	7.6	8.9

Source: Computed by Ingco and Nash (2004) from COMTRADE date tapes.

economies than manufacturing exports. This trend in turn reflects the idiosyncratic nature of the present multilateral trade regime.

Some developing economies, like China and several Asian economies, made successful niches in the global trade scenario, particularly in the trade of manufactured goods. These EMEs have turned in a stellar performance. In 2004 China overtook the US as the world's largest exporter of advanced-technology products like laptop computers, information technology products, cellular phones and digital cameras. In 2003, the US was the global leader in this category with exports of $137 billion, followed by China with $123 billion. In 2004, China notched up another first. It exported $180 billion worth of high-technology equipment in 2004, compared to the US exports of $149 billion, making China the leading global economy in the exports of high-technology products (Das, 2006a).

TRANSFORMING GLOBAL ECONOMIC AND TRADE SCENARIO

Growth endeavors and globalization during the 1980s and 1990s gradually transformed the global economic scenario. First, many developing countries are no longer insignificant import markets and have also became substantive exporters. Both their market size and export volume have began to matter. The EMEs, and among them the newly industrializing economies (NIEs)[21], deserve a particular mention in this regard. More than 25 of the developing economies earned the status of the EMEs and integrated well with the global economy (Das, 2004a). This changed situation was evident during the Uruguay Round. For the first time at least the EMEs were brought into the fold of the GATT. They were expected to adhere to the reciprocity principle[22] of the GATT system because the industrial economies felt that at their level of development they could do so. This was the time to re-establish a new equilibrium among the CPs.

The EMEs *en masse* have made impressive strides. They undertook a laudable task of integrating with the global economy during the last two decades (Das, 2004a). This sub-group of economies contributed to the rapid global growth performance of the 2000–5 period. Rapid real GDP growth in China – the largest EME – India and some of the other EMEs was part of this performance (Das, 2006b). The oil and commodity price hike did slow down the global economic growth rate. The lax monetary policies in the mature industrial economies, particularly over the 2000–5 period, *inter alia* helped the EMEs to come into their own. By 2005, this group of economies began changing the relative global balance of economic power in a discernible manner. *The Economist* (2006a) called this phenomenon 'coming of age'. In 2005, the EMEs produced a little more than half of world output measured at purchasing-power parity. They also accounted for more than half of the increase in global GDP in current-dollar terms. Due to adoption of sound macroeconomic policies, the majority of EMEs can look forward to sustaining rapid long-term growth. Extrapolation is a chancy business. However, if this relative growth rate is sustained, by 2025 the EMEs will account for two-thirds of global output (*The Economist,* 2006a). Over the decade of the 1990s, Brazil emerged as a competitive exporter in agricultural trade, China in manufactures and India in services. These three EMEs have been trying to carve a niche of their own on the global economic and trade scenario.

China and several EMEs have successfully come forward as large traders (pp. 22–3). Following the same streak, more EMEs can reasonably be expected to gain greater momentum in the near future. Their recent success has caused concern in the mature industrial economies. Together they have made another noteworthy contribution to the global economy. Integration of the EMEs, particularly Brazil, China and India, into the global economy has given the biggest boost to the global supply since the industrial revolution. Similarly, integration of global labor markets has made its impact over the global economy. Low-wage labor producing manufactured goods and services in the EMEs and exporting them globally, including to the industrial economies, has cut the cost of goods and kept the rate of inflation under tight control. In the industrial economies, the possibility that jobs could move offshore has helped hold down wages. Although demand from EMEs, particularly China and India, has fueled the surge in oil and commodity prices, the newcomers' effect, on balance, has been to restrain inflation in the industrial economies.

Participation of the developing economies in the multilateral forum is progressively becoming more consequential during the 2000s. The so-called Group-of-Twenty (G-20) was born before the Cancún Ministerial Conference. The G-20 coalition included some developing country members of the Cairns Group (Argentina, Brazil and Thailand) which were interested in improving market access for their agricultural exports. It also included other developing countries (India, Mexico, Bolivia and Ecuador) which were concerned with defending their domestic markets from import surges. The G-20 not only played a meaningful role in Cancún Ministerial Conference (Chapter 4) but also at the WTO meeting in Geneva, held in the last week of July 2004, which put together the July Package or the July Framework Agreement, which revived the moribund Doha Round (Chapter 5).[23] For the members of the G-20, one lesson learned at Cancún was that, to avoid later frustrations, they need to approach future ministerial conferences, MTNs and other important WTO meetings with well beefed-up teams of trade economists and better preparations in terms of research for negotiations.

THE DOHA ROUND AND GLOBAL POVERTY ALLEVIATION

As alluded to earlier in this chapter (pp. 2–3), one of earnest expectations from the ongoing Doha Round is to achieve the first MDG of cutting down income-poverty by a half by 2015. The long-term trend has demonstrated that the number of absolute poor in the world has been rising. During the nineteenth and twentieth centuries the number of poverty-stricken people in the world constantly rose (Bourguignon and Morrisson, 2002). There was a small reversal in this trend after 1970, and this number fell by just over 200 million. Measured in 1985 PPP terms, the number of poor declined by 350 million (Sala-i-Martin, 2002). Impressive as this achievement seems, there were still 1.2 billion absolute poor in the world, or one person in five still lived in poverty (Collier and Dollar, 2002).

Over the next decade, policy mandarins in economic and financial ministries and treasuries, professionals in international organizations, particularly the international financial institutions (IFIs), analysts in the academic world and think tanks and in the large international non-governmental organizations (NGOs) are going to be concerned with how to link poverty alleviation endeavors in the global economy with the multilateral trade regime. They will look for means for relating the two activities. They will seek ways of upgrading the multilateral trade regime in a meaningful manner so that it may underpin the objective of achieving the first MDG.

Indirect linkage between poverty alleviation and trade

Trade expansion can indeed play a consequential role in poverty alleviation by driving economic growth in the developing economies. As elucidated on pp. 4–7, developing economies that adopted the strategy of export-led growth have succeeded in integrating with the global economy better and grow faster – at least in the long-run – than those that did not. This in turn reduces the number of those living below the poverty line. However, it is possible the short-run results could be just the opposite. Due to structural adjustment costs, the immediate impact on the poor in the short term may be negative. This holds *a fortiori* for the economies that lack the resources, institutions or infrastructure to facilitate changes, or the social safety net to cushion the negative impact.

The GATT/WTO system has contributed to growth during the post-war period in two principal ways. First, as stated earlier by providing rule of law in world trade, this in turn provided greater predictability in trade and investment (pp. 7–12). Second, it nurtured and promoted trade liberalization by instituting trade negotiations, and by influencing domestic macroeconomic and external sector policies. Even if the poor do not benefit directly from economic growth, it creates resources that the public policy-makers can thoughtfully devote to poverty alleviation.

However, economic theory suggests that trade can certainly favorably affect the poor through its positive effect on the GDP and per capita income in an economy. Trade liberalization and expansion have both static and dynamic impact over the economy and creates optimal conditions for rapid growth through flows of better ideas, technology transfer, goods, services and capital. More importantly, trade expansion underpins growth through better resource allocation in the domestic economy. However, it cannot be ignored that growth is a necessary, not a sufficient, condition for poverty alleviation. Even when trade liberalization and expansion lead to rapid GDP growth, it does not and cannot ensure improvement in income inequality in the economy. But higher GDP growth decisively enhances the probability of poverty alleviation.

Household survey results for several surveys are available. By synthesizing the results of these household surveys one can conclude that a 1 percent increase in real per capita income reduces the incidence of poverty by 2 percent.[24] Elasticity of poverty with respect to growth was found to be higher in absolute terms in the developing economies where the degree of income inequality was lower, and higher where income inequality was higher.

Reducing in wage inequality is one way of alleviating poverty through trade expansion. As wage inequality decreases as a consequence of trade expansion, poverty levels are known to decline. Liberalization of multilateral trade in line with the mandates of the DDA is widely expected to contribute to alleviating poverty and achieving the MDGs.[25] However, there are other valuable policy issues that need not be ignored. Sound macroeconomic policy is perhaps the most important one of them all. Adequate physical infrastructure and institutional infrastructure are the other complementary policies whose support is indispensable.

It should be noted that while the linkage between poverty alleviation and social sector reforms – education, health, land reform, micro-credit, infrastructure development and governance – is direct, trade and poverty alleviation are not directly linked. This is not to deny the channels linking poverty alleviation with multilateral trade liberalization. However, while it is good to be optimistic in this regard, it is better to be realistic. Stressing the implicitness of the linkage Winters (2003) noted that emphasizing the strength of the link between poverty alleviation and MTNs would be an error that could endanger either or both of the two important tasks. 'Each task has important dimensions independent of the other and could become distorted by too close an association. Furthermore, raising undue expectations about the immediacy of the poverty-relieving benefits of trade liberalization might discredit the process when those expectations are frustrated'.

Principal Channels

There are three principal channels through which liberalization of multilateral trade in line with the mandate of the DDA can contribute to poverty alleviation in the developing economies. First, lowering trade barriers in the area of trade in agriculture, especially but not exclusively in industrial countries, is certain to provide impetus to poverty alleviation endeavors in the developing economies. Most of the world's poor live and work in rural areas; poverty is largely a rural phenomenon in developing economies. Second, non-agricultural market access (NAMA) is another important conduit that has a large potential for poverty alleviation. In this area, trade barriers in the developing economies also need to be addressed, within the mandate of the DDA. Third, trade in services, particularly the so-called Mode-4 services (or movement of natural persons), has enormous poverty alleviation potential. This is a sensitive, and therefore politically demanding, area of trade liberalization. It entails temporary movement of natural persons from the developing to industrial economies with an objective of providing services. These three channels warrant careful thought by policy mandarins and analysis by economists and trade analysts.

The Stolper–Samuelson theorem can provide meaningful guidance over trade liberalization leading to poverty alleviation. In the medium- and long-term, increases in returns to labor and capital employed in one sector – one having comparative advantage – should logically attract more resources to that sector. It would also raise gains for labor and capital going to this particular sector. If this sector of the economy is relatively labor-intensive, a rise in the prices of the output of this sector is sure to raise the economy-wide wages of labor. It would benefit all wage earners, skilled and unskilled, and also those directly or indirectly employed in the sector in question. Several Asian economies provide an illustration; the wage gap between the skilled and unskilled workers narrowed in the decades following trade liberalization in Korea, Taiwan, Singapore and Malaysia, although evidence in the Philippines was found to be mixed (Das, 2005a).

Rises in economy-wide wages and a reduction in the wage gap are more likely to be the long-term impacts of trade liberalization. While this holds as a generalization, empirically linking multilateral trade liberalization to poverty amelioration requires a multi-region analytical approach. As most household surveys are country specific, they are not the most ideal tools for multi-region models used for trade policy analysis (Reimer, 2002). To circumvent this problem, most empirical studies that quantify the impact of trade liberalization over poverty focus on the impact on the average or per capita income.

Estimating the Impact of Trade Reforms

According to the most recent estimates made by Chen and Ravallion (2004), of the 6.16 billion global population, 1039 million people live below the poverty line globally if the reference poverty line is defined as $1.08 dollars a day, and 2736 billion if it is defined as $2.15 a day. The largest proportions of population living below the poverty line are to be found in South Asia (31.3 percent) and sub-Saharan Africa (36.9 percent). China has made the most impressive strides in reducing the proportion of population living below the poverty line. Between 1981 and 2001, this proportion declined from 63.8 percent to 16.6 percent.[26]

For analysing the impact of multilateral trade reform at a global level, applied general equilibrium (AGE) models were found a useful tool in the past. Whally (1985) and Martin and Winters (1996) put this tool to good use in the context of the Tokyo Round and the Uruguay Round, respectively. AGE models capture the detailed interactions across the many agents of an economy, which includes producers, consumers, public entities, investors and exporters. Despite their level of representation, they present a stylized representation of an economy. For instance the version of model used for WB (2002) represented economic activity by only 20 goods and services sectors. This analysis decomposed the world economy into 15 regions and 20 economic activities. The model was calibrated to the latest release of the Global Trade Analysis Program (GTAP) dataset with a 1997 base year.

According to World Bank (2002) estimates, success in the Doha Round would lift 320 million out of absolute poverty. That is, it could cut the number of people living in poverty by 8 percent per year by 2015. Besides, it can potentially lift global income by $2.8 trillion by 2015. Of this, $1.5 trillion would accrue to the developing economies.[27] Hertel *et al.* (2004) developed a micro-simulation model to assess impact of trade liberalization on household income. They posited that 'in the short run household incomes will be differentially affected by global trade liberalization, depending on their reliance on sector-specific factors of production'. Their methodology was applied to an assessment of the consequences of global trade liberalization in the following sectors: merchandise tariffs, agricultural export subsidies, and quotas on textiles and apparel. This study focused on Indonesia and concluded that the national headcount measure of poverty declines following global trade liberalization both in the short- and long-term. In the long run the poverty headcount in Indonesia fell for all strata of poverty. Increased demand for unskilled workers lifted income for the formerly self-employed, some of whom moved into the wage labor market. Thus viewed, successful rounds of MTNs do have a discernible favorable impact over the incidence of poverty.

SUMMARY AND CONCLUSIONS

The global community has repeatedly demonstrated its strong commitment to economic growth and poverty amelioration. Its latest manifestation was the Millennium Development Goals (MDGs), particularly the first one that aims at halving income-poverty by 2015. Two more global conferences, held in 2002, strengthened the same commitments, namely, the United Nations Conference on Financing for Development, held in Monterrey, Mexico, and the World Summit on Sustainable Development, held in Johannesburg, South Africa. This chapter argues that like the MDGs, the global community needs to adopt the policy objective of economic growth and poverty alleviation by means of an ambitious program of multilateral trade policy reforms. To be sure, such a reform program will need to have an ambitious vision of coordinated global policy action. Its ultimate objective would be to buttress the MDGs. The DDA can be an effective tool for achieving the first MDG.

A stupendous stock of knowledge exists on the trade growth nexus. Notwithstanding disagreements among researchers and theorists, comprehensible policy preference for outward-orientation growth strategy has emerged in the public policy-making community over the last three decades. On the multilateral side, the trading system has evolved over the preceding six decades of its existence from a small regime covering a limited area of global trade to a large one, with much wider scope and nearly universal membership. The edifice of the WTO was created on the foundation of the GATT, a much smaller organization in terms of coverage of trade rules and membership. Multilateral trade discipline has helped to improve macro-economic and trade performance of the member economies. A multilateral system of common rules and a mutually agreed code of conduct among the WTO members can and does reduce uncertainties among trading partners by placing boundaries on the policies adopted by members.

Trade barriers have a high welfare cost and the multilateral trade regime has been endeavoring to bring them down in a steady and methodological manner. The multilateral trade regime has evolved through various 'rounds' of MTNs. So far eight rounds of MTNs were held under the sponsorship of the GATT, while the present on-going Doha Round is being conducted under the aegis of the WTO. There were marked variations in the coverage of different rounds. It is noteworthy that the evolution of the multilateral trade regime was essentially unbalanced, uneven and took place in fits and starts, and it certainly became more intricate and complex with the passage of time.

By the late-1970s, a group of developing economies had become traders of significance. More middle-income developing countries began to trade and proactively participate in the multilateral trade regime in the 1980s. During the decade of the 1990s, developing economies recorded an average merchandise export growth rate which was one-third higher than that of the industrial economies. Many of them emerged as successful exporters of manufactures. Their growth endeavors and progressive globalization during the 1980s and

1990s helped to alter the global economic and trade scenario. Many developing countries were no longer insignificant import markets and became substantive exporters. Both market size and export volume began to matter for the first time. The EMEs, among them the NIEs, deserve a particular mention in this regard. More than 25 of the developing economies earned the status of the EMEs and integrated better with the global economy than the other developing economies. This changed situation was evident during the Uruguay Round. For the first time at least the EMEs were brought into the fold of the GATT as something of equal trading partners of industrial economies.

It should be noted that while the linkage between trade and poverty alleviation are not direct, one cannot deny that there are indirect channels linking poverty alleviation with multilateral trade liberalization. Estimates suggest that successful culmination of the on-going Doha Round of MTNs can lift 320 million out of absolute poverty. That is, it could cut the number of people living in poverty by 8 percent per year by 2015. Besides, it can potentially lift global income by \$2.8 trillion by 2015. Of this, \$1.5 trillion would accrue to the developing economies.

NOTES

1. The United Nations Conference on Financing for Development was held in Monterrey, Mexico, from 18–22 March 2002, and the World Summit on Sustainable Development was held in Johannesburg, South Africa, from 26 August to 4 September 2002.
2. Although most-favored nation (MFN) sounds like a contradiction, implying some kind of special treatment to a particular trade partner, in the WTO jargon it means non-discrimination. That is, treating all trade partners under the WTO regime equally. Each WTO member treats all the WTO members as 'most-favored' trading partners. If any country improves the market benefits to one trading partner, it is obliged to give the same best treatment to all the other WTO members so that they all remain 'most-favored'. However, historically MFN did not mean equal treatment.
3. Principal among the early studies are Little *et al.* (1970), Balassa (1971) and Krueger (1978).
4. Reference here is to the well known researches of Paul Romer (1986), Robert Lucas (1988) and Grossman and Helpman (1991).
5. See, for instance, Dollar (1992), Sachs and Warner (1995), Harrison (1996) and Edwards (1998).
6. The Uruguay Round was the eighth round of MTN. It was launched in September 1986 and culminated in April 1994, with the signing of the Marrakesh Agreement. At the time of the launch 86 Contracting Parties (CPs) participated in it. When it was completed, this number had increased to 123.
7. In November 1947, delegations from 56 countries met in Havana, Cuba, to consider the ITO draft. After long and difficult negotiations, some 53 countries signed the Final Act authenticating the text of the Havana Charter in March 1948. There was no commitment, however, from governments to ratification and, in the end, the ITO was stillborn, leaving GATT as the only international instrument governing the conduct of world trade.
8. The majority of the WTO agreements are the result of the multilateral trade negotiations during the Uruguay Round (1986–94). They were signed at the Marrakesh Ministerial Conference on 15 April 1994, in Marrakesh, Morocco. The so-called 'Final Act' signed in Marrakesh was like a cover note. Everything else was attached to it. Foremost was the

agreement establishing the WTO, which served as an umbrella agreement. Annexed were the agreements on trade in goods and services, as well as agreements on intellectual property, dispute settlement, the trade policy review mechanism and the plurilateral agreements. The Marrakesh Agreement was developed out of the General Agreement on Tariffs and Trade (GATT), which it included. However, the WTO supplemented the GATT with several other agreements on such issues as trade in services, sanitary and plant health measures, trade-related aspects of intellectual property rights, and technical barriers to trade. The Marrakesh Agreement also established a new, more efficient and legally binding means of dispute resolution.

9.   So far six Ministerial Conferences have taken place under the sponsorship of the WTO. They were held in Singapore (9–13 December 1996), Geneva (18–29 May 1998), Seattle (30 November to 3 December 1999), Doha (10–14 September 2001), Cancún (10–14 September 2003) and Hong Kong SAR (13–18 December 2005).

10. The decision to launch it was taken during the fourth Ministerial Conference, held in Doha, Qatar, 9–13 November 2001.

11. While there are numerous literature surveys, one of the most recent and eminently readable one is *Trade, Growth and Poverty: Selective Survey*, by A. Berg and A. O. Krueger (2003). Giles and Williams (2000) provided another comprehensive survey of more than 150 export-growth applied papers. They described the changes that have occurred over the last two decades, in the methodologies used empirically to examine for relationships between exports and economic growth, and provided information on the current findings. The 1990s saw an abundance of time series studies that focused on examining for causality via exclusions restrictions tests, impulse response function analysis and forecast error variance decompositions. They found that that the results of studies examining export-led growth based on standard causality techniques were not typically robust to specification or method.

12. Fifty countries are presently designated by the United Nations as 'least developed countries' (LDCs). Of these, 32 were the members of the WTO in mid-2006. The list is reviewed every three years by the Economic and Social Council (ECOSOC) of the United Nations. In its latest triennial review in 2003, the ECOSOC used the following three criteria for the identification of the LDCs, which were proposed by the Committee for Development Policy (CDP): (a) a low-income criterion, based on a three-year average estimate of the gross domestic product per capita (under $750 for inclusion, above $900 for graduation); (b) a human resource weakness criterion, involving a composite Augmented Physical Quality of Life Index (APQLI) based on indicators of: (i) nutrition; (ii) health; (iii) education; and (iv) adult literacy; and (c) an economic vulnerability criterion, involving a composite Economic Vulnerability Index (EVI) based on indicators of: (i) the instability of agricultural production; (ii) the instability of exports of goods and services; (iii) the economic importance of non-traditional activities (share of manufacturing and modern services in GDP); (iv) merchandise export concentration; and (v) the handicap of economic smallness (as measured through the population in logarithm); and the percentage of population displaced by natural disasters.

13. When it came into effect in January 1948, the General Agreement on Tariffs and Trade had 23 signatories, namely, Australia, Belgium, Brazil, Burma, Canada, Ceylon, Chile, China, Cuba, Czechoslovakia, France, India, Lebanon, Luxembourg, the Netherlands, New Zealand, Norway, Pakistan, Southern Rhodesia, Syria, South Africa, the United Kingdom and the United States.

14. The Uruguay Round was launched in the modish holiday resort town of Punta del Este, Uruguay, in September 1986.

15. See footnote 6.

16. The First Ministerial Conference of the WTO was held in Singapore in 1996. During this conference Ministers from WTO-member countries decided to set up three new working groups: (a) on trade and investment, (b) on competition policy, and (c) on transparency in government procurement. They also instructed the WTO Goods Council to look at possible ways of simplifying trade procedures, an issue sometimes known as 'trade facilitation'. Because the Singapore conference kicked off work in these four subjects, they have become known as the 'Singapore issues'.

17. Enshrined in Article I of the GATT, and subsequently the WTO, the most-favored-nation (MFN) principle is the cornerstone of the multilateral trading system. It is Article II of the General Agreement on Trade in Services (GATS) and Article IV of the Agreement on Trade-Related Aspects of Intellectual Property Rights (TRIPS). According to this principle countries cannot normally discriminate between their trading partners. The expression most-favored-nation (MFN) sounds like an oxymoron. It suggests some kind of special treatment for one particular country, but it means non-discrimination, that is, treating everybody equally. Each member of the WTO treats all the other members equally as 'most favored' trading partners. If a member country improves the benefits that it gives to one trading partner, it is obliged to give the same 'best' treatment to all the other WTO members so that they all remain 'most favored'. The expression MFN originated in the nineteenth century, when its meaning was just the opposite of what it is at present. A number of MFN treaties were signed during this period. Being a 'most favored' trading partner was like being in an exclusive club, because only a few countries enjoyed the privilege.
18. Refer to Das (2001), in particular Chapter 1.
19. This part draws on Chapter 6 of the *Global Economic Prospects* (2004) published by the World Bank. See pp. 205–31.
20. Emerging-market economy (EME) was a term coined by Antoine W. van Agtmael of the International Finance Corporation in 1981. It is loosely defined as a market economy with low-to-middle per capita income that participates globally by implementing reform programs. Such economies represent 20 percent of the world economy. Countries whose economies fall into this category vary from very big to very small. They are usually considered emerging because of their fast-clip growth rate and the reforms undertaken by them. Hence, even though China is deemed as one of the world's economic powerhouses, it is lumped into the EME category alongside much smaller economies with a great deal fewer resources, like Tunisia. Both China and Tunisia belong to this category because both have embarked on economic development and reform programs, and have begun to open up their markets and 'emerge' onto the global economic scene. EMEs are considered to be fast growing economies. One key characteristic of the EME is an increase in both local and foreign investment, both portfolio and direct. A growth in investment in a country often indicates that the country has been able to build investors' confidence in the domestic economy. Moreover, foreign investment is a signal that the world has begun to take notice of the emerging market, and when international capital flows are directed toward an EME, the injection of foreign currency into the local economy adds volume to the country's stock market and long-term investment to the infrastructure.
21. The NIEs group comprises Chile, Hong Kong SAR, Korea, Singapore and Taiwan.
22. In a trade agreement, the negotiating parties make reciprocal concessions to put their trade relationships on a basis deemed equitable by each. The principle of reciprocity is extremely old, and in one form or another it is to be found in all trade agreements. The concessions exchanged by the negotiating parties are, however, in different areas.
23. At the time of writing, the G-20 has the following 21 members: Argentina, Bolivia, Brazil, Chile, China, Colombia, Costa Rica, Cuba, Ecuador, Egypt, Guatemala, India, Indonesia, Mexico, Nigeria, Pakistan, Paraguay, Peru, Philippines, South Africa, Thailand and Venezuela. The role of collegial leaders of G-20 was played by Brazil, China, India and South Africa.
24. See Bigsten and Levin (2001), Cline (2004) and Dollar and Kraay (2001).
25. Refer to two recent works of Winters (2000b) and McCulloch *et al.* (2001).
26. See Chen and Ravallion (2004), Table 2 and Table 3.
27. See the World Bank (2002), Chapter 6.

2. Necessity for a development round

> To my mind the development of the poorer countries is very much the concern of the WTO, but it is a concern which is limited by its remit, which is to facilitate trade. Those of us who believe in global economic integration and the benign effects of trade think a multilateral system can help create equal opportunity and through equal opportunity the development of better opportunities for the poor.
>
> (Peter Sutherland, 2004)

INTRODUCTION

That the Uruguay Round (1986–94) was a landmark in the systemic process of evolution of the multilateral trade regime is universally acknowledged. After some initial nervousness and uncertainties, the developing economies participated in the Uruguay Round, although not in the most adroit manner. In the end they did not think that the final outcome was favorable to them and their trade-related interests. This chapter addresses the question why in the process of its evolution it was necessary for the World Trade Organization (WTO) to have a new round of multilateral trade negotiations (MTNs) and that it should be a development round. This chapter logically tees off with the significance of the Uruguay Round in the multilateral trading system and moves on to the ongoing Doha Round of MTNs and its objectives, rationale and wide-ranging policy space.

As regards the structure of this chapter, the second section begins with the enormous achievements of the Uruguay Round and explains why the developing economies did not get enough out of it. The third section covers the successful launching of a fresh round of MTNs with an ambitious agenda and policy space. The fourth section addresses the issue of striking a balance between the needs and interests of different country groups in the MTNs, and adjusting the new Doha Round modalities accordingly. More starkly, the fifth section deals with the much needed course correction for the multilateral trade regime, for which the Doha Round could be an instrument. Areas of specific focus for redressing the imbalances in the multilateral trade regime have been indicated in the sixth section. That trade in services is one potential area with substantive developmental gains is widely acknowledged; progress or lack thereof is the focus of the seventh section. The final section provides a summary and conclusions.

SYSTEMIC EVOLUTION: PARTICIPATION BY THE DEVELOPING ECONOMIES

As alluded to in Chapter 1 (pp. 19–21), during the mid-1980s the developing countries' participation in the multilateral trade regime intensified significantly. They even formed a Group-of-Ten (G-10) which was led by Brazil and India.[1] It was active in the initial phase of the Uruguay Round, which was launched in September 1986. This development came about rapidly, if somewhat abruptly. The G-10 did not go down in history as a successful coalition. It did not have negotiating strength, could not achieve much and eventually splintered. This section delves into these issues as well as how the developing economies emerged from their first major experience of full participation in an MTNs.

Accelerating Participation of the Developing Economies

Consider the questions why the participation of developing countries accelerated during this period, and why this conceptual transformation took place in the developing economies? Why did they turn away from the import-substituting industrialization (ISI) strategy toward a more outward-oriented, export-led, liberal economic regime? An oft-cited reason is the demonstration effect of the economic achievements of Japan and the so-called Asian tiger economies. The other reasons were the debt crisis of the early 1980s, the apparent failure of central planning and the socialist model of growth and the emergence of export lobbies in developing countries that created domestic constituencies in some large- and middle-income developing economies for the adoption of outward-oriented growth strategy. The economic downturn of the early 1980s had rendered the developing economies vulnerable, driving them to the upcoming round of MTNs in the hope of some economic relief through trade expansion. Also, during this period various protectionist measures, known as the gray-area measures, were on the rise against those developing economies that were beginning to be successful exporters (Chapter 1, pp. 19–21). The developing countries saw a logical defense in adopting multilateralism, hoping to protect their trade interests. By participating in the MTNs they had a reasonable chance of influencing the new trade rule formulation exercise.

Before the launch of the Uruguay Round, many developing economies had begun undertaking unilateral trade liberalization in their domestic economies. This was the first major step by several developing economies toward full participation in the global economy, the multilateral trade regime and the MTNs. One of the noteworthy pre-Uruguay Round developments was that after long drawn negotiations – which were not always agreeable – developing economies were persuaded by the industrial economies to include the so-called new issues, namely, trade in services, Trade Related Intellectual Property Rights (TRIPS) and Trade Related Investment Measures (TRIMS) in the forthcoming MTNs. Led by the United States, interest from the industrial economies in the new issues was high. However, the G-10 countries were bitterly averse to the inclusion of the new issues in the Uruguay Round and kept resisting their inclusion in the MTNs until quite late. The US took an equally hard line and did not support the launch of a new round of MTNs without the new issues. Eventually the developing economies agreed conditionally. As a *quid pro quo* the developing countries asked for the inclusion of trade in agriculture and textiles and apparel, two of the most distorted sectors of world trade, to be brought under multilateral trade discipline. Such give and take in agenda formulation was unprecedented in MTNs.

Ineffectual Group-of-Ten Leadership

Strong aversion of the developing economies, represented by the G-10, to the new issues, particularly to inclusion of services, did not go very far. Under pressure from the US and the other large traders, they eventually caved in. Although they were able to influence the MTN agenda, inclusion of the new issues in the Uruguay Round smacked of failure for them. The developing economies saw that their developing-country-based coalition did not have a great deal of weight in the MTNs, and was close to ineffectual. Led by Colombia and Switzerland, another group called Café au Lait emerged, which brought together a coalition of both developing and industrial countries. Its success was represented by the fact that its draft proposal became the basis of the agenda of the Uruguay Round. Unlike the G-10, Café au Lait succeeded because it used integrative bargaining strategy. The G-10 had tried to resist the agenda prepared by the General Agreement on Tariffs and Trade (GATT) squarely and tenaciously on the strength of their demand for distributive justice. Instead, Café au Lait forwarded its detailed proposal based on extensive research on the potential issues that were needed to be taken up and fairly extensive discussion among the contracting parties (CPs) – both developing and industrial. The agenda proposal prepared by the Café au Lait had an issue-based focus that suggested fairness of the process. Therefore, they succeeded in making a significant contribution to the final agenda.

The other country group that was active and successful during this period was the Cairns Group of countries[2] that exported agricultural and agro-industrial products. This group also had joint membership of developing and industrial countries and was devoted exclusively to liberalization of agriculture within the framework of the GATT. Its demand conformed to the dominant institutional norms, that is, trade liberalization. Its position was absolutely legitimate and within the framework of multilateralism. It constantly applied negotiating pressure for, first, inclusion of trade in agriculture into the GATT discipline and second its liberalization in a systematic manner, which placed the EU and the US on the defensive. This was something unprecedented and had happened for the first time under the GATT regime. During the negotiations, the Cairns Group repeatedly threatened to block negotiations until substantive commitments were made in liberalizing trade in agriculture by the EU and the US.

Members of the G-10 observed this negotiations dynamic. Changing country group alignments and emerging negotiations dynamics provided a lesson to the G-10, its coalition model and negotiations strategy. Unlike the G-10, Café au Lait and the Cairns Group succeeded phenomenally and received the fulsome support of the CPs, including the developing economies. The G-10 saw that trade-offs and integrative bargaining were far superior to claims of distributive justice. It also observed that integrative bargaining directly affected outcomes of the negotiations. It was also evident that pragmatic issue-based coalitions that combined developing and industrial countries were functional, particularly when the CPs adhered to reciprocity and multilateralism. Consequently the emphasis of the developing economies on special and differential treatment (SDT) temporarily weakened during the Uruguay Round.

Was the Uruguay Round a Landmark?

Economists, trade analysts and practitioners regard the Uruguay Round, the last round of multilateral trade negotiations under the old GATT regime, as a milestone for good reasons. Compared to the preceding seven rounds, the Uruguay Round was the most ambitious and comprehensive. Although it was beset by serious disagreements and delays, frequently came to the brink of collapse and took four more years to be completed than originally planned, its achievements were the largest of any GATT round. It not only produced the most fundamental reforms but also discernibly widened and deepened the multilateral trade regime. It was the most fundamental event in the multilateral trade regime since the genesis of the GATT in 1948. It introduced multilateral trade discipline into a far wider coverage of products and a larger number of countries than ever before. When it ended, it was a testimony to a wider and deeper commitment to trade liberalization by the multilateral trading community.

Among the greatest accomplishments of the Uruguay Round were bringing trade in agricultural and agro-industrial products under multilateral discipline as well as creating of the General Agreement on Trade in Services (GATS) and the WTO. Built on the old foundation of the GATT, the new organization strengthened the multilateral trading system with substantially stronger procedures for settling trade disputes than those of the GATT. Unlike its predecessor, the WTO also had a mechanism for reviewing the trade policies of the member countries called the trade policy review mechanism (TPRM), which would contribute to greater transparency in trade policy. In addition, the WTO promoted greater involvement of the trade ministers of the member countries in the rule-making procedures.

Although Uruguay Round commitments did not result in a large reduction in protection in agriculture, its reincorporation into the multilateral trade discipline was a meaningful development. It irreversibly changed attitudes of the trading economies, both importers and exporters. It also laid a groundwork for future trade liberalization in agriculture. The Uruguay Round marked a turning point in the involvement of the developing economies in the MTNs, which was reflected in their extensive tariff bindings, participation in agreements on trade policies to liberalize trade restrictions of various kinds and general acceptance of the rights and obligations that went with full membership of the newly created WTO.

It would take us too far afield to enumerate the various agreements reached during the Uruguay Round, albeit some of the most remarkable developments can be mentioned briefly. During the Kennedy Round (1964–7) and the Tokyo Round (1973–9) of MTNs, all the liberalization commitments were made by the industrial economies. The developing countries *en masse* benefited from them because of the most-favored-nation (MFN) principle, making them a 'free rider' of the GATT system. However, the negative aspect of this was that the developing countries lost out because industrial economies excluded the trade sectors of interest for the developing economies from the MTNs (Chapter 1, pp. 14–16). Special protectionist agreement like the multi-fiber arrangement (MFA), which was an anathema to the spirit of the GATT, was allowed to maintain quantitative restrictions on trade in textiles and apparel. This is a large and low-technology industrial sector, in which many developing countries had comparative advantage. The status of trade in textile and apparel changed during the Uruguay Round. An Agreement on Textile and Clothing (ATC), one of the several struck during the Uruguay Round, brought this sector into the realm of the multilateral trade discipline. The CPs agreed to bring trade in textiles and clothing under the multilateral trade regime in stages, by 1 January 2005. The developing countries signed all the agreements, even the TRIPS agreement which was *prima facie* detrimental to their interests. They accepted it as a cost of obtaining concessions in the areas of their interest, like agriculture and textiles and apparel.

During the Uruguay Round, the developing economies participated in formulating new rules of the multilateral trading system (see Chapter 5). They also made significant market access offers in conventional areas of tariff protection on manufactures, as well as in areas that were new to trade liberalization processes, like trade in agricultural products and services.

Being latecomers to the multilateral trading system, the quality of participation of the developing economies was far from optimal. As latecomers they began as the rule-followers not the rule-makers and largely as agenda-followers not the agenda-setters. One major transformation that occurred was that after the Uruguay Round, the developing economies – small and large – no longer played the role of sideliners. They began engaging themselves in rule – and agenda formulation exercises of the MTNs. For the first time the developing economies collectively called for global redistributive justice in the multilateral trading system. Their influence on the multilateral trading system has undeniably been on the rise ever since.

By embracing the Uruguay Round agreement in its entirety the developing countries assumed full rights and obligations of the WTO, the newly created institution.[3] This stupendous commitment in effect gave them a new voice in influencing the design of multilateral trade agenda and a right to participate in the running of the multilateral trading system. It would be unrealistic and improbable to expect them to gain from every aspect of their participation. There were areas in which they clearly did not gain or lose. Empirical studies that attempted to size up gains and losses inferred that on balance the developing economies benefited from the Uruguay Round.[4] If the GATT/WTO system has evolved in fits and starts, this certainly was its brisk growth period. Notwithstanding its incessant procedural problems, the Uruguay Round finally produced the most profound reforms in the substance of multilateral trade regime.

Hangover of the Uruguay Round

Although developing economies' interest in international trade was on the rise in the mid-1980s, the majority had felt unconvinced and less confident about participating in a full-fledged round of MTNs. Despite initial hesitations and diffidence, their decision to engage actively in the Uruguay Round was to all appearances voluntary. However, Deardorff and Stern (2003) disagree with the view that their participation in the Uruguay Round was really a unilateral decision. They believe that the developing economies were 'brought on board by promises that were misleading or not likely to be kept' by the industrial economies.

Although they were a highly disparate group, disagreed with each other on a wide range of issues and frequently worked at cross-purposes, the developing economies made their presence felt in the Uruguay Round negotiations. Notwithstanding the disagreements among them, developing economies made several forays to influence the outcome of the Uruguay Round in their favor. For various reasons, their success in this endeavor was rather limited, if not completely dubious. Furthermore, as the developing economies were participating for the first time in a round of MTNs, their negotiating and participation skills were short. In addition, in several subjects under negotiation their analytical and technical skills were grossly insufficient and their understanding meager. Their negotiating strategies had not developed to achieve any objectives that they were aiming for. Little wonder that the G-10 was not very successful in achieving its objectives.

Hoekman (2004) noted that after the Uruguay Round, the developing economies observed that the 'single undertaking' subjected them to most of the disciplines and agreements, although after the transition periods have expired.[5] They also realized somewhat belatedly that many of the agreements they had signed had little benefit for them. The so-called 'grand bargain' of the Uruguay Round had a high cost to the developing economies. Also, 'in case of some agreements the perception rapidly emerged that benefits were highly skewed towards rich countries'.

Proper stocktaking at the end of the Uruguay Round revealed to the developing countries that in their zeal to participate in issue-based coalitions they lost their limited collective negotiating strength. They also belatedly found that 'issue-based coalitions had short lives, high transaction costs, and offered limited bargaining leeway. Second, in return for a promise of concessions on agriculture and textiles and clothing in the future, developing countries had bound themselves to a considerably intrusive system of rules' (Narlikar, 2006). What was worse was that while liberalization of trade in agriculture and phasing out of the MFA were placed on the agenda, they were not made a part of the general rules of the GATT-1994. They were merely treated as a set of sector-specific agreements. Trade in agriculture was not significantly liberalized and it continued to be an insurmountable roadblock to progress even in the Doha Round.

Another post-Uruguay Round surprise that awaited the developing economies was regarding the unanticipated cost of implementing the Uruguay Round commitments. In many cases they were exorbitant, particularly for the small developing countries. Finger and Schuler (2002) computed the cost of the implementation of the customs valuation agreement for one small developing country, Jamaica. Total cost of training of personnel, computing equipment and database and additional staff was going to cost Jamaica $840000. If the cost of implementing other Uruguay Round agreements is added up for only one developing country, this cost becomes excessively high – enough to deter the government from implementing the agreements.

The resulting 'Uruguay Round hangover' led to a great deal of skepticism among the developing countries regarding the benefits of WTO membership.

Consequently, policy-makers in many developing economies and in the non-governmental organizations (NGOs) began to view the prospects of adhering to additional agreements and disciplines in the multilateral trading system with a high degree of skepticism, even mistrust. Hoekman (2004) made a valid point when he observed, 'The Uruguay Round hangover has made them very aware of the downside of signing on to agreements that are ill understood and that have little if any backing by domestic stakeholders. Indeed, many developing countries are now actively seeking to improve their "terms of trade" in the WTO'. Thus viewed, the final outcome of the Uruguay Round was of dubious benefit for the developing economies. The developing economies also learned from the Uruguay Round that their calls for distributive justice were not going to produce any results in future MTNs. Another lesson was that their unilateral liberalization of the mid-1980s and eagerness to participate in the MTNs failed to deliver the promised goods. The realization came home that they were rash in taking on reciprocity.

TINKERING WITH THE EVOLUTION: RIGHTING THE WRONGS OF HISTORY

As the earlier rounds of MTNs focused on the issues of interest to the industrial economies, a good deal of institutional and academic dialog took place on the need for a round on the issues of interest to the developing economies. The 1995–2001 period, which was the intervening period covering the completion of the Uruguay Round and the launch of the Doha Round, was focused on an elongated intellectual dialog and policy debates on the need to redress the imbalance in this regard.

That there was an imperious need to integrate various sub-groups of developing economies fully into the multilateral trading system was emphasized by many trade analysts. Various sub-groups among the developing economies have differing expectations from the global trading system. Extensive suggestions of a future development round, having a development and developing-country oriented agenda, centered on the issues of concern for various sub-groups of developing economies, were ubiquitous. Each proponent of a development round posited an appropriate agenda that would meet the needs and demands of different groups and sub-groups of developing economies. Each one put forward a new contour of the multilateral trade regime. Organizational changes in the WTO and those in its operations and emphases were also suggested by academic scholars and practicing trade economists.[6]

In 1999, during the Third Ministerial Conference of the WTO, in Seattle, attempts to launch a new round of MTNs were aborted because of deep-seated disagreements among the members on *inter alia* the agenda. Not only many member countries but also trade analysts and practitioners did not support the proposal of launching a new round of MTNs so soon after the completion of the Uruguay Round, particularly before many of the commitments made in Marrakesh in 1994 were even close to implementation. It could not be ignored that the Uruguay Round took four years of preparation and seven more years after that to complete. Besides, if launched in 1999, the new round of MTNs would have superseded the built-in agenda of the Uruguay Round in agriculture and services.

As alluded to above (pp. 38–40), many developing economies were highly discontented about the final outcome of the Uruguay Round. They were candidly questioning their role and purpose in the multilateral trade regime. Furthermore, this was also the period when globalization was being seriously questioned, systematically misunderstood and acerbically criticized. It was borne out by the street theater in Seattle during the Third Ministerial Conference, which is universally considered a symbol of comprehensive failure of the GATT/WTO system. There were a host of clear reasons behind the discord, dissention and ultimate collapse in Seattle, which have been analysed in numerous scholarly writings.[7] It caused apprehension among the WTO members regarding its institutional soundness and ability to reach consensus on trade and economic policy issues. The failure in Seattle created a concern about the general institutional capabilities of the multilateral trading system, even the stability of the global economic framework. However two years later, members of the WTO reached a consensus regarding launching a new round of MTNs. The Doha Round of MTNs was launched in Doha, the capital of Qatar, following the Fourth Ministerial Conference of the WTO.

Breakthrough in Doha: Launching a New Round of MTNs

After surfeit of disagreements and controversies in Seattle, the agreement to launch the Doha Round among the 142 WTO members came through during the Doha Ministerial Conference during 9–13 November, 2001. The Doha Round, driven by the Doha Development Agenda (DDA), was widely regarded as something of a breakthrough. First under the aegis of the WTO, at the time of the launch, this round of MTN was scheduled to conclude in January 2005. Launching a new round bolstered confidence in the WTO as a multilateral negotiating forum for traders and in the multilateral trading system.

A systemic leap that was made in Doha was that the WTO members took the intellectual debates about the need to redress the imbalances seriously and acted on them. They agreed to take the 'the development dimension seriously across the board', although some cynically thought of it as mere post-Seattle spin (Lamy, 2003).[8] The Doha Ministerial Declaration candidly acknowledged that the benefits of trade needed to be more widely distributed among the members of the WTO (WTO, 2001a). The Doha Round of MTNs was christened the development round by the WTO secretariat. The DDA made growth and development the principal focus of this round of MTNs. Pascal Lamy (2006b), the Director General of the WTO,[9] conceded that this was done in recognition of the fact that 'there remains, in today's multilateral trading systems, rules and disciplines, and imbalances that penalize developing economies – and this must be corrected'.

The basic intention in naming it a development round was to try to improve the multilateral disciplines and commitment by all members of the WTO in such a manner that they 'establish a more level playing field and provide developing countries with better conditions to enable them to reap the benefits of trade liberalization'. The Doha Declaration document showed that many aspects of developing country needs were paid attention to, in particular their implementation related requirements. The Doha Ministerial communiqué document uses words like 'development' and 'developing' 63 times in 10 pages and 52 paragraphs' (WTO, 2001a). This could not mean mere lip service by the members. It is safe and fair to assume that at the time of the launch it was expected that the final outcome of the Doha Round will have discernible developmental implications. Since then, the governments of the industrial countries repeatedly pointed to the Doha Round as evidence of their commitment to create a more equitable pattern of globalization (Watkins, 2003). Peter Sutherland (2004) aptly remarked that 'the Doha Round would be a crucial test for multilateralism'.[10]

Three-Pronged Challenge

The priorities of a development round were obvious. The first, and vitally important, task for the developing economies during the development round was mentioned in the Doha Declaration alluded to above, that is, to work towards achieving a rebalancing of the multilateral trading system in such a manner that the newly evolving multilateral trade rules establish a level playing field and support economic growth in an effective manner. However, they needed to work for more than merely rebalancing the multilateral trade regime. The other two crucial and closely related challenges that they faced were: first, convincing and inducing the large trading industrial economies as well as China to improve market access for their export products, and second, starting a domestic campaign to educate and persuade domestic stakeholders regarding the payoffs from an export-led growth strategy. This would be followed by domestic macroeconomic policy reforms in synchronization with external sector reforms, which in turn would be locked in through the requirement of the WTO discipline.

Designing and implementing a triple-pronged strategy on the lines indicated above would indeed take time and concerted effort. However, it would be worthwhile adopting a pragmatic and comprehensive strategy in this regard. It will potentially have much larger payoff than the uni-dimensional strategy followed by many developing economies in the past. The developing economies are *demandeurs* in this regard and have high stakes in using the multilateral trading system to their benefit. It includes the benefits of adopting sound macroeconomic policies, based on rigorous neoclassical economic principles and the so-called Washington consensus.[11]

Wide-ranging Agenda Space

After prolonged deliberations before and during the Fourth Ministerial Conference of the WTO, members agreed on a wide-ranging array of negotiating areas in the MTNs. While the principle areas in the DDA are agriculture, manufactures and services, the comprehensive list includes the following issues: implementation-related issues; agriculture; services; market access; TRIPS; trade and competition policy; trade and investment; government procurement; trade facilitation; WTO rules; dispute settlement understanding; trade and environment; electronic commerce; small economies; trade, debt and finance; transfer of technology; technical co-operation; least-developed countries; special and differential treatment (SDT); and organization of the work program (WTO, 2001a). Such a wide spread of the agenda space made the Doha Round another comprehensive round of the MTNs, comparable to the Uruguay Round.

As the WTO (more correctly its predecessor the GATT) as an institution, and the multilateral community of trade ministers and trade delegations, had had the experience of bringing the extensive Uruguay Round to a successful conclusion, albeit after seriously staggering several times, they had the confidence to launch into another comparably extensive round of MTNs with equally wide-ranging scope, and had several subject matters for in-depth negotiations. The Doha Ministerial Conference was decisively influenced by lessons learned from the debacle in Seattle in many ways. In addition, in 2001 the global economy perceived a coming recession, which intensified the interest of the world trading and business communities and the WTO member governments in launching a fresh round of MTNs. Failure in Seattle had left a pall of frustration and disillusionment regarding the multilateral trading system, and the WTO members were raring to come out of it.

It is widely agreed in the community of trade analysts, economists and practitioners that liberalizing markets for trade in agriculture, in manufactured products and services can buttress global economic growth and development as well as potentially having a salutary influence over the developing economies, in particular the absolute poor in these economies. It was hoped that the new round of MTNs would deliver substantive results in terms of further trade liberalization in both goods and services. What the global economy needed was something more than a lowest-common-denominator text of politically safe but commercially meaningless diplomatic verbiage.

Furthermore, during the planning phase of the DDA, attention was paid to the need of delivering more to developing economies than they received from the eight GATT rounds of MTNs in the past for the reasons discussed above (pp. 5–6 and Chapter 1). It was expected that liberalization of multilateral trade in agriculture and non-agricultural market access (NAMA) would receive a great deal of attention from the industrial countries, which in turn would benefit the poorest in the developing economies. Although not a part of the 'Single Undertaking', a reform of Dispute Settlement Understanding (DSU) and addressing the vulnerability of least-developed countries (LDCs)[12] were also agreed to be taken up during the new round of MTNs by the participating trade ministers during the Doha Ministerial Conference.

It is often assumed that a great deal of trade liberalization has taken place since the birth of the GATT in terms of tariff slashing. No doubt average unweighted tariffs are exceedingly low in the industrial economies (6.1 percent), but they are still high for some regions. For instance, South Asian (30.7 percent) and Middle Eastern and North African (19.3 percent) economies still have high average unweighted tariffs.[13] Notwithstanding the achievements of the eight rounds of MTNs, reducing tariff barriers in many areas of trade and in many country groups is still critical. Hoekman (2004) estimated that a 50 percent global tariff cut will have a much greater positive effect on exports and welfare of the developing economies than a 50 percent cut in subsidies. The reason is that tariffs for subsidized products continue to be very high. They frequently take the form of non-transparent specific duties.

A Developmental Round: Abiding by the Basic Principles

Thus viewed, a good deal of thought and planning went into the Doha Round, which is the ninth round of MTNs under the aegis of the WTO. Steered by the DDA, it promised a novel and unprecedented direction to the MTNs and called for a new mindset among negotiators from both industrial and developing economies. A transformation of a basic nature was to be introduced into the multilateral trade regime through the Doha Round. As the Doha Ministerial Declaration emphasized, the development dimension was being taken earnestly by the WTO members. Developmental concerns formed an integral part, not only of the Doha Ministerial Declaration, but also of subsequent July Package (31 July 2004) or the so-called July Framework Agreement. The General Council of the WTO,[14] which is the WTO's highest-level decision-making body in Geneva, rededicated the WTO members to fulfilling the development dimension of the DDA, which placed the needs and interests of developing economies and LDCs at the heart of the Doha Work Program. It was time for the members to banish the ghosts of mercantilism and set these negotiations firmly on the path to achieving the valuable objectives of the round as well as the shared goal of global economic growth and poverty amelioration.

The evidence of members' commitments to the objectives of the Doha Round abounded. It was reflected not only in the July Framework Agreement but also in the other stages of the Doha Round. The General Council reiterated the 'importance of the role that enhanced market access, balanced rules, and well targeted, sustainably financed technical assistance and capacity building programs can play in the economic development of these countries' (WTO, 2004). Furthermore, in paragraph 2 of the Hong Kong Ministerial Declaration (2005) trade ministers of the 149 participating countries again restated their emphasis on the importance of the development dimension in every aspect of the Doha Work Program and recommitted themselves to making the Doha Round 'a meaningful reality' in terms of the results of the negotiations on market access and rule-making as well as in terms of 'specific development-related issues' (WTO, 2005b). Good intentions, appropriate thinking and correct values of the member countries could not be more evident and better expressed.

For the developing economies, gains from trade integration are acknowledged to be far larger than any probable increase in external official developmental assistance flows. A pro-development outcome of the Doha Round is sure to provide a good number of developing economies with an opportunity and incentive to use trade expansion proactively as a growth lever. It will also go a long way to establishing the development credibility of the present trade regime in general as well as the WTO in particular.[15] A pro-development outcome of the Doha Round would also go a long way to achieving the cherished MDGs of the global community.

REBALANCING THE COUNTRY GROUPS AND THE MULTILATERAL TRADE REGIME

For the reasons given in Chapter 1, over most of the GATT period the industrial economies not only overwhelmingly dominated the multilateral trade, they also dominated the MTNs, and with that their agenda-making procedures. The Quadrilateral (or Quad) countries[16] comprised three trade superpowers of that period. They dominated global trade in terms of value and volume, and enjoyed a clear supremacy over the multilateral trading system even during the Uruguay Round period as the strongest negotiators, having considerable negotiating weight. The global economy has undergone a considerable transformation since then and several other country groups have emerged that are making their presence felt. Important in this regard are the emerging-market economies (EMEs), and among them the newly-industrialized economies (NIEs) (Chapter 1, pp. 23–4). In the early 2000s, China emerged as the third largest trading economy and is widely regarded as the future economic superpower (Das, 2006b). Not only have these new country groups emerged but they have also integrated well with the global economy.

Failure is a great teacher. One lesson from the skewed outcome of the Uruguay Round (Chapter 1) and from the Seattle debacle was that the agenda-making process of the MTNs acquired far more significance than ever before. Consequently, the WTO members deliberated more on the broad framework of the Doha Round and its agenda. They were assigned far more time and attention by the members than any in the past. The members relentlessly struggled to strike a balance between the interests, priorities and tangible outcome of an MTNs for the developing and industrial economies alike. The former group was diverse and sub-divided. The trading and economic priorities of various sub-groups of developing economies are known to be markedly different. The focus of the issues covered in the agenda accommodated interests of various participating country groups, which made the agenda as wide-spread as indicated above (pp. 43–4).

While Quad and the other industrial economies controlled the multilateral trading system in the past, presently the developing economies dominate at least the membership of the WTO in terms of the sheer number. As stated in Chapter 1 (pp. 21–3), more than three-fourths of the present members and over 25 percent of the accession candidates are developing economies, whose diversity ranged from People's Republic of China (hereinafter China) to the Kingdom of Tonga. The developing economies tended to see strength in numbers. Besides, the WTO league tables of the 30 largest exporters and importers published annually now comprise the NIEs and several EMEs in high places. Also, China which acceded to the WTO during the Doha Ministerial Conference, was the third largest exporter and importer in the world in 2004, after Germany and the US. It was also the third largest importer in the world after the US and Germany, in that order, making it a large and globally significant trading economy.[17] China's global economic significant has been on the rise, therefore it was invited to the Group-of-Seven (G-7) meeting held in Boca Raton, Florida, in February 2004.

Over the last two decades, the EMEs did a laudable task of integrating with the global economy (Das, 2004a). Given the increasing economic interdependence between the mature industrial economies and the EMEs, a larger, more representative group of finance ministers would be a more useful and representative group for deliberations on global economic, financial and trade issues. The old G-7 concept (founded in 1978) is progressively becoming outdated and irrelevant. One suggestion to expand it came from Paul Martin, the erstwhile Finance Minister of Canada in 1999.[18] He proposed that the G-7 needed to be upgraded to a new Group-of-Twenty (G-20). His view was that the global economic system could not possibly treat the interests and priorities of the the EMEs and NIEs, the Group-of-Ninety (G-90)[19] economies, as merely marginal. Stubbornly adhering to the long-standing principle of G-7 and not moving nimbly and adapting to the changing global economic realities is sure to lead to global economic disarray.[20] An amber signal is essential here. This proposal of G-20 is different from the one that was born before the Cancún Ministerial Conference in 2003. The 20 countries named in this proposal of G-20 were different from the G-20 that was born later in Cancún.

Integrating Goods Markets

As the group of developing economies moved up the economic and technology ladder, they not only became economies of global importance but many of them have also undertaken an appreciable task of integrating with the global economy. Consequently goods market integration increased significantly over the decade of the 1990s. It essentially takes place through trade flows, with larger trade flows implying greater goods market integration. Goods market integration is estimated using data for bilateral trade flows, which are easily available. Price dispersion is another method of estimating it, with smaller price differentials between trading economies implying greater goods market integration. Several recent empirical studies have used price dispersion to quantify goods market integration across a large number of economies.[21] They used prices of a large number of goods (more than 90) across a large (say, 100) number of cities. The goods chosen were generally highly disaggregated. These empirical studies concluded that the pattern of goods market integration increased markedly during the last decade. In addition, the regional integration arrangements (RIAs) were found to have a positive effect over goods market integration.

That disregarding priorities and preferences of different country groups have disastrous results was brought home by the Seattle Ministerial Conference. Therefore, members who consciously sought agreement and harmony between industrial and developing economies paid explicit attention to the agenda of the Doha Round. Under the present set of circumstances, the notion of disregarding the priorities and trade interests of various sub-groups of the developing economies in an MTN agenda would indeed be sub-optimal.

It would amount to creating a flawed economic and trading system. Wisdom lies in addressing and integrating those priorities squarely into the MTN agenda because they are likely to produce systemic benefits, and contribute to the systemic vigor. A multilateral trade regime is a global public good. All the consumers of this global public good stand to gain from an inclusive approach.

Striking a Balance in Modality

In any MTN exercise determining and agreeing to a set of modalities is the core of negotiating endeavors. The term modality implies precise numerical formula, targets and a timetable for implementation of trade liberalization agreements. In determining modalities, issues and sectors have to be paid careful, calculating and conscientious attention. An equal amount of careful attention needs to be paid to what is referred to as the 'negotiation modalities'. In the contemporary trading world, balancing negotiation modalities has enormous significance. In the past a lack of balance in negotiation modalities frequently jeopardized the MTNs and Ministerial Conferences. It is certain to do so in the future as well.

Determining what comprises a legal obligation needs to be done in such a manner that none of the trading country groups feel that they are being considered of secondary importance and, therefore, are being marginalized by the multilateral trading system. The debate around the issue of intellectual property rights provides an interesting example. For sure, an MTN agenda must include the protection of intellectual property rights in which the industrial economies are interested, but at the same time it should not ignore the issues of current and potential concern to developing economies, such as property rights to knowledge embedded in traditional medicines, and access to life-saving drugs and pharmaceuticals by the developing economies (Stiglitz, 1999a; Das, 2001). Striking a balance on such delicate issues can often mean the difference between a successful round of MTNs and an unsuccessful one.

The term 'negotiation modality' in the context of tariff negotiations takes on a specific nuance and needs to be elaborated upon. Both in GATT-1947 and GATT-1994, the member governments were mandated to enter into negotiations to reduce tariff and non-tariff barriers (NTBs).[22] Negotiations were expected to be conducted 'in reciprocal and mutually advantageous basis'.[23] Article XXVIII *bis* goes on to clarify that they 'may be carried out on a selective product-by-product basis or by application of such multilateral procedures as may be accepted' by the negotiating member countries. Conventionally, the CPs or the WTO members carried out negotiations on a product-by-product basis, and also devised mutually agreeable formulas for tariff reduction, NTB elimination and trade liberalization. An assortment of instruments and techniques were deployed to this end. Application of a particular method or negotiation modality also involves agreement on important related aspects, that is the base rate and staging. The base rate means the tariff level taken as a base for applying the agreed upon tariff reduction formulae, while staging means the period over which the tariff reduction would be phased (Hoda and Verma, 2004).

A balance on the above-mentioned lines can not be struck until the member delegations take into account the institutional disadvantages that many developing economies have in participating meaningfully in the MTNs. For instance, while 19 of the 42 African WTO members are not even represented at the WTO headquarters in Geneva, the average number of trade officials from each one of the OECD countries is 70. In addition to the differences in the level of growth of the members, Stiglitz (1999b) correctly drew attention to the 'suspicions born of a legacy of past power imbalances'. The developing and industrial economies play on an uneven playing field, which for historical reasons is tilted against the former. Developing economies face greater volatility in their economies and under certain circumstances trade liberalization can also become a source of volatility. They find it relatively more difficult to deal with economic adjustments which are a consequence of trade liberalization. A closely related fact is that developing economies either do not have social safety nets or have very weak ones. Unemployment has been a persistent problem in a majority of them. Thus regulations and liberalization measures that *prima facie* look even and fair to both the country groups may have very different and unequal consequences for the developing economies.

EVOLUTIONARY PROCESS: DO WE NEED A COURSE CORRECTION?

In the six decades since the creation of the GATT/WTO system, the global economy has evolved out of recognition. Some evidence of which was given in the earlier part of this chapter. Therefore, the current evolution of the WTO needs to be given a serious reconsideration to accommodate the on-going progression and alteration in the global economy. Furthermore, as the developing economies were late in becoming active in the GATT/WTO system, it permitted an uneven development of the GATT/WTO regime (Chapter 1, pp. 10–12). The Doha Round is an opportune moment for making certain systemic corrections to rebalance the WTO architecture.

Rebalancing the WTO Architecture

The scope of negotiations and negotiation modalities in the Doha Round need to be expanded in such a manner that mutually beneficial bargains can be struck between the participating country groups, resulting in enhancement of global welfare. Mattoo and Subramanian (2003) proposed a vigorous and coherent, albeit achievable, set of alterations and expansion in the WTO architecture, based on the following five matter-of-fact principles:

1. The coverage of the improved global trade architecture must be comprehensive, including not only trade in goods and services but also factors of production. The negotiations in services are needed to be given adequate importance.
2. The new WTO architecture must enforce national treatment[24] or non-discrimination, both *de facto* and *de jure*, between domestic and foreign products and suppliers of services, after they have entered the domestic market. This one measure will contribute enormously to the strength of the multilateral trade regime.
3. While there can be some flexibility in allowing restrictions on the entry of foreign goods and suppliers of services, they must be negotiated and bound at current levels. In allowing the restrictions, only the most efficient instrument, namely tariffs, should be used. Inefficient instruments, like quotas, must be avoided.
4. Regulatory harmonization needs to be attempted only in a narrow range of situations where lack of harmonization is spawning negative externalities. For securing regulatory changes' compensation is a superior instrument to sanctions.
5. Regional integration agreements (RIAs) need to be allowed as long as interests of the non-members of the RIA are protected.

These broad principles need to be explained. The first principle proposes expansion of the WTO and the GATS under the existing multilateral discipline. The GATS and the Council for Trade in Services (CTS) are open to all the WTO members. To be sure, bringing service transactions within the ambit of the global trade discipline was a major step forward, but the system must not stop after taking the first step. It must function to achieve progressive trade liberalization in services. The neoclassical argument supporting liberal trade in goods and services, including the factor of production, is that it would lead to efficiency gains at a multilateral level and eventually enhance global welfare. The GATS *inter alia* covers trade in factors of production, that is, capital and labor. The industrial economies had insisted on inclusion of the trans-border movement of capital, while the developing economies had insisted on the inclusion of the temporary movement of labor for delivering services. These are worthy suggestions for the consideration of the new WTO architecture. Their inclusion in the modern multilateral trade regime must not be deferred.

Inclusion of the movement of factors of production in the WTO regime would *inter alia* augment the scope and negotiating space in the WTO system in present and future rounds of MTNs. It would expand the issues of interest of the developing economies, particularly the EMEs. Therefore, it should logically lead to a greater possibility of mutually beneficial negotiations between the developing and industrial economies. Opportunities for labor mobility are extra beneficial for the developing economies because they offer a distinct possibility of dwarfing the gains from improvement in market access in goods. Winters (2000a) and Winters *et al.* (2002) computed gains from labor mobility using a computable general equilibrium (CGE) model. According to their estimates, if industrial economies allow inward movement of unskilled temporary workers equivalent to 3 percent of their workforce, it would generate global welfare gains worth $150 billion per annum. There are two important features associated with these gains. First, both developing and industrial economies share in these gains, and second, gains are larger if labor mobility of both low-skilled and high-skilled workers is permitted. Mattoo and Subramanian (2003) also point out that these gains 'dwarf the estimated gains from complete liberalization of trade in goods and any of the initiatives currently contemplated under the Doha Development Agenda'. While the DDA covers investment in paragraphs 20 through 22 of the Doha Ministerial Declaration (WTO, 2001a), it excludes temporary movement of labor, which is a stark asymmetry in the DDA. To offset this imbalance the WTO needs to encompass the temporary movement of labor, so that this anomaly is offset in the WTO architecture. This issue has become a little more complex than it was after the tragic events of 11 September 2001. If it cannot be included in the Doha Round, it can be made an intermediate-term target for deliberation and negotiations.

The second improvement in the WTO architecture would come through adoption of unfettered national treatment. For maximizing efficiency, national treatment in trade in goods and services should be completely unrestricted. In the case of trade in services, the mode of delivery and the point of delivery must be immaterial. To be sure, this would be a demanding requirement for both developing and industrial economies and many of them would find countenance challenging. Nevertheless, this principle quintessentially provides support to sound multilateral trade policy, therefore, and adopting it is necessary to allow a certain degree of flexibility. In the case of the GATT-1947 and GATT-1994 national treatment is a general obligation (Article III), which applies to goods post-entry. That is, economies were not allowed the flexibility to impose restrictions after the entry of the traded good. As opposed to this, in the GATS national treatment is applied both pre-entry and post-entry. But it is not a general obligation and countries have the flexibility to apply it to the selected sectors and modes of entry. The GATS needs to expand the application of national treatment. Application of the GATT principle to the GATS in this regard would indeed strengthen national treatment under the GATS. Enhanced transparency in domestic trade policy is one of the important advantages of applying of national treatment. Flexibility in the matter of domestic subsidies to producers may be tolerated for a while because they are the least inefficient instrument for remedying domestic distortions.

Third, in allowing WTO members restrictions on the entry of foreign goods and suppliers (in case of services) some freedom can be tolerated. Additionally, members can be allowed to choose sectors in which to allow foreign direct investment (FDI) and temporary movement of labor, albeit these freedoms need not be totally unrestricted. In this regard, application of the GATT principle of choosing only the less-inefficient instrument for restricting market access would indeed circumscribe this freedom on market restriction.

Fourth, regulatory harmonization in the WTO system is desirable, but only if the final outcome is global welfare enhancement. Furthermore, if it is, it should be encouraged, attempted and achieved with the help of a compensating instrument or rewards, not with sanctions or threats. There are situations in which both economic and non-economic externalities exist and members would be enticed towards regulatory harmonization of their own accord. In situations where there are no such externalities, there is little reason to harmonize the regulatory differences. In addition, the WTO system should be flexible enough to respect national trade-offs in this regard. For instance, the EU's choice of higher safety standards for beef or developing economies' option for lower environmental standards must be respected by the WTO system. In the latter case, one would expect that the developing economies would try and emulate the industrial economies as they move up the development ladder with the passage of time.

Finally, small regional or sub-regional groups that plan to form RIAs and seek shallow or deep economic integration must remain free to do so. Under Article XXIV of the GATT-1947 they have been free since the birth of the global trading system.[25] The integrating regional economies voluntarily choose to harmonize or mutually recognize each other's standards. What is important is how to accommodate those trading partners that did not participate in the RIA and are outsiders. In the absence of a mutual recognition agreement (MRA) an outsider may be discriminated against, which in turn would result in trade diversion from the non-members of the RIA. This is important because successful RIAs like the EU can form MRAs with little effort. They cannot do so with the developing economies like Egypt or the Philippines, making them potential victims of trade diversion. To minimize this problem Mattoo and Subramanian (2003) suggested using the approach taken by the GATS Article VII, which 'allows countries to harmonize or mutually recognize standards, provided such arrangements are not used as a means of discrimination and outsiders with substantially similar standards are afforded an opportunity to negotiate similar agreements'. This provision provides a pragmatic openness *vis-à-vis* the non-member countries.[26]

Skewing the Benefits of the Doha Round

That an apparent imbalance in the contemporary multilateral trading system's rules and disciplines existed, and continues to exist, and needs to be corrected is widely acknowledged (Lamy, 2006b). What policy actions need to be taken to normalize the one-time, and still persisting, tilt in the multilateral trading system toward the industrial economies? Deardorff and Stern (2003) have made several noteworthy, effectual and spirited policy recommendations regarding the substance and process of the multilateral trade regime. The first one relates to the decision-making process in the WTO. The Seattle failure amply demonstrated that the Green Room process of yesteryear – which worked during the GATT era – is no longer an appropriate negotiating and decision-making tool for the WTO. The Green Room process worked to exclude smaller trading economies, particularly the developing economies. It has outlived its utility in the contemporary period. What is needed is establishment of a formal decision-making process, which should be devised so that the developing economies realize that the trade issues of interest to them are not being ignored and that they are 'represented in a manner that is commensurate with the importance' that these economies have in the global trade and multilateral trading system. In one word, the process has to be an inclusive one.

One recent and functional improvement in this area is organizing 'mini-Ministerial meetings' of a sub-set of WTO members, say, approximately 25 of them. Such meetings have the advantage of facilitating rapid negotiations and fruitful decision-making on difficult issues, which is not feasible in the presence of the entire membership of the WTO. While organizing the 'mini-Ministerial meetings', care should be taken in selecting the representative economies. It should be done in such a manner that the decision-making process not only becomes fully representative of developing country interests but is also seen to be by the stakeholders.[27] This is sure to inspire confidence in the developing member economies. They will perceive themselves as having a voice in the multilateral trading system as well as having ownership of the system. That the concept of mini-Ministerial is a functional one is evident from the fact that they are in vogue. Two of them were organized in quick succession (in Davos and in Geneva) after the Hong Kong Ministerial Conference of 2005.

Due to the presence of stringent protectionist measures, trade in agricultural products has continued to be a bone of contention. Deardorff and Stern (2003) made strong, if somewhat blunt and no-nonsense, policy recommendations on trade in agriculture, affecting the whole gamut of agricultural policies in the industrial economies. These recommendations are forthright and logical from the perspective of a trade theorist. The authors would prefer to see a clear commitment by industrial economies not only to eliminate agricultural export subsidies completely but also to reduce their agricultural output, which is the result of heavy subsidization of their agricultural sector. In their view, this must be done without any further delay, particularly in areas of export interest of the developing economies. High tariffs on agricultural imports in the industrial economies and other policies that depress the world market prices of agricultural products must also be eliminated. Global market prices of agricultural products are artificially depressed by subsidized farm production in the industrial economies as well as high import tariffs and other trade barriers. Many developing countries are adversely affected by these policies, and the burden is disproportionately borne by the rural populations in the developing economies. The industrial economies also need to submit a clear and explicit schedule for adhering to these correctional moves in their policy. Although before the launch of the Doha Round this set of recommendations would have seemed like chasing an impossible target, it is no longer so. After the failure of the Ministerial Conference in Cancún in 2003, the industrial economies did make an offer to eliminate agricultural export subsidies. Negotiations on agriculture are of special interest to developing economies and should affect the whole range of agricultural policy structures in the industrial economies. The final objective of these Doha Round negotiations should be to ensure that these policies do not continue to distort global agricultural trade and undermine the ability of developing economies to exploit their comparative advantage in this vital sector.[28]

Market access in industrial products is another crucial area of negotiations, which is sure to have far-reaching implications for global trade. During the Doha Round, all the WTO members need to commit to NAMA, particularly to eliminate their most restrictive trade barriers, tariff escalation, quotas and the so-called high tariffs or 'spikes',[29] not to mention non-tariff and market entry barriers. This is one of the important development- and developing-country-related issues of the DDA.[30] There has been a pressing need to rationalize tariff escalation and rules of origin (ROO) because they are acknowledged to be strongly biased against the developing economies. In the contemporary world trade scenario, the highest trade barriers – particularly tariff spikes – exist predominantly against labor-intensive export products from the developing economies, particularly against textiles and apparel. These barriers come in the way of the developing economies pursuing their comparative advantage, and run counter to what David Ricardo (1772–1823) recommended two centuries ago.[31] In the present-day multilateral trade regime labor-abundant economies feel handicapped in exporting labor-abundant products. What is worse is that the trade barriers against these products in the developing economies are more restrictive and cover a larger range of products than those in the industrial economies, constraining trade between developing economies.

Furthermore, market access for manufactured products is frequently constrained by administered protection, which includes measures like safeguards, countervailing duties and anti-dumping duties. It is widely acknowledged that these measures are often applied in an unjustifiable, if not totally illegitimate, manner. The WTO rulebook regarding administered protection need to be rewritten in such a manner that they are not abused as protectionist devices to limit market access (see Chapter 7). Most often the anti-dumping laws are unjustly used for protection of specific industries. It has become customary to use these administered protection measures whenever a specific industry has to be protected. Although trade covered by administered protection is not large, these measures continually pose a threat to free trade.

Many developing economies need assistance in complying with their WTO obligations. In the Doha communiqué, paragraph 38 directly, and paragraphs 40, 42, and 43 indirectly, deal with the provision of technical assistance and capacity-building programs (WTO, 2001a). 'Technical cooperation and capacity building' mentioned in the Doha communiqué implies preparing developing economies, particularly low-income ones as well as LDCs, for integrating into the multilateral trading system. The WTO needs to set up a formal mechanism of providing this assistance and explore the means to finance it. That being said, the WTO is a small organization; its secretariat has limited professional strength and financial resources. Its 2004 budget was SFr 162 million and its total (professional and non-professional) staff strength was 600. In 2006, the budget increased marginally to SFr 175 million, and staff strength to 635. This budgetary amount is smaller than the travel budget of the International Monetary Fund. With such a professional and financial resource base, it would indeed be difficult for the WTO to meet the obligation of providing such public goods. Negotiators need to deliberate and decide on how to fulfill this institutional requirement and earmark resources for an institutional facility.

Bearing in mind the constraints faced by developing economies, WTO members reaffirmed special and differential treatment (SDT) for the developing economies in paragraph 44 of the Doha communiqué. Although SDT implies exemption from market liberalization, it should be taken to imply 'acknowledgement of the adjustment cost of liberalization and a plan to provide assistance with bearing those costs' (Deardorff and Stern, 2003). It should include the technical and financial assistance noted in the preceding paragraph.[32] It would not be feasible in the short term but this issue must be debated during the Doha Round and the realistic possibility of such assistance for the LDCs may be explored.

Broad Aspects of Tariff Slashing Modalities

The first four GATT rounds followed Article XXVIII *bis* of the GATT-1947 closely and adopted a product-by-product modality of tariff slashing, without being imaginative or venturesome about it. Even in the fifth Dillon Round (1960–1) little progress was made toward bringing in innovative ideas in the modality. In the basic framework of tariff slashing negotiations, reciprocity was an important consideration, although Article XXVIII *bis* did not specify how it was to be quantified. Therefore, strict reciprocity was followed in the first five rounds under the sponsorship of the GATT. All the CPs of the GATT, developing and industrial, exchanged tariff concessions on the basis of reciprocity during the Dillon Round.

However, in the mid-1960s the concept of reciprocity underwent a change. In view of the macroeconomic and financial problems faced by the developing economies, the principle of reciprocity was dropped and non-reciprocity was accepted as a norm for negotiations between developing and industrial economies. On later examination, some adjustments were made in this arrangement. It was felt that while strict reciprocity may not be expected from the developing economies, they need to make concessions to the industrial economies, which were consistent with their individual development, financial and trade needs. As an afterthought, zero reciprocity from the developing economies was no longer considered acceptable by the industrial economies.

The product-by-product tariff cuts principle resulted in only small reductions in tariffs, and there was general discontent among the CPs about it. Besides, as the number of CPs participating in the negotiations was rising, product-by-product modality was growing increasingly cumbersome and unwieldy to operate. Therefore, the modality adopted during the Kennedy Round (1964–7) had to be innovated. For the first time the product-by-product modality was replaced by a linear tariff reduction. A working hypothesis of 50 percent tariff cuts was accepted by the industrial economies, which quickened the pace of tariff reduction. The linear approach was applied to the industrial products, while the modality of product-by-product tariff slashing continued to be applied to the agricultural products. The linear tariff reductions applied only to the negotiations between industrial economies. Complete non-reciprocity was still granted to the developing countries, but only in a limited manner.

The tariff slashing modality further changed in the Tokyo Round (1973–9) and the CPs from the industrial economies agreed to deploy a formula for general application, which was based on the principle of the higher the tariff rate the greater the cut. Although a number of formulae were proposed, final agreement was on the Swiss proposition. The Swiss formula was as follows:

$$Z = AX/A + X$$

where
X = initial tariff rate
A = coefficient and maximum final tariff rate
Z = resulting lower tariff rate at the end of period

Coefficient A was frequently assigned the value equal to 14 or 16. The CPs had an option to choose the value of A; 16 resulted in slightly lower reduction than 14. As agreed in the Kennedy Round, the developing economies did not use the formula at all.

Several new negotiating modalities were proposed for the Uruguay Round by the members of the Quad and Switzerland, with each proponent certain about the superiority of its proposal. There was no agreement on which modality to finally adopt. Deliberations, discussions and foot dragging continued until the mid-term review in Montreal, after which a general principal was accepted that a target overall reduction in tariffs should take place. The target was fixed at 33.3 percent. Determining the modality to reach the target was left to the individual CPs. In principle, the target reduction was applied to the developing economies but the expectation from them was that they should increase the coverage of their bound tariff schedules.[33] The public policy-makers in the developing economies were having a change of heart during – even before the launch of – the Uruguay Round. Many developing economies began to take the initiative unilaterally, liberalizing their trade policy regimes. In the context of wide-ranging macroeconomic reforms, trade barriers began to come down or were eliminated. Despite not being under pressure to commit to the 33.3 percent target, many developing economies made generous concessions in their tariff rates. Korea was regarded as the champion because it overshot the targeted rate. At this point, the principle of non-reciprocity lost its relevance for the developing economies completely. Four Latin American economies (Argentina, Brazil, Chile and Mexico) had 100 percent of their tariffs bound soon after the Uruguay Round ended. In Thailand the bound tariff rates had soared to 64 percent at the end of the Uruguay Round; its pre-Uruguay Round bound rate was 1 percent. However, negotiations on reducing international tariff peaks by 50 percent were only partially successful.[34]

Tariff Slashing Modality in the Doha Round

In paragraph 16 of the Doha Ministerial Declaration, the WTO members agreed:

to negotiations which shall aim, by modalities to be agreed, to reduce or as appropriate eliminate tariff peaks, high tariffs and tariff escalation, as well as non-tariff barriers, in particular the products of particular interest to developing countries. Product coverage shall be comprehensive and without *a priori* exclusions. The negotiations shall take fully into account the special needs and interests of developing and least-developed country participants, including through less than full reciprocity in reduction commitments, in accordance with the relevant provisions of Article XXVIII *bis* of GATT-1994 ... To this end the modalities to be agreed will include appropriate studies and capacity-building measures to assist least developed countries to participate effectively in the negotiations. (WTO, 2001b)

The mandate given by Paragraph 16 of the DDA is fairly explicit.

The Negotiating Group on Market Access (NGMA) met several times after the Doha Ministerial, but members had differing positions and no agreement on modalities was in sight. After several proposals and counter proposals, the Chairman of the NGMA submitted a draft of the 'Elements of Modalities for Negotiations on Non-Agricultural Products' in May 2003, but consensus eluded this attempt as well. Several well thought out and result oriented modality proposals were put forth by the US, Hong Kong SAR, Japan, Korea, the EU, MERCOSUR countries,[35] the People's Republic of China and India, in that order (Hoda and Verma, 2004). Some of them were variations of the Swiss formula of the Tokyo Round. Disagreements regarding the base rates, implementation period and staging continued until early 2004. Not all the modality proposals can be taken up for discussion here because of the lack of space.[36]

Tariff slashing was a sensitive area of negotiations. The EU and the US were in favor of adopting a 'blended formula', which was fiercely opposed by the Group-of-Twenty (G-20) coalition for being against developing countries interests. After prolonged negotiations, the WTO members reached an agreement in this regard on 1 August 2004, in the July Framework Agreement, which contains frameworks and other agreements. The text of the General Council's decision on the Doha Agenda Work Program noted that a single approach for developed and developing country members meets all the objectives of the Doha mandate, and noted that 'tariff reductions will be made through a tiered formula that takes into account their different tariff structures'. To ensure that such a formula will lead to substantial trade expansion, the following principles will guide its further negotiation:

- Tariff reductions will be made from bound rates, not the applied rates. Substantial overall tariff reductions will be achieved as a final result from negotiations.
- Each Member (other than LDCs) will make a contribution.

Operationally effective special and differential provisions for developing country members will be an integral part of all elements.

• Progress in tariff reductions will be achieved through deeper cuts in higher tariffs with flexibilities for sensitive products. Substantial improvements in market access will be achieved for all products.

The number of bands, the thresholds for defining the bands and the type of tariff reduction in each band were not specified in the July Framework Agreement. The role of a tariff cap in a tiered formula with distinct treatment for sensitive products was also left for future evaluation (WTO, 2004b). Thus, much in the 'tiered formula' approach 'remains under negotiation' (paragraph 30), which implies that its development impact is almost impossible to appraise. This lack of detail hides major divisions between importing and exporting countries in developed and developing countries which were very difficult to reconcile. The agreement includes references to 'sensitive products' designed to take into account the interests of the EU and Japan and 'special products' designed to take into account the food security, development and poverty concerns of developing countries. Loopholes of this kind have been abused in the past. This scenario warrants only cautious optimism.

AREAS OF SPECIFIC FOCUS FOR REDRESSING THE IMBALANCES

Notwithstanding the notable achievements of the eight rounds of MTNs in multilateral trade liberalization, much remains to be done in several areas of multilateral trade, particularly for offsetting the imbalances in gains from the earlier rounds of MTNs. However, a successful culmination of the Doha Round can result in sizeable welfare gains to the participants, irrespective of the country group or sub-group they belong to. The past rounds of MTNs succeeded in achieving tariff cuts, reduction or elimination of NTBs and liberalizing trade by other means. Tariff slashing was most notable in manufactured goods. At the time of the genesis of the GATT average tariffs on manufactured goods was 40 percent. By the time Tokyo Round was completed (in 1979), this rate had fallen to 6 percent and when the implementation of recommendations of the Uruguay Round was completed (end of 2005), they fell further to 4 percent. The Uruguay Round agreement also succeeded in binding tariff rates in all the industrial economies as well as larger traders among the developing economies. Since the completion of the implementation of Uruguay Round recommendations, tariff-free trade is plausible for some products (for example, information technology-related goods). In the same vein, international trade can be reasonably expected to benefit from the Doha Round of MTNs.

The structure of tariffs is another problem that adversely affects market access, and tariff-related distortions persist. Tariff peaks and escalation continue to create serious hurdles (pp. 53–6). Economies that tended to upgrade their structures by moving up the technological ladder soon discovered that tariffs were lower on the low-technology, labor-intensive products than on higher-technology, capital- or knowledge-intensive goods. This kind of tariff escalation between product categories was a disincentive to the developing economies and their technological advancement endeavors (IMF/WB, 2002).

Indubitably, tariffs still influence and distort multilateral trade patterns. They *pari passu* distort the resource allocation patterns in the domestic economy. These distortions are substantially higher in many developing economies because tariffs are significantly higher in them than those in the industrial economies. Notwithstanding the recent improvements, average MFN tariffs are the highest in South Asia, Latin America, North Africa and sub-Saharan Africa, in effect impeding trade, including intra-developing country trade. Early during the Doha Round, it was realized that the tariff rate on manufactured goods traded between the developing economies continue to be twice as high – or frequently more than twice as high – as for trade in similar goods between industrial economies.

Negotiations on agriculture would certainly demand a good deal of time, endeavors and skills, because agriculture has continued to be the most illiberal area of multilateral trade, having exceedingly high tariffs, no matter which country group one chooses. Even in 2001, tariff rates varied widely among countries, ranging between 36 percent and 63 percent (IMF/WB, 2002). The situation in agriculture has been further complicated by having quotas and tariffs operating together, that is, having differential tariff rates inside and outside quotas. For instance, an importing country may set a tariff rate of 15 percent for the first 150000 units of a certain grain. Once this limit is reached, the tariff rate is raised to 50 percent. Tariff peaks are particularly high and frequent on several exports of developing country interest, such as textiles and apparel, leather, rubber and footwear, travel goods and transport equipment. Likewise, tariff escalation most affects developing country exports in products like tobacco, leather, cocoa, wood and paper.

Two areas of special focus in the DDA are the so-called 'environmental goods'[37] and textiles and apparel. The former line of products were targeted by the WTO members because they are instrumental in improving the environment, a global public good as well as a local public good, and therefore are badly needed in most countries. Thus far trade in environmental instruments follows the usual pattern of tariffs, that is, high when traded between the developing economies and relatively lower when traded between the industrial economies. Lowering of tariffs in this sector would encourage their use in more developing countries and spread the environmental protection technology. Second, as stipulated in the Uruguay Round Agreement on Textiles and Clothing (ATC), the Multifiber Agreement (MFA) expired on the last day of 2004. Free trade in textiles and apparel is of enormous commercial interest to many developing economies, small and large. Many of them faced stiff constraints trading under the MFA quotas regime, which was as irrational as it was illiberal. How trade in textiles and apparel will evolve under the post-MFA WTO regime and what will be the new rules of the game is of interest to all of them (WTO, 2005c; Das, 2005b).

LIBERALIZATION OF TRADE IN SERVICES

The proportion of services in the global economy has expanded markedly in the recent past, and services account for almost 70 percent of production in the industrial economies. They have also become progressively important in the high- and middle-income developing economies at the expense of agriculture and manufacturing. Over the preceding two decades, trade in services has increased at a more rapid rate than that in goods, and is expected to continue to do so in the foreseeable future.

Multilateral trade in commercial services crossed the $2 trillion mark, reaching $2.13 trillion in 2004.[38] The value of world exports in commercial services increased by 11 percent in 2005, compared to 19 percent in 2004. Its dollar value was $2.4 trillion in 2005. One notable characteristic of trade in services is that it is overwhelmingly dominated by the industrial economies. In 2004, they accounted for 74.9 percent, while the developing economies accounted for 22.7 percent. The LDCs accounted for the rest. However, the share of developing countries has been slowly but steadily increasing. The most dynamic segment of trade in services for the developing economies is the category called 'other commercial services', which comprises construction, insurance, financial services, computer and information services, cultural and recreational services, and other business services. This category represents 47 percent of total exports of services and has recorded double digit growth in the recent years. Two developing economies, China and India, are significant exporters of services in this category and accounted for 8 percent of total multilateral exports in this category in 2004.

Another noteworthy attribute of trade in services in developing countries is that it is highly concentrated. The 12 leading exporters of services among the developing economies accounted for 70 percent of total services exports from this country group. Developing economies need to become more competitive in dynamic services like business services and computer and information services. These are among more promising services areas, having possibilities of significant development gains. Rapid future expansion is also expected in these services areas. Liberalizing trade in services, particularly under Mode-4 (or movement of natural persons), is regarded as highly beneficial to the developing economies. It is also expected to significantly alleviate poverty in the developing economies.

Development Implications of Trade in Services

The service sectors possess growth-generating traits, particularly for the developing economies. Liberalization of trade in services would benefit both developing and industrial economies and is also expected to contribute more to growth than further liberalization in goods (Lucke and Spinanger, 2004). In the developing economies, a shift toward strengthening the services sector in the economy takes place with a rise in per capita income. At lower levels of per capita income such a shift is much slower, if it takes place at all. Pace and sequencing of trade liberalization in services in the developing economies need to be carefully determined because they contribute in a significant manner to developmental gains. They also impact upon the final outcome of liberalization. Second, mere adoption of liberalization is not enough; these endeavors need to be supported by flanking policies to strengthen domestic capacities in services. Third, for service sectors to emerge in a strong and viable manner, the creation and support of a competitive environment in the domestic economy is crucial. Fourth, an appropriate institutional development and a regulatory framework are usually regarded as preconditions for meaningful trade liberalization in services; both of which are time consuming to develop. Fifth, developing countries cannot take the beneficial outcome of services trade liberalization for granted. The structure of the global market in services will have a decisive bearing on the outcome of domestic services trade liberalization. The external trading environment many well be the primary determinant of success in the liberalization endeavors of the developing economies.

The GATS came into effect in 1995. It was founded on the same basic principles as those of the GATT. Two of its fundamental principles are: most-favored-nation (MFN) treatment, that is, non-discrimination between exporters, and national treatment, that is, treating imports and domestic suppliers equally inside the national market (Chapter 1). Unlike trade in goods, trade in services is usually restricted by regulations rather than by tariffs. Therefore, liberalization negotiations proceeded on the basis of all-or-nothing commitments to liberalize services trade in particular sectors, modes of supply and protective instruments. Since its inception some progress was made in negotiations in the service sectors of interest to the industrial economies.

This activity must be broadened. Negotiations on services must push ahead under the Doha Round and all-round progress needs to be made, without ignoring the services in which developing economies have comparative advantage, namely, construction, maritime shipping, outsourcing, particularly business-process outsourcing (BPO) and movement of natural persons. On their part, developing economies need to pursue these negotiations in a thoughtful manner in the labor-intensive services areas where they have comparative advantage. How these negotiations will be conducted in the Doha Round and what modalities will be devised and adopted is an unknown. Therefore, developing economies need to prepare carefully and pragmatically, bearing in mind the tangible final outcome of what they are negotiating. For instance, liberalization of movement of only high-skilled persons would result in limited gains for these countries. Conversely, as set out above, the short-term movement of low-skilled persons is sure to spawn enormous benefits for the developing economies, making the GATS an instrument of significant benefits for them.

Services trade liberalization usually has short-term adjustment costs, which could often be considerable. Developing economies need to plan to adjust them. Becoming internationally competitive takes time. Therefore, in the early stages of development, service sectors may need a certain degree of protection before they can be methodically liberalized.

Plausible Welfare Gains

In January 2000, WTO member governments launched a new round of negotiations to promote progressive liberalization of trade in services. The GATS agreement stated that the negotiations 'shall take place with a view to promoting the interest of all participants on a mutually advantageous basis' and 'with due respect for national policy objectives and the level of development of individual members'. Economic theory indicates that, under certain conditions, developing countries can expect significant welfare and income effects. The static effects originate from specialization and factor utilization. At the same time, there are dynamic effects emanating from capital formation and technology dissemination. The market-based competition model for liberalization used for trade in services is based on the same theoretical assumptions that apply to trade in goods.

That multilateral trade liberalization in the services sectors results in welfare gains has been demonstrated by numerous empirical studies. Although they show an overall positive impact, estimates of worldwide welfare gains from liberalization differ widely. They range from $90 billion to $688 billion, depending upon the depth of reduction in trade barriers. The distribution of gains between the developing and industrial countries was found to be in proportion to their GDP (UNCTAD, 2006.) Hertel and Keeney (2006) estimated that reduction in barriers to trade in services under the aegis of the Doha Round would result in enormous welfare gains for both developing and industrial economies. Services trade liberalization may boost potential welfare gains from the Doha Round by as much as 80 percent. However, the distribution of these gains was found to be uneven, with the lion's share going to the industrial economies.

Rationale Behind Sluggish Trade Liberalization

Under all the four modes, commitments under the GATS remained shallow and modest for several reasons.[39] First, there were both economic and political issues retarding negotiations in trade in services. Second, the subject of trade in services is relatively new in trade and technically complex. Many issues are difficult to comprehend. Therefore, initially developing countries were not very enthusiastic about liberalization of trade in services and did not want extension of multilateral system to this area of trade. To liberalize trade, many innovations had to be considered, like the application of trade rules to 'non-border' measures such as investment approval or granting work permits. Second, decision-making in many countries required coordination between different ministries as well as between federal and lower-level government agencies. Also, business associations and chambers of commerce had to be involved in it. Third, among the developing economies aversion to trade-related obligation in services was generally strong. The knowledge gap in services and trade in services as well as the potential effects of liberalization constituted an obstacle to participation in the negotiations in GATS negotiation in an effective and result-oriented manner. This knowledge gap was also responsible for the inability to define and implement pro-development domestic policies in the services areas (UNCTAD, 2006). Therefore, views of different constituencies in this regard varied widely. In sum, given the ignorance about the GATS, 'the Agreement has become a convenient rallying point for dyed-in-the-wool skeptics to express their general frustration with market mechanisms, private ownership, globalization, and other prevailing evils' (Adlung and Roy, 2005).

SUMMARY AND CONCLUSIONS

Compared to the preceding seven rounds, the Uruguay Round was the most ambitious and comprehensive and is widely regarded as a milestone of the GATT/WTO regime for good reasons. It principal accomplishments include bringing trade in agricultural and agro-industrial products under multilateral discipline as well as the creation of GATS and the WTO. Due to the 'single undertaking' the developing economies were subjected to all the disciplines and agreements of the WTO. The developing economies realized somewhat belatedly that many of the agreements had little benefit for them. Also, in case of some agreements the perception rapidly emerged that benefits were highly skewed towards industrial countries.

The post-Uruguay Round period gave rise to an elongated intellectual dialogue and policy debates on the need to redress the imbalance in the multilateral trade regime. Many trade analysts also emphasized that there was a need to integrate various sub-groups of developing economies fully into the global trading system. After a surfeit of discord, dissensions and controversies in Seattle, the launch of the Doha Round, driven by the DDA, was widely regarded as something of a breakthrough. The development dimension was given a great deal of importance during the Doha Ministerial Conference in 2001. It was acknowledged that the benefits of trade needed to be more widely distributed among the members of the WTO. The basic intention in naming the Doha Round a development round was to try to improve the multilateral disciplines and commitment by all members of the WTO in such a manner that they establish a more level playing field and provide developing countries with better conditions to enable them to reap the benefits of trade liberalization. Members agreed on a wide-ranging array of negotiating areas for the Doha Round.

During the GATT period, the industrial economies had historically dominated the multilateral trade, and they also dominated the MTNs, and with that the agenda making procedures. In particular, the Quad countries had enormous influence over the multilateral trade regime. They dominated the global trade in terms of value and volume, and enjoyed a clear supremacy over the system even during the Uruguay Round period as the strongest negotiators, having large negotiating weight.

The agenda making process and the broad framework of the Doha Round was given far more time and attention by the members than any in the past. It took into account the needs, interests and preferences of a large group of countries. In the six decades since the creation of the GATT/WTO system, the global economy has evolved out of recognition. Therefore, the current architecture of the WTO needed to be given serious reconsideration to accommodate the evolution and alteration in the global economy. Furthermore, the developing economies were late in becoming active in the GATT/WTO system, which permitted an uneven development of the GATT/WTO regime. The Doha Round has been an opportune moment for making certain systemic corrections.

For the purpose of balancing the WTO architecture, the modalities and scope of negotiations in the Doha Round needs to be expanded in such a manner that mutually beneficial bargains can be struck between the participating country groups, resulting in enhancement of global welfare. A vigorous and coherent set of alterations and expansion in the WTO architecture must be made so that the one-time tilt in the multilateral trading system toward the industrial economies can be corrected. One method could be to use the instrument of the Doha Round to skewing benefits toward the developing economies.

Liberalization of trade in services can potentially have a great deal of development implications. If the negotiations in GATS progress reasonably well, the developing economies may benefit from it because they do have comparative advantage in several service sectors.

NOTES

1. The Group-of-Ten (G-10) comprised Argentina, Brazil, Cuba, Egypt, India, Nigeria, Nicaragua, Tanzania, Peru and Yugoslavia.
2. The 18 members of the Cairns group are Argentina, Australia, Bolivia, Brazil, Canada, Chile, Colombia, Costa Rica, Guatemala, Indonesia, Malaysia, New Zealand, Pakistan, Paraguay, the Philippines, South Africa, Thailand and Uruguay.
3. The World Trade Organization was officially born on 1 January, 1995.
4. See Martin and Winters (1996) and Stern (2000).
5. The concept of 'single undertaking' has been interpreted in different manners. It dawned in 1986 during the Punta del Este Ministerial Declaration, which preceded the launching of the Uruguay Round. This Ministerial Declaration explained it as follows: 'The launching, the conduct and the implementation of the outcome of the negotiations shall be treated as parts of a single undertaking.' In the WTO lexicon Single Undertaking implies that virtually every item of the negotiation is part of a whole and indivisible package and cannot be agreed separately. The single undertaking was regarded as a major structural innovation by trade economists, a new regime principle. It began to be treated as a basic normative principle of the multilateral trade regime.
6. See, for instance, Winters (2000a, 2000b), Rodrik (2001) and Hoekman *et al.* (2003a, 2003b, 2003c).
7. Das (2000) and Das (2001) provide a succinct analysis of this ignominious failure.
8. See address by the erstwhile Commissioner for Trade for the European Union (EU) Pascal Lamy, 'Can the Doha Development Agenda live up to its name?' delivered in Cancún on 10 September 2003.
9. He was confirmed as the Director General of the WTO in September 2005.
10. Peter Sutherland was the Director General of both the General Agreement on Tariffs and Trade and its successor World Trade Organization.
11. The term 'Washington Consensus' is considered synonymous with 'neo-liberalism' and 'globalization'. John Williamson propounded the concept as a set of neo-liberal policies, which in turn referred to the lowest common denominator of policy advice that was being given by the Washington-based Bretton Woods twins to Latin American countries in 1989. This policy advice essentially entailed: fiscal discipline, a redirection of public expenditure priorities toward fields offering both high economic returns and the potential to improve income distribution (such as primary health care, primary education, and infrastructure), tax reforms (to lower marginal rates and broaden the tax base), interest rate liberalization, a competitive exchange rate, trade liberalization, liberalization of inflows of foreign direct investment, privatization, deregulation (to abolish barriers to entry and exit) and secured property rights.
12. Fifty countries are presently designated by the United Nations as 'least developed countries' (LDCs). Of these, 32 were the members of the WTO in mid-2006. The list is reviewed every

three years by the Economic and Social Council (ECOSOC) of the United Nations. In its latest triennial review in 2003, the ECOSOC used the following three criteria for the identification of the LDCs, which were proposed by the Committee for Development Policy (CDP): (a) a low-income criterion, based on a three-year average estimate of the gross domestic product per capita (under $750 for inclusion, above $900 for graduation); (b) a human resource weakness criterion, involving a composite Augmented Physical Quality of Life Index (APQLI) based on indicators of: (i) nutrition; (ii) health; (iii) education; and (iv) adult literacy; and (c) an economic vulnerability criterion, involving a composite Economic Vulnerability Index (EVI) based on indicators of: (i) the instability of agricultural production; (ii) the instability of exports of goods and services; (iii) the economic importance of non-traditional activities (share of manufacturing and modern services in GDP); (d) merchandise export concentration; and (e) the handicap of economic smallness (as measured through the population in logarithm); and the percentage of population displaced by natural disasters.

13. The source for these statistics is Hoekman (2004), Table 2.2.
14. The General Council meets regularly to carry out the functions of the WTO. It has representatives (usually ambassadors or equivalent) from all member governments and has the authority to act on behalf of the ministerial conference which only meets about every two years.
15. See WTO (2005a).
16. During the GATT period four members of the Quadrilateral (or Quad) were Canada, the European Union, Japan and the United States.
17. Refer to Table 1.5, p. 21, *International Trade Statistics 2005,* published by the WTO.
18. The Group-of-Seven (G-7) was founded in 1978 by French President Giscard d'Estaing and German Chancellor Helmut Schmidt. Paul Martin, the erstwhile Canadian Finance Minister, is credited with founding the Group-of-Twenty (G-20) in 1999 which comprised ten industrial economies and ten EMEs. The first group was composed of the G-7 economies, plus Australia, Russia and the President of the EU. The second group included Argentina, Brazil, China, India, Indonesia, Korea, Mexico, Saudi Arabia, South Africa and Turkey. With the passage of time, G-7 has become inadequate to address the economic challenges of the global economy. The G-20 is more representative group of finance ministers that has attracted worldwide attention as a useful forum for discussing and negotiating policies on global economic issues (Bradford and Linn, 2004).
19. The G-90 is an umbrella grouping of WTO member countries, which comprises the Caribbean and Pacific (ACP), the Least Developed Countries (LDCs) and the African Group (AU). In 2006, 64 of the G-90 countries were the members of the WTO.
20. The concept of this Group-of-Twenty (G-20) was born during the Cologne Summit of the G-7 on 18 June 1999. The leaders of the G-7 industrial economies declared their intention to work together to establish an informal mechanism for dialogue among systemically important countries within the framework of the Bretton Woods institutional system. The intention of the G-7 leaders was to broaden the dialogue on the crucial economic and financial issues related to the global economy. The objective was to promote cooperation to achieve stable and sustainable global economic growth that benefits all. It was formally created at the 25 September 1999 meeting of the G-7 Ministers. It was launched with fanfare in December 1999 in Berlin, where the first meeting of the G-20 took place. Representatives of the European Union (EU), International Monetary Fund (IMF) and World Bank, were made a part of G-20. The French and Italian governments were opposed to the concept of this G-20. The reason they gave was that it would undermine the authority of the IMF. Instead, they supported the new International and Monetary Financial Committee (IMFC). The USA and Japan were very much in favor of the new body. Britain, while supportive, was somewhat reserved, for fear that the G-20 might undercut in practice the prominence of the new IFMC, which Britain's finance minister Gordon Brown was initially chosen to chair. Canada threw its weight in favor of G-20. This was largely because it wished to see a broader consultative structure that was more formalized, linked to other supranational institutions, and less controlled by the USA. The G-20 was chaired for its first two years by Canadian Finance Minister Paul Martin, who declared that the mandate of the G-20 was to 'promote discussion and study and review policy issues among industrialized countries and emerging

markets with a view to promoting international financial stability'. Its initial 18 country members consisted, in addition to the G-7, of Argentina, Australia, Brazil, China, India, Mexico, Russia, Saudi Arabia, South Africa, South Korea and Turkey. Canada hosted the second meeting in 2000. It was decided that the chair would rotate among participants with two-year terms, and with the initial chairs being chosen from among the G-7 countries.

21. See, for instance Parsley and Wei (2001), Rogers (2001) Hufbauer *et al.* (2002) and IMF (2002).

22. In the economics of international trade, the two expressions, namely, the GATT-1947 and the GATT-1994, are frequently used. The difference between the two is that that the latter is the revised version of the original GATT Agreement of 1947. The text of the Agreement was significantly revised and amended during the Uruguay Round and the new version was agreed upon in Marrakesh, Morocco. Apparently, the GATT-1994 reflected the outcome of the negotiations on issues relating to the interpretations of specific articles. In its renewed version, the GATT-1994 includes specific understandings with respect to GATT Articles, its obligations and provisions, plus the Marrakesh Protocol of GATT-1994.

23. Refer to GATT-1994, Article XXVIII *bis*, in GATT (1994).

24. The concept of national treatment is as basic to the WTO system as the most-favored-nation (MFN) principle. A tariff reduction at the border would provide absolutely no benefit if the imported goods are later discriminated against in the market place (beyond the border) by the host government by way of a differential sales tax, or other requirements of inspection, packaging, and so on. It is the principle of giving others the same treatment as one's own nationals. The requirement of national treatment prohibits against negative discriminatory treatment of imports. Imports cannot be accorded less favorable treatment than products of national origin. The GATT and WTO Article III requires that imports be treated 'no less favorably than the same or similar domestically produced goods' once they have passed customs. General Agreement on Trade in Services Article XVII and Agreement on Trade-Related Intellectual Property Rights Article III also deal with national treatment for services and intellectual property protection, respectively.

25. For the logic behind it, see Das (2004b), Chapter 2.

26. This section draws on Mattoo and Subramanian (2003).

27. See, for instance, Deardorff and Stern (2003) for details, and also Miller (2003).

28. See also Brown *et al.* (2003).

29. Relatively high tariffs, usually on 'sensitive' products, amidst generally low tariff levels are known as tariff peaks. For industrial countries, bound tariff rates of 15 percent or above are generally considered as international peaks or spikes. As opposed to this, when tariffs are three times, or greater, than the domestic mean tariffs they are called national peaks.

30. See Laird *et al.* (2006) for a detailed treatment of this problem.

31. David Ricardo's theory of comparative advantage was propounded in 1817.

32. Seekers of more information should refer to Deardorff and Stern (2003) and Brown *et al.* (2003).

33. Tariff binding is defined as a commitment not to increase a rate of duty beyond any agreed level. Once a rate of duty is bound, it may not be raised without compensating the affected trading partners. Tariff binding is enshrined in Article II of GATT-1994.

34. Bound tariff rates of 15 percent and above are known as international peaks or tariff spikes. As opposed to this, when tariffs are three times, or greater, than the domestic mean tariffs they are called national peaks.

35. Its full name is Mercado Comun del Sur or the common market of the south. Its membership includes Argentina, Brazil, Paraguay and Uruguay.

36. Hoda and Verma (2004) provide details regarding each proposal culled from the WTO documents.

37. Such as catalytic converters, air filters, etc.

38. Source of these statistics is *International Trade Statistics 2005*, World Trade Organization, Geneva, Table 1.

39. The four modes of trade in services are as follows: Mode-1 relates to cross border trade; Mode-2 to consumption abroad; Mode-3 to commercial presence; and Mode-4 to presence of natural persons.

3.   Special treatment and policy space for the developing economies in the multilateral trade regime

Patience and perseverance have a magical effect before which difficulties disappear and obstacles vanish.

(John Quincy Adams)

INTRODUCTION

This chapter dwells on the diversity-driven special treatment of the developing economies in the multilateral trade regime. The concept of 'special and differential treatment' (SDT) materialized early during the General Agreement on Tariffs and Trade (GATT) period. During the life-time of the GATT the concept of the SDT developed in several stages. Developing countries were given non-reciprocal preferences under SDT by the industrial economies. Whether the former group benefited from the SDT, and by how much, remained opened to debate. The developing economies used SDT for *inter alia* securing preferential access in the markets of the industrial countries. The SDT took varying forms and was related to different trade issues. There were numerous categories of preferential market access schedules given to developing countries under different agreements and arrangements. In recent years the SDT intensified for the low-income developing countries and the least-developed countries (LDCs)[1] were granted enhanced preferential market access by the industrial economies under the Generalized System of Preferences (GSP), a large category of market-access schedule.

In the next section the concept of SDT and its intellectual origins are traced, while the third section focuses on various beneficiary country groups. Trade liberalization on a most-favored-nation (MFN) basis has been eroding the non-reciprocal preferences enjoyed by the low-income developing countries; their concern in this regard is analysed in the fourth section. The issue of hierarchies of beneficiaries is the focus of the fifth section. Small and low-income developing economies are the new entrants to the multilateral trade stage; how the trade regime can accommodate them is taken up in the sixth section. SDT is an important part of negotiations in the Doha Round and the seventh section elaborates on the progress made in this area. The pressing need for enhancing the development relevance of the WTO and devising a development-supportive policy space are discussed in the eighth and ninth sections. Whether the Doha Round is true to its name and progressing toward being a development round or not is discussed in the tenth section. Whether the innovative concept of MFN-based liberalization can be adopted in the Doha Round is analysed in the eleventh section. The last issue taken up in the chapter is the intra-developing country trade, which is the focus of the twelfth section. The last section provides a summary and conclusions of the chapter.

SPECIAL AND DIFFERENTIAL TREATMENT

The members of the World Trade Organization (WTO) range from very high-income to very low-income countries. Likewise, in terms of stages of growth, institutional development, resources and capacity constraints they cover a large spectrum. The WTO does not have a definition of developing economies, although some supranational institutions, like the World Bank, not only provide a closely worded definition of developing economies but also of various sub-groups among them. In the case of the WTO, it is the member that decides and declares its status itself. Members announce for themselves whether they are 'developed' or 'developing' countries. However, other members can challenge the decision of a member to make use of the WTO provisions available to developing countries. Given the fact that members have a wide diversity in economic and institutional resources, their ability and willingness to incur costs associated with implementing of new multilateral trade rules also varies radically. So does their ability to derive benefit from new multilateral trade rules. There are two more costs, namely, the implementation and adjustment costs of new regulations. They are almost always borne by the developing economies because these rules essentially represent the status quo in the mature industrial economies and are passed on to the developing economies as the best practices.

Over the decades, the traditional approach in the multilateral trade system for the developing economies was to seek benefits under the SDT. This was part of the process of evolution of the multilateral trade regime and can be traced back to the period when negotiations for the International Trade Organization (ITO) were going on (Narlikar, 2006). What does the term SDT precisely entail? It captures the GATT/WTO provisions that: (a) allow high-income countries to grant preferential access to their markets to some developing economies; (b) allow developing economies the right to limit reciprocity in MTNs to levels commensurate with the development require-ments of this group of countries; (c) give them exemption from some WTO obligations, many of which are transitory and some permanent; (d) give them extra time periods to comply with them; (e) allow them greater freedom to use otherwise restricted trade policies; and (f) provide technical assistance and help in institution building so that the WTO obligations can be fulfilled and negotiated decisions implemented. The basic philosophical premise behind the provisions of SDT is simple and logical. The developing economies are provided SDT on the premise that industrial development in them needs assistance for some time in both their home market (by way of protection) and in their export markets (by way of preferences in the form of lower tariffs and non-tariff barriers).

Intellectual Foundation of the Special and Differential Treatment

The SDT is an obvious deviation or departure from the all-important MFN principle of the GATT/WTO. The history of SDT is as old as the GATT/WTO system itself. It existed not only since the inception of the GATT but also had a significant history in the multilateral trading system. Raúl Prebisch and Hans Singer were the intellectual fathers of the concept of SDT. They argued that during the 1950s and 1960s the exports of the developing economies were concentrated in the area of primary products and commodities, which were characterized by volatile prices and steadily deteriorating terms-of-trade. Therefore, they (along with Ragnar Nurkse) propounded the strategy of import-substituting industrialization (ISI), supported by high rates of protection for infant domestic industries in the developing economies. When they proposed the strategy of ISI, it appeared eminently logical. The rationale that infant industries needed protection from international competition is reflected in 'policy space' argument, which posits leeway in the implementation of WTO regulations for the developing economies.

Although the infant industry argument is accepted by economic theory, this group of economic theorists applied it a little too comprehensively and indiscriminately. Consequently, in the economies that followed the ISI strategy, the infant industries remained infants for decades – until many of them touched their middle ages. This strategy was avidly followed by South Asian and Latin American economies in the 1950s and beyond. The second premise behind the SDT was that trade liberalization under the MFN clause was not enough for the small and low-income developing countries to be able to expand their trade, and thereby accelerate their growth rates. These developing economies needed preferential market access in the industrial country markets through instruments like SDT. To that end, various programs under the auspice of the GSPs were considered necessary.

In the international fora such as the United Nations General Assembly and subsequently in the United Nations Conference on Trade and Development

(UNCTAD) the developing economies lobbied for an equitable outcome in the GATT system, rather than mere equitable processes, so that preferential treatment would be institutionalized for them. As the GATT did not have institutional mechanisms like majoritarian voting and coalition-building, these efforts had to take place outside the GATT. These opinion-building efforts achieved some measure of success in the form of Article XVIII of GATT-1947.[2] In the initial stages SDT was limited to the provisions of Article XVIII, which allowed developing economies to void or renegotiate their commitments as well as being limited to infant industry protection. The modification that took place in 1954–5 was the inclusion of Article XVIIIb, which further allowed the developing countries' use of Quantitative Restriction (QRs) for balance-of-payments reasons. These were significant epistemic and institutional developments and for the first time the developing economies were able to introduce a concept of fairness in the GATT system.

Developing economies continued their endeavors to have the objective of growth and development included in the agenda of the supranational institutions. The 1960s were designated as the UN Development Decade. This turned out to be a fruitful period for the developing economies when they achieved more success in this area. The second defining moment in the development of the concept of SDT came during the Kennedy Round (1962–7), when Part IV on the benefits to and obligations of the developing economies was introduced in the Articles of Agreements of the GATT-1947. Added in 1965, Part IV of the GATT was exclusively devoted to trade and development. It provided for discriminatory 'advantages' for developing countries during the MTNs. The Committee on Trade and Development (CTD) was also established. It is noteworthy that much of the language of Part IV suggested good intentions rather than obligations.

Article XXXVI of Part IV acknowledged the wide income disparities between the developing and industrial economies and emphasized the need for rapid economic advancement in the developing economies by means of 'a rapid and sustained expansion of the export earnings of the less-developed contracting parties'. The developing economies were explicitly relieved of any requirement to reciprocate the benefits provided by the industrial economies. Recognition of the principle of non-reciprocity by the industrial economies was an unprecedented measure. The term GSP was devised by the UNCTAD in 1968; it was first used as 'generalized, non-reciprocal, non-discriminatory system of preferences'.[3] In 1971, a waiver was adopted to legitimize temporarily – for ten years – the GSP under the GATT system.

Enabling Clause

The third important period in the life of SDT came during the Tokyo Round

(1973–9). What SDT entails was further clarified and made a formal element of the multilateral trading system in 1979, when the so-called Enabling Clause was introduced. The official name for this provision is 'Differential and More Favorable Treatment, Reciprocity and Fuller Participation of Developing Countries'. It established that the developing economies were exempted from Article I, the MFN clause of the GATT-1947.[4] The Enabling Clause legally established the principle of non-reciprocity in trade negotiations, in turn, facilitated more favorable treatment and preferential market access for the developing countries in the mature industrial economies. In negotiations in different rounds of MTNs, reciprocity was limited for them to levels 'consistent with development needs', as specified in the Enabling Clause. In addition, they were provided with greater freedom to use trade policies than the GATT rules otherwise permitted. At this stage, the cost of implementation of WTO agreements was made part of SDT. The Enabling Clause effectively made GSP a permanent feature of the multilateral trade regime, and further extended discriminatory preferences to the UN designated LDCs group.

With prescience, the Enabling Clause required that, as economic development gathers momentum, the developing economies would try to improve their capacity to reciprocate concessions gradually. This was christened the process of 'graduation'. Subsequently, several preferential trade agreements (PTAs) were created under the Enabling Clause.[5] The 'Graduation Principle' was an important associated with the Enabling Clause. The Enabling Clause was to be understood as an impermanent measure devised for a specific objective. It clearly implied that the developing economies had to assume their normal reciprocity in multilateral trade liberalization when the time came to do so. The MFN and reciprocity were the fundamental principles of the GATT and their waiver was granted only for supporting the economic growth process.

These objectives were covered by Article XVIII of GATT-1947, and subsequently GATT-1994. Conceived in a considerate and accommodative manner, Article XVIII not only made it possible for the developing economies to use their trade policies in pursuit of economic development and industrialization but also imposed a weaker discipline on them than on the industrial economies in several areas of GATT/WTO regulations. It also encouraged industrial countries to take into account the interests of the developing economies in the application of the GATT discipline.

Discriminatory System of Preferential Market Access

In principle the SDT is a system of preferences, which by its very definition has to be discriminatory. Historically, efforts to operationalize SDT essentially centered on preferential market access through the GSP. To this end, there has been a long-standing trend of unilateral discriminatory liberalization, which was operationalized through offering tariff- and quota-free market access for the small and low-income developing economies, particularly the LDCs. This group comprises economically vulnerable countries. If fully implemented, the discriminatory liberalization schemes could certainly make the SDT more effective than it was in the past.

There is a basic systemic flaw in the SDT, which prevented it from helping the absolute poor globally. Unilateral market access could not be offered to the developing economies that do not fall under the small, low-income developing countries and the LDC category, because it would have been a political impossibility in the industrial economies.[6] Therefore, the absolute poor of the global economy cannot benefit from the SDT because a large proportion of them live in South Asia and Sub-Saharan Africa. While all of these economies come under the category of developing economies, not all of them are low-income developing economies and LDCs. This means that the absolute poor can only benefit if trade liberalization is made multilaterally, in a non-discriminatory manner.

MEAGER BENEFITS OF SPECIAL AND DIFFERENT TREATMENT

Over time, non-reciprocal trade preferences became part of the relationship between the developing and industrial economies in the multilateral trade regime. In the recent period such preferences have deepened, particularly for the LDCs and Africa, Caribbean and the Pacific (ACP) economies. Noteworthy among the SDT schedules are the Everything-But-Arms (EBA) initiative by the European Union and its parallel that the United States came up with, namely, African Growth and Opportunity Act (AGOA). This however is not the end of the list of SDT schedules (pp. 76–8). The SDT schedules exempt imports of certain range of products from tariffs.

Theoretically this concept was logical, meaningful and significant, but in practice it did not engender substantial benefits to the beneficiary developing economies. There were several causes behind this failure. The preferential market access schedules under SDT were designed voluntarily by the industrial economies, which chose both the eligible countries and products for their respective schedules. It was observed that, for one thing, the selected countries generally lacked the capacity to export the products that they were selected to export. Second, countries and products which had export potential were excluded from the schedules. Third, when the market preferences were granted, the preference schedules were laden with restrictions, product exclusions and administrative rules in the form of documentary requirements.

They coalesced to constrain exports under different market access schedules.

Schemes like the EBA and AGOA could potentially have a good deal of favorable impact over exports of the beneficiary economies, but those benefits are primarily conditional upon the supply-side capabilities in these economies. Supply-side constraints did seriously limit potential use of SDT schedules. In addition, documentary requirements by the preference granting countries for ascertaining the origin of exports, or the so-called rules of origin (ROO) requirements, have tended to work as a real administrative barrier and significantly reduced the utilization rate of the GSP schedules. This has applied most to some sectors of large exports, like textiles and apparel. Third, most LDCs failed to benefit from the GSP schedules because of the costs and uncertainties created by product exclusion (Brenton, 2003). Fourth, the strategy of granting non-reciprocal market access to LDCs under various GSP schedules was not enforceable commitments under the WTO. Consequently, many of these schedules merely worked as exhortations. They did not go beyond 'best endeavor' promises that were subjected to numerous restrictions.

Fifth, overall coverage of these schedules was only a tiny part of the exports of small and low-income developing economies. Experiences under various GSP schedules revealed that the eligible countries were able to utilize only a small part of the preference granted to them. Their utilization rate was quantified. The exports of eligible countries under various preferential schemes formed a very small part of the EU and US imports. Over the preceding three decades, they ranged between 0.9 percent and 0.4 percent of total annual imports of the EU and the US (WB, 2004). Sixth, the preference schedules were characterized by trade diversion, that is, they diverted trade with the ineligible developing countries. Finally, the preferential market access schedules did not benefit the target groups of population called the absolute poor of the world.[7]

While there was a large number of eligible recipients of SDT's benefits, not all of them benefited from it. Numerous studies have shown that while some developing economies benefited from non-reciprocal preferences to a significant degree, others did not benefit at all (Ozden and Reinhardt, 2003; Grossman and Sykes, 2005). As regards the developing economies that did benefit, the foremost group was a small sub-set of relatively more advanced developing economies of Asia, which acquired the status of emerging-market economies (EMEs) over the years. The supply-side scenario in this small group of countries was better developed than in the other small, low-income developing economies. Also, the export revenues generated were put to good use by them. This group not only had the wherewithal to export the products but also met the administrative requirements of the GSP-granting countries well. Preparation of the required documents by the preference-granting countries was efficiently met by them. This sub-set of economies did not allow ROO to become an effective barrier. It was observed that liberal ROO requirements were a critical factor for eliciting a strong response from the potential beneficiary economies, particularly in products like textiles and apparel.[8]

A large number of countries were bunched together as recipients of SDT benefits in terms of market access. According to the statistics compiled by the World Bank (2004), in 2001 there were 130 countries and customs territories that were eligible for the SDT. According to the International Monetary Fund this number was 144 in 2006 (IMF, 2006). Of these, ten countries accounted for 77 percent of the US non-oil imports under its GSP. The same ten countries accounted for 49 percent of all GSP imports from all the industrial countries that were providing GSP. Occasionally a small developing country did benefit substantially from preferential market access where domestic prices were raised above the world market prices by tariffs, subsidies or other trade distorting mechanisms. For instance, Mauritius which exports sugar and enjoys preferential access to the EU markets benefited a good deal from this opportunity. However, these benefits to Mauritius came at a high cost to the EU taxpayers and consumers (WB, 2004).

A comparison of beneficiary countries that were eligible for the US GSP, and those that recently graduated from it, revealed that the latter category outperformed the former in terms of export performance. Countries that were no longer on the GSP eligibility list had a higher export to GDP ratio, as well as a higher export growth rate in real terms. One explanation of the success of the countries that graduated from the US GSP-eligible list that seems rational is that it appears that GSP provided a stimulus to their export industries. Causality must be carefully attributed, but GSP seemingly helped the graduating countries in engendering supply-side capabilities, which strengthened with the passage of time and turned these small developing economies into successful trading economies. The flip side of the coin is that mere GSP eligibility cannot turn them into successful exporters. Reforming their macroeconomic policy structure must have played a decisive role in this endeavor.

HIERARCHIES OF BENEFICIARIES AND PREFERENTIAL MARKET ACCESS

In the hierarchy of beneficiaries from preferential market access, the most preferred countries are those that are part of a regional integration agreement (RIA) with the preference-granting economy, which is usually a mature industrial economy. Trade partners in an RIA commonly have close trade and economic ties. This trade relationship is usually reciprocal in nature. The

LDCs, which enjoy unilateral preferences or free market access, come next in terms of importance. Other small developing economies with which the preference-granting economies have GSP relationship are the last. GSPs are unilateral in nature and are devised for large country groups of beneficiaries by policy-makers in the preference-granting economy.

Several unilateral preferential market access programs were devised under the GSPs by the industrial economies as well laid out, structured and customized programs that were intended to be carefully implemented. Each one of them had characteristic features regarding eligibility criteria, product coverage and administrative rules, in important areas like ROO. Together these criteria determine which developing countries are excluded and which can benefit from the customized unilateral preferential market access schedule. The programs devised and implemented by the US include the AGOA, the Caribbean Basin Initiative and the Andean Trade Promotion Act, as well as several unilateral and reciprocal trade agreements with Israel and Jordan. Likewise the principal EU programs include the Cotonou convention which includes the ACP countries and the EBA initiative targeting the LDCs. The EU has also entered a large number of unilateral and reciprocal trade agreements with the North African, Middle Eastern and the Mediterranean economies.[9]

The characteristic features of the unilateral and reciprocal trade agreements differ in several important respects. For instance, some sectors (such as textiles and apparel, processed foods, and so on) are treated as 'sensitive' items and usually excluded from the GSP. These sensitive sectors of trade are included in some unilateral and reciprocal trade agreements. Exports of bananas, rice and sugar were not covered under the EBA. By 2009, the EBA initiative will cover all the exports of the target group of countries. All the protectionist measures will be eliminated for imports into the EU economies from the 50 LDCs. However, an unseen restriction in this was that the products that matter most to LDCs (rice, sugar and bananas) were not to be liberalized until after 2006. Their liberalization would begin in 2007 and end in 2009. Second, under the unilateral and reciprocal trade agreements administrative requirements tend to be more relaxed in comparison to the more comprehensive GSP schemes, particularly regarding the ROO.

The attention of the preference-granting economies was repeatedly drawn toward the meager benefits from the GSP schedules in the world trade and other fora. It led to some improvements in the implementation of these programs in recent years. However, despite these improvements, as alluded to earlier (pp. 74–6), the overall imports into the industrial economies under various preferential schemes have continued to remain diminutive, almost insignificant. An exception in this regard are textiles and apparel exports from small African economies that came under the AGOA of the US, which recorded significant gains. In 2001, imports by the Quad countries from the

GSP beneficiary economies amounted to $588 billion, of which $298 billion were subject to normal trade and non-trade restrictions, while $184 billion came under various preferential trade programs. That is, the coverage of these programs was 38.9 percent of the eligible exports, which in turn received market access preference. In 1991, this proportion was 51.1 percent. Thus the proportion of coverage of eligible exports declined during the decade of the 1900s (Inama, 2003). A similar quantitative study by Haveman and Shatz (2003) produced comparable, although slightly different, evidence of coverage.

SMALL DEVELOPING COUNTRIES IN THE MULTILATERAL TRADE REGIME

As sovereign countries, a large number of small and low-income developing countries and LDCs are now members of the WTO. In mid-2006, of the 50 designated LDCs by the United Nations, 32 had membership of the WTO. Eight more were in the process of accession.[10] Together this group dominates the WTO membership. Cambodia became the 148th member of the WTO and the Kingdom of Tonga 149th, both of which were LDCs.

With growing numbers, this category of countries acquired a good deal of influence in the multilateral trade system and its decision-making process – even some negotiating weight. During negotiations, like any sovereign nation, they decide about what is in their short- and long-term interest and demand that those interests are fairly reflected in the WTO decisions and agreements. During the Fifth Ministerial Conference in Cancún, and the subsequent WTO meeting in Geneva in July 2004, this sub-group of small developing countries held together as the Group-of-Ninety (G-90) and was led by Rwanda.[11] The G-90 became an umbrella grouping of WTO member countries, which comprised Africa, Caribbean and Pacific (ACP), the LDCs and African Group (AG). This is the largest country group in the WTO system. In 2006, 64 of the G-90 countries were members of the WTO.

Two interesting characteristics of small and low-income developing countries and LDCs tend to stand out. First, their economies and trade volume are small, if not tiny. By definition, each of them accounts for 0.05 percent, or less, of multilateral imports of goods and services. Realistically, such a small trader has little to offer in terms of market access concessions to its trading partners during the MTNs. This precludes this group of small developing countries from any serious reciprocal bargaining, which is considered central to the WTO operations. Second, the interests and trade-related requirements of this group of WTO members are imperfectly aligned with the extensive agenda of the multilateral trade system. In addition, as these small economies enjoy preferential market access to the industrial country markets (pp. 74–7), further multilateral liberalization in the Doha Round may well erode rather than enhance the market access of these countries. Many of them would reap few benefits from multilateral broadening of the WTO mandate, which includes MFN liberalization. Owing to these two characteristic differences from the principal trading economies, small and low-income developing economies stand out as an unusual and exclusive group in the multilateral trading system.

Evolution of a Pro-Development Stance

As it is dominated by various categories of developing economies, there is an imperious need for the evolving multilateral trade regime to take a pro-developmental direction. While many are small traders, they are in the WTO in a large numbers. The new systemic reality of the multilateral trade regime is diametrically opposed to that of the early decades of the GATT system. The evolving multilateral trade regime will need to adapt to the expectations and needs of these country groups. In addition, the contemporary intellectual and political environment strongly favors a 'fair' Doha Round outcome for these country groups. In this *mise-en-scène*, the evolving multilateral trading system is faced with the challenge of equilibrating two important and seemingly incompatible issues. First is pragmatically accommodating the interests and needs of the small and low-income developing country group and, second, ensuring rapid, efficient and expeditious progress in the Doha Round.

In this context, Stiglitz and Charlton (2005) judiciously observed that the primary principle of

> the Doha Round should be to ensure that the agreements promotes development in the poor countries. To make this principle operational the WTO needs to foster a culture of robust economic analysis to identify pro-developmental proposals and promote them to the top of the agenda. In practice this means establishing a source of impartial and publicly available analysis of the effects of different initiatives on different countries. This should be a core responsibility of an expanded WTO Secretariat.

The other objective of this analysis would be to reveal that if any WTO agreement 'differentially hurts developing countries or provides disproportionate benefits to developed countries', it should be regarded as unfair and be considered inappropriate for and incompatible with the Doha Development Agenda (DDA). In the final analysis the DDA should promote both *de facto* and *de jure* fairness.

To be sure, the MFN liberalization route is considered both efficient and innovative for the Doha Round (see pp. 92–4), but the multilateral trading system 'faces the classic conflict between efficiency and distribution' (Mattoo and Subramanian, 2004). If the MFN-based liberalization is the most efficient for reallocation of global resources, it also leads to adverse distributional effects on economies that have been granted the benefit of preferential market access. As the WTO has followed the GATT tradition of arriving at decisions by consensus, this situation is further deformed and exacerbated by the fact that the small and low-income WTO member countries in this group have as much say in ensuring the progress of the Doha Round and creating an efficient multilateral trading system as large industrial economy members. Without this say, the multilateral trading regime cannot be regarded as democratic and egalitarian. To resolve this knotty, if paradoxical, situation Mattoo and Subramanian (2004) proposed devising a transfer mechanism for compensating the small and low-income WTO members that stand to lose by further liberalization of the multilateral trade regime.[12]

Liberalization and Integration Endeavors

It is widely recognized that small and low-income developing countries stand to gain in the long term from trade liberalization and integration into the multilateral trade regime. There are short-term macroeconomic adjustments, which in turn lead to immediate adjustment costs. The short-term adjustment costs are reflected in variables like output, employment and current account. The total welfare effect of trade liberalization on small developing economies can be decomposed into a transitional effect related to macroeconomic adjustment and a steady-state effect associated with long-run changes in resource allocation. Using a dynamic general equilibrium (DGE) model, Choudhri *et al.* (2006) show that the short-term macroeconomic adjustment cost is small relative to the efficiency gains in the long-term. Under the fixed exchange rate, the short-term cost was estimated at about one tenth of the long-tem gains. The DGE model also shows that the short-term costs can be reduced by a flexible price level targeting policy rule.

There is another kind of short-tem cost for the small and low-income developing economies. It is widely acknowledged that they would also have difficulties of an institutional nature in meeting some of the multilateral obligations. Important among those are difficulties in meeting obligations related to establishing a system of monitoring and ensuring the protection of patents and other intellectual property rights, implementing high sanitary standards such as fumigation of fruits and vegetables for exports, certification that products are in compliance with international standardization codes and modernization of customs procedures. Also, opening domestic financial services markets for foreign firms would surely put a strain on the domestic regulatory and supervisory capabilities in this group of countries (IMF,

2006). These difficulties can be mitigated by help from the large industrial economies. Also, the international financial institutions (IFIs) can be of assistance. A new concept of 'aid for trade' is now being discussed to lighten this burden of meeting institutional obligations. Under this concept, the small and low-income developing economies are to be provided technical assistance for capacity building, along with financial assistance to defray adjustment costs.

The so-called July Package or the July Framework Agreement, which was reached on 31 July 2004, after the failure of the Cancún Ministerial Conference, called on the IFIs, particularly the International Monetary Fund (IMF), to provide technical assistance to the small and low-income developing countries in trade facilitation. Furthermore, in 2005 the joint Development Committee of the IMF and the World Bank, endorsed the strategy of proactively supporting the small and low-income developing countries in strengthening their trade infrastructure, with a view to support their liberalization and integration endeavors. During the Sixth Ministerial Conference in Hong Kong SAR in mid-December 2005, a work program was established to determine ways in which the aid for trade initiative could be operationalized. At this point, a higher level of financial assistance was also planned for this purpose.

SPECIAL AND DIFFERENTIAL TREATMENT IN THE DOHA ROUND

Subsequent rounds of MTNs reaffirmed faith in the SDT, which included both the Uruguay and the Doha Rounds. The DDA was clear about reaffirming the importance to the SDT for the multilateral trade regime and referred to it as 'an integral part of the WTO agreement' in the Doha Communiqué in paragraph 44. The SDT figures at several places in the Doha Communiqué. The objective of the DDA in this area is clearly laid down in paragraph 2 of the Communiqué as:

> we shall continue to make positive efforts designed to ensure that developing countries, and specially the least-developed among them, secure a share in the world trade commensurate with the need of their economic development. In this context, enhanced market access, balanced rules, and well-targeted, sustainably financed technical assistance and capacity-building programs have important roles to play. (WTO, 2001a)

Recognizing that the SDT did not succeed in imparting many benefits to the target group of beneficiaries, in Paragraph 44 participating members called for a review of the SDT schedules so that their provisions could be strengthened 'making them more precise, effective and operational' so that they are able to fulfill their objectives (WTO, 2001a). As the benefits of SDT were provided through enhanced market access, balanced rules and well-targeted, sustainably financed technical assistance, a good case exists for rethinking all three channels so that the benefits can be directed more precisely at the target groups that need them most. Affirming the good intentions of the negotiators, in paragraph 14, the Doha Communiqué provided a deadline, March 2003, for reestablishing the new modalities of the SDT. The deliberations and dialogues on this issue continued through 2002 and 2003.

Notwithstanding the upbeat commitments expressed in firm language in the Doha Communiqué during these deliberations, the WTO members were not only deeply divided on important SDT matters, but also had opinions that were significantly far apart from each other. They could not near a consensus or an agreement of any kind. The deep division between WTO members on the scope and design of SDT was indubitably the reflection of a wide distance between them in terms of income levels, stages of growth, capacity and institutional constraints, national policies and investment priorities. The foregoing sections have pointed to differences in each member's ability and willingness to bear the burden of cost associated with implementing of WTO rules and the payoff from these rules.

Official Commitments to Special and Differential Treatment

After the failure of the Fifth Ministerial Conference in Cancún, the so-called July Framework Agreement was formulated in 2004, in which the General Council, highest-level decision-making body of the WTO in Geneva, reaffirmed that provisions for SDT are an integral part of the WTO agreements. The Council not only reaffirmed the DDA objective of strengthening them but also recommended making them more 'precise, effective and operational'. The CTD began a review of SDT. The Council instructed the CTD to expeditiously complete the review of all the outstanding agreement-specific proposals regarding SDT and report to the General Council, with clear recommendations for a decision, by July 2005. The CTD, within the parameters of the Doha mandate, was asked to address all other outstanding work, including on the cross-cutting issues, the monitoring mechanism and the incorporation of SDT into the architecture of WTO rules. However, the CTD after several meetings failed to make concrete recommendations to the General Council. Members continued to have strong and fundamental disagreements on several issues.

The General Council reviewed and recognized the progress that has been made since the beginning of the negotiations of the Doha Ministerial Conference in expanding Trade-Related Technical Assistance (TRTA) to small and low-income developing countries and economies in transition. In furthering this effort the Council affirms that such countries, and in particular the LDCs, should be provided with enhanced TRTA and capacity building assistance, to increase their effective participation in the negotiations, to facilitate their implementation of WTO rules, and to enable them to adjust and diversify their economies. In this context the Council welcomed and further encouraged the improved coordination with other agencies, including under the Integrated Framework (IF) for TRTA for the LDCs and the Joint Integrated Technical Assistance Program (JITAP) (WTO, 2004). This did give an impression that the SDT is being taken up for serious review and at the end of the Doha Round should emerge stronger than ever in the past.

The Hong Kong Declaration of 18 December 2005, once again reaffirmed that the provisions for the SDT are an integral part of the WTO Agreements (WTO, 2005b). In paragraphs 35 through 38 of the Hong Kong Ministerial Communiqué members expressed their determination to fulfill the DDA mandate, spelled out in paragraph 44 of the Doha Ministerial Declaration as well as in the July Framework Agreement, that all SDT provisions would be reviewed with a view to 'strengthening them and making more precise, effective and operational'. Official recognition was given to 'lack of progress' in the Hong Kong Declaration, accordingly the CTD was instructed to 'expeditiously complete the review of all outstanding Agreement-specific proposals and report to the General Council, with clear recommendations for decision by December 2006'.

Refining and Strengthening the Special and Differential Treatment

In view of the fact that the SDT did not spawn large benefits for the target country groups, academics and policy-makers have debated over what future shape the SDT should take so that it is able to meet the expected goals.[13] In its various official pronouncements, the on-going Doha Round negotiations gave an additional importance to this debate, because this *inter alia* is being seen as an opportunity to refine the SDT system. As alluded to above, while the WTO members have found agreement on SDT elusive (p. 81), there is some degree of agreement among analysts and researchers on the new shape of STD. Their recommendations are thoughtful and comprehensive and are summarized as follows. First, a bold unilateral measure like a general reduction in all MFN tariffs in the industrial economies on labor-intensive exports of the small and low-income developing economies to 5 percent by 2010 and 10 percent on agricultural exports will indeed be able to reduce some of the veritable impediments like the ROO-related documentation requirements. The target date of achieving Millennium Development Goals (MDGs) is 2015. By this time all tariffs on exports of manufactured products from the developing economies should be eliminated.

Second, like the first recommendation, industrial economies need to unilaterally expand market access for LDCs, and simplify the ROO requirements. This will be able to circumvent some of the problems presently faced by the GSP schedules.

Third, in keeping with the spirit of the first and the second recommendations, developing economies on their part should slash their tariff barriers on the basis of an agreed formula-based approach. This would amount to their reciprocation to the measures taken by the industrial economies. It will help in keeping the multilateral trade regime balanced.

Fourth, paragraph 2(d) of Article I of the GATS identifies international trade in the supply of services through the presence of natural persons in a foreign country, when both the country of origin and the recipient country are members of the GATS. This is known as Mode-4 of providing services. Industrial economies should make binding commitments in trade in services to expand a temporary excess of services providers by a specific proportion of the workforce, say, 1 percent. Judged by the present level of temporary access, this indeed is a large measure and will realistically take some time to implement in a phased manner without disturbing the domestic economies in the industrial countries.

Fifth, acceptance of the principle of policy space for the developing economies under the WTO discipline would go a long way in helping many small and low-income developing economies. They may be permitted to decide whether to implement a new set of WTO rules, as long as their non-implementation does not significantly impair the trade interests of other WTO members.

Sixth, the developing economies on their part need to accept the core discipline of WTO on market access, including undertaking liberalization commitments. It may, however, be done in a differentiated manner across the entire spectrum of developing economies.

Seventh, the multilateral trade system needs to explore feasible channels of meeting the special institutional development needs of low-income developing economies and LDCs.

Eighth, the industrial economies need to meet the trade-related technical assistance needs of the small and low-income developing economies.[14]

Although none of the above proposals are novel and revolutionary, these or similar expansions of SDT have been discussed in the past. However, if they are deliberated, promoted and adopted during the Doha Round, the final outcome would indeed be supportive of development in the small and low-income developing economies and the LDCs. The name DDA would then ring true.

EROSION OF NON-RECIPROCAL PREFERENCES

The preference recipient countries, particularly WTO members from the ACP group and LDCs, have an additional concern about the erosion of non-reciprocal trade preferences during the Doha Round. As the industrial economies slash their tariffs on imports from all of their trading partners under the multilateral trade liberalization on an MFN-basis, the value of trade preferences previously granted to these country groups will decisively erode, adversely affecting the competitiveness of their exports.[15] To that extent these small and low-income developing countries believe that the MTNs render them vulnerable. To be sure, loss due to preference erosion – which will drive down the competitiveness enjoyed exclusively due to GSP – will partly be offset by expanding multilateral market size and higher world prices. However, some of these economies apprehend serious losses in their export markets and expect setbacks in their export revenues. They have become indifferent to general MFN trade liberalization by lowering tariffs and elimination of quotas and have begun resisting and resenting the MFNs. This conflict has pitted a small number of low-income and some medium-income economies against the interests of the other developing economies.

It has been pointed out in the preceding sections that, first, not all the developing countries gained a lot from the GSP schemes that were devised for them. Second, empirical research on preference erosion has concluded that apprehension of erosion from MFN liberalization is grossly over-stated. A comprehensive study of the non-reciprocal preference recipient countries inferred that these countries as a group did not lose from preference erosion following MFN-based trade liberalization in the Doha Round, although significant gains and losses underlie the estimates of the average (Low and Piermartini, 2005). The beneficiaries of GSP schemes of the Quadrilateral (or Quad) countries[16] plus Australia enjoy a net gain of $2 billion in terms of the value of adjusted preference margins on non-agricultural products using a Swiss formula, with a coefficient of 10. Almost all LDCs either lose from preference erosion or are unaffected by it because their exports are MFN tariff-free. Their loss was estimated at $170 million, not high by any normal standard. However, the most significant effect of preference erosion was found on LDCs exporting textiles and apparel.

Using elaborate cross-country analysis, Alexandraki and Lankes (2004) quantified the impact of preference erosion and inferred that it is a source of vulnerability for a small set of countries that have enjoyed deep preferential access to the markets of the Quad, have an undiversified export base, and a heavy export dependence on the Quad markets alone. The ability to absorb the impact of preference erosion will necessarily depend upon an economy's competitiveness in the affected sectors and their macroeconomic robustness. Computations in this empirical exercise revealed that the magnitude of potential shock in a realistic realizable scenario was small. It ranged between 0.5 percent and 1.2 percent of the total exports of the countries for the sample countries, and was dependent upon the elasticity of export supply. This small impact of preference erosion was also spread over time, in accordance with the liberalization schedule established under the Doha Round. However, for a small sub-set of economies the shocks of preference erosion could be significant. Estimates show that small island countries that enjoyed deep preferences in the Quad markets due to historic, cultural or geo-political reasons in the EU (in the case of banana and sugar exports) and the US (in the case of sugar exports) suffered most under the MFN liberalization under the Doha Round.

ENHANCING DEVELOPMENT RELEVANCE OF THE WTO

If the task of enhancing the development relevance of the WTO has fallen on the Doha Round, it took it on without any ambiguity. Paragraphs 1 and 2 of the Doha Ministerial Declaration make members' steadfast commitment to this objective abundantly clear (WTO, 2001a). In paragraph 1, it noted that the 'multilateral trading system embodied in the World Trade Organization has contributed significantly to economic growth, development and employment throughout the past fifty years'. It also emphasized that 'international trade can play a major role in the promotion of economic development and the alleviation of poverty'. In paragraph 2, members put the 'needs and interests' of the developing economies 'at the heart of the Work Program adopted in this Declaration'. Paragraph 2 also mentioned the contribution that trade can make to 'the alleviation of poverty'.

The Doha Ministerial Declaration also included several other trade-related development objectives like duty-free and quota-free (DFQF) market access for the export products of the LDCs (paragraph 42), an 'Integrated Framework' for trade-related technical assistance (paragraph 43), improved, strengthened and more effective SDT (paragraph 44), as well as a work program for fuller integration of small and vulnerable economies into the multilateral trading system (paragraph 35). Thus viewed, the DDA placed development concerns at the core of the deliberations. Putting in order an agenda was a necessary condition but not sufficient to enhance the development focus of the WTO. The challenge that followed was to achieve an outcome that supported economic growth and poverty alleviation through MTNs.

Designing Development-supportive Policy Space

Policy space, alluded to above (pp. 71–2), implies greater flexibility for the trade policy implementation by the developing economies, or leeway to pursue policies that would otherwise be subject to strict multilateral discipline. A choice may be given to small and low-income developing economies in the implementation of a specific set of new trade regulations, as long as this does not impose significant negative spillovers on other WTO members (Stevens, 2002). This measure has also been mentioned above in suggestions to refine the SDT. Cautiously utilized, policy space could indeed be development supportive. However, there is one possibility of a negative impact. If the small and low-income developing economies are allowed indiscriminate use of policy space, one possible direct result would be a qualitative decline and deterioration of the multilateral trade regime. It will result in uncertainty in the multilateral trade regime, rendering it undependable, eventually discouraging major trading economies to make commitments in the first place.

A segregation of core and non-core WTO disciplines would be of help in addressing the concern where policy space can be allowed to the small and low-income developing member economies. In an evolving multilateral trade regime, WTO members could clearly delineate which are the core principles that are indispensable, and central for a healthy and efficacious multilateral trade regime. These fundamental principles include the MFN clause, transparency, non-use of quotas, the binding of tariffs, willingness to lower trade barriers and eliminate non-tariff barriers over time in a planned manner in the context of MTNs and cannot be diluted in any manner. They form the foundation of the contemporary multilateral trade regime and any deviation from or dilution of commitment to these core principles will weaken the multilateral trade discipline. This is an outcome that is to be avoided at all costs. As opposed to these, the non-core disciplines could be made eligible for policy space of the small and low-income developing country members. The ideal instruments for identifying a non-core rule for an individual member country could be the Trade Policy Review Mechanism (TPRM)[17] under the WTO and the committees that oversee the operation of specific agreements.

Hoekman (2005a) proposed that in the process of its future evolution the WTO needs to adopt a country-specific and agreement-specific approach. Implementation of new multilateral trade rules should be made a function of a member's domestic economic policy priorities. This is the country-specific approach. While a worthy concept, it will create new and additional demands on the institutional resources of supranational institutions. According to this proposal, WTO disciplines should be implemented in conformity with, and in support of, the attainment of national developmental goals. 'A process of multilateral monitoring and surveillance, with input by international development agencies, would be established to ensure that decisions are subject to scrutiny and debate' (Hoekman, 2005a).

An agreement-specific approach would entail *ex ante* setting of specific criteria on an agreement-by-agreement basis, it needs to be determined whether a member country could be allowed to opt out of implementing a new WTO regulation for a pre-determined period. The decision in this regard could be taken on the basis of threshold criteria like the stage of growth, administrative capability, institutional development and country size. Low-income developing economies need to be allowed to opt out of resource intensive agreements. Emphasis in this approach is on the economic indicators, which should be the exclusive determinants. It is based on differentiation among the developing countries, rather than treating them as a monolithic group. This approach is not sweeping and generalized. It is thoughtful and takes the developing economies on a case-by-case basis and rejects the old tradition of country classification with which multilateral organizations feel comfortable. This approach is comprehensive, and would provide the DDA with a developmental orientation and enhance the development credibility of the WTO as an institution.

Although numerous academics and practitioners have addressed this issue, a Group of Seven Wise Men, such as the famous Fritz Leutwiler Group of eminent persons appointed by the then Director General of the GATT Arthur Dunkel in 1983, can be appointed once again to analyse these issues and provide a set of objective and functional recommendations that would bring the multilateral trading system closer to the DDA mandate.[18] This Eminent Persons Group remarked in 1985 that fundamental changes were taking place in the global economy and that they are not only inevitable but also to be welcomed as a driver of economic growth. They concurred that trade liberalization led to sustained growth and regarded protectionism as a serious growth-retarding factor. These conclusions were as correct then as they are now. The group had also argued that trade policy-making should be opened up to public scrutiny so that an intelligent and inclusive public debate could occur on vital collective choices affecting national as well as global wealth and welfare. Enlightened debate on these issues required independent research and analysis that could be fed into a broad public policy debate on the costs and benefits of trade policy choices. The present global economic circumstances call for another identical set of incisive thinkers that can provide new direction to the multilateral trade regime.

CHECKS AND BALANCES FOR A DEVELOPMENT ROUND

Oftentimes road to hell is paved with good intentions. To ensure that the

Development Round remains a development round, the WTO members need to run some checks and balances over what has been transpiring in the MTNs. Stiglitz and Charlton (2005) devised four litmus tests to determine whether the negotiations, agreements and decisions are pro-development or not. These four principles are: (a) the agreement's future impact on development should be assessed objectively, if there are possibilities of it being negative, then it is unfit for inclusion in the DDA; (b) the agreement should be fair; as well as (c) fairly arrived at; and (d) the agreement should be confined to trade-related and development-friendly areas, and not venture outside into non-trade-related areas on the pretext that they have an indirect bearing on trade.

Economic Analysis of the Impact

Little economic analysis has been done in the past to examine the potential impact of individual WTO agreements on member country or country groups. Analytical studies that were attempted did not penetrate into the core of negotiations, which largely remained based on prevailing orthodoxies. They were also influenced by lobbying from strong interest groups. For quantifying the potential impact of each agreement, computable general equilibrium (CGE) exercises can indeed be useful. They are an excellent tool of quantifying the potential impact. Modeling frameworks like Global Trade Analysis Project (GTAP) and its variations have been in frequent use by scholars and professional economists for the purpose of reckoning the impact. The GTAP project is coordinated by the Center for Global Trade Analysis, which is housed in the Department of Agricultural Economics, Purdue University. The Center for Global Trade Analysis undertakes applied general equilibrium (AGE) modeling, and provides services to other AGE modelers as well as supranational organizations using AGE-based analysis. The objective of GTAP is to improve the quality of quantitative analysis of global economic issues within an economy-wide framework. Since its inception in 1993, GTAP has rapidly become a common 'language' for many of those conducting global economic analysis. Economists at the University of Michigan and Purdue University have a great deal of experience, spanning over a decade, in running these comprehensive simulation exercises. Given the availability of this technique, the WTO Secretariat could be assigned the responsibility of conducting general equilibrium incidence analyses, which they can produce with the help of academic scholars in this area. These empirical studies can quantify the impact of different proposals on different countries or country groups. However, it should be ensured that the CGE and AGE models used remain sensitive to this differentiation.

Fairness of an Agreement is a Problematic Concept

The fairness of agreements is as important as it is problematical and conflict-ridden. It is basically a tricky concept. The economic circumstances of each one of the 149 sovereign member countries of the WTO are different, therefore, each WTO agreement impacts upon each of the members in a different manner.[19] In terms of net gains measured as percentage of GDP, if any agreement that hurts one country group and benefits the other, it is considered unfair by the one that is hurt. Fairness also has an element of progressiveness, that is, largest benefits of an agreement should accrue to the poorest group of member developing countries. So defined, fairness has not been a part of the multilateral trading regime thus far. This concept of fairness applies to the entire package of WTO agreements, not to individual agreements. The package has to be viewed and adjudged in its entirety. In case of individual agreements, there necessarily has to be some leeway for give and take, one agreement giving more to one group of members, while the other agreement giving more to another group. This effect of the WTO agreements is inevitable, therefore, one needs to look at the bottom line in this regard and reckon which country, or country group, is benefiting or losing on balance.

Procedural fairness or justice is the principle that deals with the transparency of negotiations process. Historically, transparency was not part of the culture of the GATT system, which was well known for its lack of transparency. It was reflected in the Green Room process, which worked to exclude small trading economies and the developing countries. Its lack of transparency became one of the destructive features during the Seattle Ministerial Conference. It is apparent that setting an agenda will have a large bearing over the final outcome of the MTNs. Therefore, participating members having a say in the mapping of an agenda is essential. As many opinions and country positions as possible need to be taken into account before the agenda of an MTN is finalized. In the past, a lack of transparency often allowed the large and powerful trading economies to ride roughshod over the system. After the debacle at Seattle, the issue of transparency in the WTO system made visible and impressive strides. The July Framework Agreement, which was finalized on 31 July 2004, was posted on the website of the WTO immediately after finalization.

The fourth litmus test relates to defining and limiting the policy space to trade-related areas during the MTNs. Over two decades, particularly during the Uruguay Round, there was a strong tendency to expand the GATT mandate to include all kinds of assorted areas, ranging from intellectual property rights to labor standards and pollution control. For a while it seemed that any international issue which was not formerly covered by any other supranational organizations was considered right for the WTO. Attempts were made to include in the ambit of the WTO even those issues for which there were specialized or United Nations organizations, such as environment and labor issues. Stiglitz and Charlton (2005) contended that policy makers employed the prefix 'trade related aspects of' liberally and excessively in the past.

The WTO deals with a difficult and important area of multilateral economic life. It cannot possibly be made into a negotiating forum and enforcement mechanism for all and sundry issues. There is a high price to pay for expanding the policy space of the WTO. First, inclusion of many tangential issues tends to confuse and overload the WTO system, which has expanded considerably since the Uruguay Round. Second, it also stretches the analytical and negotiating resources of the member developing economies. Third, the industrial economies negotiate from a higher platform in the WTO system. Expansion of the WTO boundaries gives them an opportunity to use their superior bargaining strength and negotiating weight in trade to exploit the developing economies over a larger range of issues. The inclusion of the so-called Singapore issues in the Fifth Ministerial Conference at Cancún is a case in point. Therefore, expansion of the WTO mandate should strictly follow the principle of conservativism, and not include issues that do not have a direct relevance to multilateral trade flows.[20]

MFN-BASED LIBERALIZATION: A POSSIBLE DOHA ROUND INNOVATION

The foregoing exposition has suggested that the GSP programs so far produced only limited results for the small and low-income developing economies. In spite of the goodwill of the donor economies, the target groups are not receiving much benefit; particularly the absolute poor in the world population have not been benefiting from the various GSP schemes (pp. 73–6). The target of achieving the first MDG of halving the income-poverty levels by 2015 is not likely to be met unless the delivery vehicle is changed. As a large proportion of absolute poor live in the People's Republic of China (hereinafter China), South Asian and sub-Saharan Africa, economies in these geographical regions cannot be granted zero tariffs under GSPs, for all their exportable products. As noted on pp. 73–6, doing so would be a political impossibility due to adverse public opinion. However, there is a possibility of granting zero tariffs to the sub-Saharan economies essentially because their export volumes are tiny.

To this end, an ambitious and innovative modality could be considered during the on-going Doha Round. The old approach – before the GSPs were created under the GATT – was that the MFN-based liberalization is the best route to underpinning economic growth. It was believed that, first, it is efficient, and second, it will *inter alia* eliminate the reverse SDT, which implies the opt-outs and exemptions made by the industrial economies due to political expediency or pressure from the domestic interest groups. These are made at the expense of the exporting developing countries. Elimination of agricultural subsidies as well as the protection of textiles and apparel sector would not only be immensely beneficial to the developing countries but also benefit consumers in the industrial economies. The same observation can be made regarding the removal of tariff peaks – both international and national – on the one hand, and tariff escalation on the other.[21] This MFN-based liberalization process will advance the trade policy reform process in the developing economies and motivate them to further liberalize their macroeconomic structure.

As for the negotiating modality for such a comprehensive MFN liberalization, two steps are essential for the WTO members: first, setting up benchmarks of tariff reduction and product coverage, and second, setting up a precise timetable and having an accepted schedule for the implementation of various measures. To this end, identifying 'reciprocal commitments that make economic sense and support development' would be a challenging and time-consuming task for the members (WB, 2004). In such negotiations, the old norm of non-reciprocity can become a disadvantage for the developing economies. Hindsight reveals that non-reciprocity was overly used in the past, resulting in reductions in gains from trade by way of domestic trade policy liberalization. Besides, non-reciprocity is the reason why tariff peaks today are largely on goods produced in developing countries' (WB, 2004). Since the Uruguay Round this policy mindset in the developing economies has undergone a sea change. Further impetus to domestic trade liberalization would also be instrumental in stimulating intra-developing country trade.[22]

INTRA-DEVELOPING COUNTRY TRADE AND THE DOHA ROUND

Historically, developing economies traded with each other reluctantly and maintained high tariff and non-tariff barriers (NTBs) against each other. They traditionally preferred to focus on opening up access to the much larger industrial country markets. This portends to a missed opportunity by the developing economies, *a fortiori* for the small and low-income ones. Export market diversification is one of the most important benefits of intra-trade among developing economies. The growth rate of intra-trade among developing economies has remained low. When it did grow, it grew in fits and starts, as these economies went through their stop-and-go cycles.

Intra-trade was dominated by primary products, and accounted for 6.4

percent of multilateral trade in 1990. During the decade of the 1990s, developing economies grew at a faster clip than the industrial economies and transition economies. The growth rate of intra-developing country trade was twice as fast as that of world trade during the 1990–2001 period. Its value soared from $219 billion to $640 billion during this period. Recent long-term forecasts show that the developing economies will continue to grow faster than the industrial and transitional economies during the coming decade (2003–2015).[23] Higher GDP growth performance during the 1990s was the principal reason leading to doubling the share of the intra-developing country trade in the total multilateral trade in 2001. Thus, a possibility of this performance being repeated during the first decade of the twenty-first century is strong.

As continuance of the high GDP growth rate is forecast for the medium term for the developing economies, further liberalization under the DDA could provide an impetus to their intra-trade, and diversify their trade further. To this end, the Doha Round provides an apt opportunity to the developing economies for making concerted efforts to slash both tariffs and NTBs.

Two factors, namely, above average real GDP growth rate and substantial trade and investment liberalization, led to dynamic growth in trade expansion in the developing economies, and intra-trade benefited from it. Notwithstanding the liberalization of trade regime since the mid-1980s, the developing economies still have much higher tariffs and NTBs than the industrial economies. One measure of tariff barriers is the ratio of tariff revenue collected *vis-à-vis* the value of imports. This ratio was computed for selected developing economies. It recorded a decline from 12 percent in 1985 to 4.5 percent in 2000. Also, average applied tariffs fell from 25 percent to 15 percent over the same period. However, wide differences still persist in levels of protection, both among the developing economies and the product categories. The dollar value of total import duties collected in the developing economies in 2000 was $83 billion, which was almost 65 percent of the total global import duty collection.[24]

Using Global Trade Analysis Project (GTAP) 6.3 database (or GTAP 2004 database) Fugazza and Vanzetti (2004) computed the trade-weighted applied average tariffs in merchandise trade for different country groups against each other. Their calculations given in Table 3.1 show the trade-weighted tariffs levied by industrial countries, developing countries and LDCs. They confirm that in the area of merchandise trade the industrial economies levy 2.1 percent tariffs on imports from the other industrial economies, 3.9 percent on imports from the developing economies and 3.1 percent from LDCs. The most significant sectors contributing to higher tariffs on developing country exports are petroleum and coal products and textiles and apparel. Industrial economies face higher tariffs (9.2 percent) when they export to developing economies than do the other developing economies (7.2 percent). This is partly explained by the composition of trade and partly by preferential agreements among groups of developing economies. Agricultural trade presents a different picture. Average tariffs rates are higher in both industrial and developing economies for exports from both the country groups. However, in this sector industrial economies provide greater access to LDCs (2 percent) than to developing economies (12 percent). The reason is various GSP schemes, which apply to all the industrial economies.

Table 3.1: Trade weighted average applied tariffs by stage of development (in percent)

Exporting country group	Industrial countries	Developing countries	Least developed countries
Industrial economies	2.1	9.2	11.1
Developing economies	3.9	7.2	14.4
Least developed countries	3.1	7.2	8.3
Total	2.9	8.1	13.6

Source: Fugazza and Vanzetti (2004). Computed from WITS/TRAINS (2004) database.

Fugazza and Vanzetti (2004) also examined potential for gains from liberalizing intra-developing economies' trade. The GTAP 6.3 database had 86 countries and 65 sectors. They estimated that static annual welfare gains to developing countries were $50 billion from intra-developing country trade liberalization. As against this, liberalization of industrial economies resulted in estimated annual gains of $24 billions to the developing economies. Estimates show that all the developing regions gain from liberalization of trade among the developing economies. However, the largest beneficiaries were Korea (Republic of), Taiwan, Mexico, China and the Association of Southeast Asian Nations (ASEAN) region. Conversely, Latin American economies and sub-Saharan Africa turned out to be net losers. The negative effects were derived from the negative terms-of-trade (TOT) effect in the manufacturing sector. As the TOT effects add up to zero globally, these negative effects have a positive impact through lower import prices for the other developing economies.

CONCLUSIONS AND SUMMARY

It is a significant fact that the members of the multilateral trade regime presently range from very high-income to very low-income countries. This reality of global economic life has a bearing on the operations of the multilateral trading system. Given the fact that members vary widely in their economic and institutional resources, their ability and willingness to incur costs associated with the implementation of new multilateral trade rules also varies. So does their ability to derive benefit from new multilateral trade rules. Over the decades, the traditional approach of the developing economies, which were at lower income levels, has been to seek benefits from the industrial economies under SDT. This has been a part of the process of evolution in the multilateral trade regime.

The concept of SDT grew in three basic stages. In the first stages SDT was limited to the provisions of Article XVIII of GATT-1947, which allowed developing economies to void or renegotiate their commitments. The second defining moment in SDT came during the Kennedy Round, when Part IV on the benefits to and obligations of the developing economies was introduced in the Articles of Agreements of the GATT-1947. The third important period in the life of SDT came during the Tokyo Round. What SDT entails was further clarified and made a formal element of the multilateral trading system in 1979, when the Enabling Clause was introduced.

The SDT has operated in the developing economies, principally the small, low-income ones, for many decades. Non-reciprocal trade preferences have become a part of the relationship between the developing and industrial economies in the multilateral trade regime. In the recent period such preferences deepened, particularly for the LDCs and ACP economies. Theoretically this concept was meaningful and significant, but in reality it did not engender substantial benefits to the beneficiary developing economies. Empirical research on this issue concluded that not many developing countries benefited from the SDT. There were several reasons behind this failure. The beneficiaries of SDT, particularly WTO members from the ACP group and LDCs, have an additional concern, that is about the erosion of non-reciprocal trade preferences during the Doha Round. Empirical research on preferential erosion has concluded that apprehension of erosion resulting from MFN liberalization is over-stated.

As sovereign countries, a large number of small and low-income developing economies and LDCs are now members of the WTO. With growing numbers, this category of countries acquired a good deal of influence in the multilateral trade system and its decision-making process. During the Fifth Ministerial Conference in Cancún, and the subsequent WTO meeting in Geneva in July 2004, this sub-group of small developing countries held together as the Group-of-Ninety (G-90). This sub-group presently dominates the WTO system – albeit they are small trading economies. The new systemic reality of the multilateral trade regime is diametrically opposite to that of the early decades of the GATT system. The evolving multilateral trade regime will need to adapt to the expectations and needs of this country group.

It is widely recognized that small and low-income developing countries stand to gain in the long term from trade liberalization and integration into the multilateral trade regime. There are short-term macroeconomic adjustments, which in turn lead to immediate adjustment costs. However, the short-term macroeconomic adjustment costs are small relative to the long-term efficiency gains.

Subsequent rounds of MTNs, including both the Uruguay and the Doha Rounds, reaffirmed faith in the SDT. The DDA was clear about reaffirming the importance of the SDT for the multilateral trade regime and referred to it as 'an integral part of the WTO agreement'. As it did not spawn large benefits for the target groups, there is a pressing need for refining the SDT. Academics and policy-makers have debated over what future shape the SDT should take so that it is able to meet the expected goals. A comprehensive set of recommendations have been presented for this purpose.

The small and low-income developing economies need appropriate policy space to accommodate their requirements. They need greater flexibility for the trade policy implementation and to pursue policies that would otherwise be subject to strict multilateral discipline. It is prudent to give small and low-income developing countries a choice in the implementation of a specific set of new trade regulations, as long as this measure does not impose significant negative spillovers on other members.

NOTES

1. In 2006, the United Nations classification of least-developed countries included 50 countries, of which 30 are members of the WTO and five are observers.
2. In the economics of international trade, the two expressions, namely, the GATT-1947 and the GATT-1994, are frequently used. The difference between the two is that that the latter is the revised version of the original GATT Agreement of 1947. The text of the Agreement was significantly revised and amended during the Uruguay Round and the new version was agreed upon in Marrakesh, Morocco. Apparently, the GATT-1994 reflected the outcome of the negotiations on issues relating to the interpretation of specific articles. In its renewed version, the GATT-1994 includes specific understandings with respect to GATT Articles, its obligations and provisions, plus the Marrakesh Protocol of GATT-1994.
3. Cited in Narlikar (2006).
4. Although most-favored nation sounds like a contradiction, implying some kind of special treatment to a particular trade partner, in the WTO jargon it means non-discrimination. That is, treating all trade partners under the WTO regime equally. Each WTO member treats all the WTO members as 'most-favored' trading partner. If any country improves the market benefits to one trading partner, it is obliged to give the same best treatment to all the other WTO members so that

they all remain 'most-favored'. However, historically MFN did not mean equal treatment.

5. For instance, the Caribbean Basin Initiative (CBI), the Lome Convention, the Cotonou Agreement, the NAFTA Parity Act, the Central American Common Market (CACM) and the CARICOM Common Market, are some of the PTAs that were created under the Enabling Clause.

6. The developing economies according to the World Bank (2006) definition are divided into various sub-groups. These sub-groupings are available in *Classification of Economies* on the Internet at http://www.worldbank.org/data/countryclass/countryclass.html. Economies are divided according to 2003 per capita gross national income. The groups are: low-income developing countries have $765 or less; lower-middle income, $766–$3035; upper-middle income, $3036–$9385; and high income, $9386 or more.

7. The definition of absolute poor is based on subsistence, the minimum standard needed to live. Robert McNamara who coined this term defined it as 'a condition of life beneath any reasonable standard of human dignity'. There has been a long drawn debate in the discipline regarding whether income or consumption poverty lines should be defined in absolute or relative terms. Most international organizations define the poverty line in an absolute way as the 'level of income necessary for people to buy the goods necessary to their survival'. In keeping with this concept, the dollar-a-day line, at 1985 purchasing power parity, is being extensively used in academic researches and by policy-makers (Bourguignon, 1999). However, a broader definition of poverty is the general lack of capabilities that enable a person to live a life he or she values, encompassing such domains as income, health, education, empowerment and human rights.

8. See for instance Brenton and Manchin (2002) and Brenton (2003).

9. See Das (2004) for these details, in particular Chapter 3, as well as Schiff and Winters (2003).

10. In mid-2006, additional least-developed countries that were in the process of accession to the WTO were: Bhutan, Cape Verde, Ethiopia, Laos, Samoa, Sudan, Vanuatu and Yemen.

11. This is an umbrella grouping of WTO member countries. The Group-of-Ninety includes Africa, Caribbean and Pacific, the Least Developed Countries and the African Group (AG). This is the largest country group in the WTO system. In 2006, 64 of the G-90 countries had WTO membership.

12. See also WTO (2005b).

13. Some of the recent studies include Oyejide (2002), Hart and Dymond (2003), Hoekman *et al.* (2003a, 2003b, 2003c, 2004) and Hoekman (2005). These recommendations on SDT have been drawn from the studies enumerated here.

14. Ibid.

15. Several researchers have addressed these issues. See for instance Hoekman *et al.* (2003), Messerlin (2003) and Wolf (2003).

16. Canada, the European Union (EU), Japan and the United States (US) are the four Quadrilateral (or Quad) countries.

17. The purpose of the Trade Policy Review Mechanism (TPRM) of the WTO is to contribute to improved adherence by all Members to rules, disciplines and commitments made under the Multilateral Trade Agreements and, where applicable, the Plurilateral Trade Agreements, and hence to the smoother functioning of the multilateral trading system, by achieving greater transparency in, and understanding of, the trade policies and practices of members.

18. The recommendations of the GATT Eminent Persons Group were published in 1985 by the GATT. The Group was chaired by Fritz Leutwiler, Chairman of the Swiss National Bank and the Bank for International Settlements. Their report was entitled *Trade Policies for a Better Future: Proposals for Action*.

19. During the Sixth Ministerial Conference of the WTO in Hong Kong, (15 December 2005) members approved Tonga's terms of accession. This decision paves the way for the South Pacific Island nation to become the 149th member of the Organization. The Kingdom of Tonga will be the fourth Pacific Island State to accede to the WTO after Fiji, Papua New Guinea and the Solomon Islands. The WTO members negotiating Vietnam's accession began intensive negotiations on 9 October, 2006. They aimed at putting the final touches to the package of agreements and completing the deal by the end of October, 2006.

20. For a more detailed discussion on this issue refer to Stiglitz and Charlton (2004).

21. Bound tariff rates of 15 percent and above are known as international peaks (also tariff spikes). As opposed to this, when tariffs are three times, or greater, than the domestic mean tariffs they are called national peaks.

22. Francois and Martin (2003) deal with this issue at great length.

23. The WB (2003) forecast the real GDP growth rate for the developing economies for the 2003–2015 period is 4.7 percent per annum, while that for the industrial economies is 2.5 percent. Similarly, the medium-term forecast of the IMF (2003) for the 2003–2007 period is 5.7 percent for the developing economies and 3.1 percent for the industrial economies.

24. The source of all the statistical data used here is WTO (2003).

4. The Fifth Ministerial Conference: the wheels come off at Cancún

Never walk away from failure. On the contrary, study it carefully – and imaginatively – for its hidden assets.

(Michael Korda)

INTRODUCTION

During the Doha Ministerial Conference, the 142 members of the World Trade Organization (WTO) had agreed to make growth and development the principal focus of the Doha Round of MTNs. However, divergence in positions of developing and industrial economies existed on several significant issues, and the gap was not bridged even during the fifth biennial Ministerial Conference, held in Cancún, Mexico, from 10–14 September 2003.[1] The number of participating economies in this Conference was 146. The principal bones of contention were agricultural trade reforms, an age-old chestnut, and the so-called Singapore issues.[2] Due to serious, albeit avoidable, errors of judgment, the dissension in negotiating stands taken by the large-trading WTO members and poor conference management, wheels did come off the cart of the multilateral trading system. This chapter delves into the mechanics of comprehensive failure in Cancún.

The developing economies were active participants in the Doha Round and their negotiating preparation in the Cancún Ministerial Conference was of superior order compared to the past. Also, as a group they coordinated better among themselves and there was far less division in the negotiating positions taken by them. This chapter details the negotiations between the four principal negotiating blocs, namely, the European Union, the United States, the so-called Group-of-Twenty (G-20)[3] developing nations and the Group-of-Ninety (G-90)[4] of small and least-developed countries (LDCs)[5]. It also identifies the principal causes of the disillusionment in Cancún.

As for the structure of this chapter, we begin with the *mise-en-scène* of the Doha Round of the MTNs and its launching in the next section. The third section is devoted to divergences in the positions taken by the member economies, while the fourth section focuses on the participation of the developing economies in the Cancún Ministerial Conference. A more detailed fifth section provides the causal factors behind the setback in Cancún, while the sixth section dwells on the lessons from this failure. The seventh section provides an in-depth analysis of whether the WTO suffers from institutional flaws, and if so how they can be remedied. The final section provides a summary of the chapter and its conclusions.

WAS THE CANCÚN MINISTERIAL CONFERENCE FOREDOOMED?

Culmination of the Fifth Ministerial Conference of the WTO without an agreement at Cancún, Mexico, had little element of surprise for the cognoscenti in the area of international trade. Its successful conclusion would, indeed, have been astounding. Other than being a tough grind, at the best of times such negotiations are strongly failure-prone. Although this failure was indeed a setback to the trade liberalization efforts of the global community, such failures had occurred in the past. Of the nine Ministerial Conferences under the aegis of the GATT and the WTO, four were considered as complete failures. The all-embracing debacle in Seattle (1999) is another fairly recent example. The Uruguay Round (1986–94) of multilateral trade negotiations (MTNs) teetered at the brink of disaster for a long time and then collapsed. It had to be dexterously pulled back on its feet by Arthur Dunkel, the Director General of the General Agreement on Tariffs and Trade (GATT) during 1980–93. Originally the Uruguay Round was to be completed in three years but its deadline had to be extended several times. The Doha Round of MTNs has been heading the same way.

While the Doha Round running into the sand in Cancún was a setback to the global trading system, only an alarmist would think that it would undermine the legal and organizational foundations of the world trading system. Disappointing as the setback in Cancún was, it did not reflect a collapse of the multilateral trade regime, albeit it did inspire a penchant toward bilateral trade agreements (BTAs) and regional trade agreements (RTA) among the WTO members. Such bilateral deals are based on narrow national interests of the partner economies and have been on the rise (Das, 2004b). They are considered economically inferior. Although the United States endeavored to restart the MTNs after the Cancún failure, it was concurrently preparing to enter into a free trade agreement (FTA) with Thailand.[6] However, BTAs, RTAs and FTAs are not always an easy way out of the comprehensive MTNs. This has been demonstrated by the recent failure of negotiations between Japan and Mexico to form an FTA.

Probable Candidates for Loss from Failure

Trade analysts believed that one group of economies that stood to lose substantially from the failure in Cancún, and subsequently from the possible failure of the Doha Round, was the developing economies in general, particularly small and low-income developing countries. Even after eight rounds of MTNs under the GATT, some of the most illiberal policies in agricultural trade have persisted. In addition, several vitally important issues in non-agricultural market access (NAMA) and services still need to be negotiated. Furthermore, developing economies have their own set of protectionist measures, limiting intera-trade among themselves, which imposes a large cost on the domestic consumers and developing economies in general (Chapter 3, pp. 92–4). This was another area for the MTNs to address.

Elimination of trade-distorting policies in both industrial and developing economies could lift millions out of absolute poverty. Therefore, the Doha Ministerial Declaration had promised to 'place needs and interest (of the developing economies) at the heart of the Work Program adopted in this Declaration'.[7] A successful conclusion of the Doha Round is expected to work toward reaching the Millennium Development Goal (MDG) of cutting down income poverty by a half by 2015 (Winters, 2003). Therefore, disagreement in Cancún on negotiating 'modalities' and targets, and its subsequent failure, was a pernicious development for the developing economies first, and small and low-income developing economies second. This inability to agree and compromise in the global trade forum was likely to affect the poorest G-90 countries most. The Cancún failure was a proof that the Doha Round was not living up to its name of being a development round. A more open and equitable trading system would provide the G-90 countries with an important tool in alleviating poverty by raising their levels of economic development (Panitchpakdi, 2003).

The issues and emphases in the MTNs went on varying over the decades (Chapter 1, 13–23). Not only has the value and volume of multilateral trade undergone a marked transformation, but also its structure has changed radically since 1980. This transformation was squarely based on the changing comparative advantage of the economies participating in the multilateral trading system. In 1980, the largest volume and value of world trade was in primary products and medium-technology manufactures. By 2000, primary products became the smallest component of world trade, while high-technology products surpassed them by a wide margin. They soared from 10 percent of the total world exports in 1980 to 25 percent in 2000. During this time span, world exports had a high and positive correlation with the level of technology. While the highest growth rates were recorded in the high-technology product categories, resource-based manufactures were at the other end of the spectrum. The lowest overall growth was recorded in the primary exports category – a paltry 3.2 percent per annum.[8]

DIVERGENCES AND DIFFICULTIES IN THE FIFTH MINISTERIAL CONFERENCE

The objective set for the Fifth Ministerial Conference at Cancún was to 'take stock of the progress in negotiations, provide any necessary political guidance, and take decisions as necessary'.[9] As ministers could not agree in Cancún on the negotiating framework and future agenda, the future of negotiations on many relevant issues seemed uncertain. A valid apprehension was that the Cancún setback would not only make the Doha Round lose its momentum but could bring it to a grinding halt. For these reasons, the outcome of the Fifth Ministerial Conference was a disappointment to the entire multilateral trading community. In the end the participating trade ministers could neither summon the necessary flexibility nor the political will to bridge the gaps that separated their respective positions. Other than wide differences in negotiating positions in agricultural trade, they could not agree in Cancún *inter alia* on whether to launch negotiations on the four Singapore issues, namely: (a) trade and foreign investment; (b) trade and competition; (c) transparency in government procurement; and (d) trade facilitation.[10] The level of political sensitivity varies widely on these issues, and this caused serious disagreements among the members. The EU – the principal *demandeur* – and within it the United Kingdom, insisted that the decision to launch negotiations on the Singapore issues was taken in Doha, but the G-20 and other developing economies insisted that this was not the agreement. They asserted that these issues were to be addressed after the Cancún Ministerial Conference not during the conference. A former Director General of the GATT and the WTO, Peter Sutherland (2004), remarked that, 'Singapore issues should never have been included in the round'.

Seed of Failure

Failure in Cancún can justly be blamed for some developments in Doha two years ago. Although the Doha Ministerial Conference had a veneer of concurrence among the WTO members and it ended on a harmonious note, the deliberations before the launch of the Doha Round were marked by acrimonious disagreements between the developing and industrial economies. Impressive launch rhetoric concealed the friction and promised reductions in trade-distorting farm support, slashing tariffs on agricultural and agro-industrial products, cutting industrial tariffs in areas that developing countries cared about (such as textiles and apparel), freeing up trade in services and taking up Singapore issues for creating multilateral rules. As developments in Cancún demonstrated, this rhetoric was a mere expression of good intentions. The actions of the members did not conform to it.

After the launch of the Doha Round, members and country groups began to disown important parts of the Doha Development Agenda (DDA). For instance, the EU denied ever having promised elimination of export subsidies in agriculture. Similarly, the developing economies denied ever having agreed for talks on the Singapore issues. The position of the low-income G-90 countries was more uncomfortable, almost distressful. The majority continued to complain about their grievance over the imbalances in the outcomes of the Uruguay Round and felt no need to launch a new round of MTNs. This kind of posturing meant that brisk progress in negotiations could not be realistically conceived. The atmosphere during the preparatory phase was marked by divergence, disagreement and muddle. In Cancún, countries and country groups continued with their intransigence and grandstanding, instead of seeking and working towards compromises on which MTNs could be squarely based (*The Economist*, 2003).

A notable characteristic of disagreements in Cancún was that during the chaotic Third Ministerial Conference in Seattle, disagreements among the WTO members were all around – that is, they took north–south, east–west, north–north and south–south axes (Das, 2001). As opposed to this scenario, in Cancún the disagreements among the members followed a clear north-south axis. This was not a sudden or surprising development. The possibility of acute discord and a north–south divide was apprehended well before the Fifth Ministerial started in Cancún.[11]

The divergence in positions of developing and industrial economies existed on several significant issues. The most important ones included: (a) the negotiating 'modalities'; (b) launching of negotiations on the Singapore issue and their scope; (c) addressing the old outstanding issue of highly illiberal trade in agriculture and settling on modalities; (d) modalities for strengthening the present WTO provisions on special and differential treatment (SDT) for developing economies; and (e) addressing the implementation issue, that is, the problem of the small and low-income developing economies that were not able to implement the recommendations of the Uruguay Round. Progress in negotiations during the Doha Round had thus far been virtually absent. It missed important self-imposed deadlines – in some important cases, such as agricultural negotiations, repeatedly. Many of the sensitive trade issues and contentious political decisions were being continuously put off, and consequently the Cancún Ministerial Conference became overburdened. A large number of complicated issues had accumulated for resolution during the Conference.

Movements towards Partial Agreements: Light at the End of the Tunnel

Not all the developments in Cancún – in negotiations that were undertaken during the preparatory phase of the Fifth Ministerial Conference – were negative. There were a few hopeful, if tentative and nebulous, developments, which could be skillfully followed up. For instance, some movements were made in reaching partially agreed positions in two areas in agricultural negotiations, namely, on a formula-based approach in the reduction of agricultural subsidies and market access. Similar partial agreement evolved on NAMA.

In addition, two areas in which a bridge could possibly be built – albeit uneasily – between positions of developing and industrial economies were Trade-Related Aspects of Intellectual Property Rights (TRIPS) of which public health related issues were a part. Thus viewed, when the Cancún Ministerial Conference began, not the entire negotiations scenario was bleak and bereft of progress. Its details are discussed on pp. 108–11.

PARTICIPATION OF DEVELOPING ECONOMIES IN CANCÚN MINISTERIAL CONFERENCE

Having learned from their participation in the Uruguay Round, the developing economies were fairly well prepared and integrated into negotiations on modalities and targets in Cancún. This is reflected by several developments in Cancún. Several events happened for the first time there. The developing economies coordinated better among themselves and there was far less division in the positions taken by them than in the past. This is not to say that there was no discord among them. They knew from the beginning that trade in agriculture and the four Singapore issues needed their undivided attention. They gave a good deal of importance to cotton subsidies as well. Several middle-income developing economies in Latin America and low-income African countries were particularly focused on agricultural trade negotiations. The latter country group and the LDCs were also concerned about the Singapore issues. Twenty-two developing economies were absolutely opposed to the inclusion of the Singapore issues in the MTNs and they emphasized it in their statement, although three large developing countries (Mexico, Korea (Republic of) and Venezuela) supported it.

The initiative to form the G-20 was taken by Brazil, China, India and South Africa during the preparatory phase of the Fifth Ministerial Conference. The four large emerging-market economies (EMEs) provided collegial leadership to this group. Twenty members of this group had joined hands during the pre-Cancún period, while two more joined in after the start of the Conference. The

G-20 became a voice to reckon with in Cancún. This group represented half the world's population and two-thirds of its farmers. The Group-of-Ten (G-10) of the Uruguay Round period has been ineffectual, but the G-20 was better organized and more professional in the manner it operated. Therefore, it also came to have some negotiating weight. For negotiations on agriculture and the Singapore issues, developing countries coalesced into *ad hoc* coalitions.

Several Firsts

The agenda for agricultural negotiations had three principal pillars: domestic support, market access and export subsidies. For handling negotiations on each one of them, two developing-country ministers were chosen by the developing economies. The G-20 coalition remained together throughout the negotiations during the Ministerial Conference. Like the former G-10 it did not disintegrate under pressure. This is not to say that efforts were not made to create fissures in it by way of offering carrots to individual coalition members and threatening with sticks, the old technique. 'Despite active efforts to split the group through specific offers to individual countries, the coalition remained together' until the end.[12] In the past, such efforts to split the developing economies had met with success, albeit not in Cancún. Another first was groups of developing countries taking one stand and participating together in negotiations cohesively. In the past, such group action was limited to agenda setting or blocking coalitions.

Yet another first was the emergence of a noteworthy issue-specific coalition. This came about on cotton exporting West African countries, namely, Benin, Burkina Faso, Mali and Chad referred to as the Cotton-4, although they became five because Senegal joined them a little late (see Chapter 6). This sub-group took a stand in favor of abolishing trade-distorting subsidies granted to cotton growers in the EU, the US and China. Their grievance was just. They were being crushed by the subsidies in the industrial economies, particularly the annual $3 billion-plus that the US was paying to its 25 000 cotton growers. Supported by this subsidy the US became the world's biggest exporter of cotton. The subsidy also lowered the world market price of cotton by up to 40 percent (World Bank, 2003). Therefore, this country group demanded compensation for the three-year transition period, when these subsidies would be phased out. Although nothing came out of their proposal in Cancún, it succeeded in attracting a good deal of world attention, which resulted in support from developing and industrial economies alike. The Cotton-4 could be credited with partial success in achieving its objectives. The latest version of the Global Trade Analysis Project (GTAP) database was used to estimate the impact of slashing subsidies and tariffs on the cotton trade of the Cotton-4 economies of West Africa. Results confirmed that it is subsidy reduction rather than tariff cuts that would make by far the largest impact on the cotton-exporting countries (Anderson and Valenzuela, 2006).

CAUSAL FACTORS BEHIND THE SETBACK IN CANCÚN

Different causal factors emerged from the press reports including 'inept' chairmanship of the Ministerial Conference by Luis Ernesto Derbez, the foreign minister of Mexico. Some believed that the agenda for Cancún was 'overloaded', making it difficult for the WTO members to simultaneously negotiate several complicated issues before or during the Ministerial Conference (pp. 102–4). Some national negotiators were unwilling to go beyond the pre-determined demands of the other delegations, and seriously negotiate with the other delegations. However, for all appearances, negotiations on agriculture and the Singapore issues were the prime causal factors behind the *Tequila* sunset in Cancún. The developments that brought about failure were as follows:

Negotiations on Singapore Issues

The last day of the Fifth Ministerial was entirely devoted to the Singapore issues. Different sub-groups of developing economies, including the members of the African, Caribbean and Pacific (ACP)[13] countries and the members of the African Group (AG) came to Cancún with a well-defined position of not supporting the launch of negotiations on the four Singapore issues. In this they had support from Malaysia, although other EMEs did not take a strong position because the industrial countries had scaled back the scope of these negotiations in a realistic manner before the Cancún Ministerial started.

The US position on the four Singapore issues was that of diffidence, although it did have a strong desire to launch negotiations on trade and foreign investment-related issues. As the US firms make large foreign direct investments (FDI), US interest in protecting them with the WTO rules was natural. This observation was buttressed by the two recent BTAs that the US signed with Chile and Singapore. These BTAs included clauses on capital controls and FDI. The US interest in the other three Singapore issues ranged from lukewarm to none.

As set out above (pp. 000–0), the principal proponents of the Singapore issues were the EU, Japan and Korea. In the EU, opinion on this issue was again divided. In several large EU economies, many firms did not support a strong EU stand on the Singapore issues. The EU displayed foresight and flexibility by proposing to drop two of the four Singapore issues (namely, competition and investment) from the negotiations, and terminating the working groups on these subjects. Apparently the EU decision to make a retreat on the Singapore issues was taken late, which turned out to be a tactical error.[14] Besides, Japan and Korea remained adamantly opposed to even the delayed and renewed EU proposal. Strong opposition from the ACP group, LDCs and AU countries in this regard persisted, although India proposed that the fourth Singapore issue (namely, trade facilitation) could be taken up for negotiations at Cancún. Given the considerable diversity in positions, negotiations on Singapore issues could not be launched.

One view – many WTO members seemed to share it – was that the EU and Japan continually insisted on launching negotiations on the four Singapore issues only to divert attention of the negotiators from their own intransigence over agriculture, a politically sensitive area for the both the EU and Japan. Liberalized agricultural trade was, and was intended to be, an important focus of the Doha Round. These countries were cognizant of the fact that they have some of the most illiberal, archaic, and well-entrenched, systems of agricultural protection in the world. They were hopelessly on the defensive in this regard since the launch of the Doha Round. Political acceptance of agricultural reforms in these countries seems beyond their governments. Therefore, negotiators from the EU and Japan believed that the intransigence of three groups of developing economies, named above, on Singapore issues could easily be made a scapegoat for the failure at Cancún.

A post-Cancún view emerged on the Singapore issues, which emphasized taking them completely off the table.[15] While these issues have their developmental significance, in particular the fourth issue, they are not related – or directly related – to the core issue of market access in international trade, which is the *sine qua non* of the world trading system. These issues do not adhere to the 'tried-and-tested formula of improving economic welfare through trade negotiations that result in reciprocal reduction to impediments to international commerce' (Evenett, 2003). In addition, negotiating and implementing WTO agreements on the four Singapore issues would be complex, time consuming and expensive.

Negotiations on Agriculture

Trade in agricultural products continued to remain the most contentious area of negotiations in the MTNs. It divided negotiating delegations both before and during the Cancún conference. The Geneva process failed to narrow differences between countries on modalities and the parameters of liberalization on agriculture. The negotiators in Geneva also failed to meet the deadline of settling the modalities for agricultural negotiations by the mini-Ministerial in Montreal in July 2003. Negotiations on modalities had reached an unpromising stalemate before the Cancún conference.

Following the mini-Ministerial in Montreal, the EU and the US drew up a joint framework for the liberalization of farm trade on 13 August 2003. It was a weaker and much less ambitious proposal than was visualized at the time of the launch of the DDA in 2001. According to the August proposal, export subsidies – one of the principal bugbears – were not to be eliminated. The EU had always and strongly resisted their elimination. This proposal was structured to maintain 'existing farm programs on each side of the Atlantic, and deserved the harsh critique of the newly-formed G-20' coalition (Schott, 2004). Hindsight reveals that tabling the joint EU–US compromise proposal was an injudicious, imprudent and counterproductive move by the two hegemonic trade powers. Developing countries' reaction to it was poorly calculated by them.

The joint EU–US August proposal ended up creating complete mistrust among the developing economies and provoked the creation of a strong G-20 coalition. It responded by a counter proposal, in which the G-20 called for a larger subsidy cuts, modified the formula for tariff reductions, and squarely inserted SDT provisions. It further called for the identification of special products (SP) for the developing economies which would be exempted from tariff cuts as well as for a special safeguard mechanism (SSM). In addition, it called for an elimination of the Blue Box, rather than its amendment, as well as spending caps on the Green Box.[16] This was a substantial proposal from a new country group, and was much bolder than the EU–US proposal. For the first time, it became clear that G-20 was emerging as an important negotiating group that the EU and the US would have to contend with. While this alliance was firmly united in its demand, its members could not agree to a common position regarding their own contribution to liberalization endeavors, which justly exasperated the EU and the US.

The fair and rational grievances of the cotton-growing economies of West Africa were ignored in Cancún. There was only an indistinguishable mention of them in the draft document that had emerged halfway through the Cancún conference. While the document mentioned a review of the textile sector, it did not touch upon the issue of eliminating the cotton subsidies, let alone the issue of compensation to the five West African countries. Instead, they were advised to diversify their exports. Responding to the demand of national constituency, the US delegation led in rejecting the West African position on elimination of cotton subsidies. Eliminating cotton subsidies would have been a domestically unpopular move in the US. Besides, the chairman of the Senate agricultural committee in the US was known to be an ally of cotton growers. Consequently, frustrated West African countries vented their anger by digging in their heels when it came to supporting negotiations on Singapore issues.

Despite missed deadlines for agreeing on modalities, agriculture negotiations did progress to a limited extent. To be sure, the liberalization offer was nowhere near what was committed during the launch of the Doha Round. However, it was reported in the business press that the ministers had been prepared to discuss it further on the last day in Cancún and advance their negotiating positions, when the chairman of the conference, Luis Ernesto Derbez, decided that the negotiations were not progressing and brought them to a formal closure. If they had not been ended so abruptly, there was a plausibility of some more progress in this difficult area of trade negotiations. With the breakdown of the Doha process, the progress of negotiations on other issues – including market access for services and NAMA, implementation matters, the environment and some areas of intellectual property – stalled by default. At this point, some member countries had envisaged that political resistance to agricultural reform in the large industrial countries for agricultural reforms was strong and the Doha Round would necessarily be extended beyond the originally stated deadline of January 2005. This assumption made their own commitments in the MTNs lax and unhurried.

Inept Conference Management

The Ministerial Conference, during both the preparatory phase in Geneva and during the Conference in Cancún, was managed in a far superior manner than that in Seattle. Participating members were notified of the Green Room meetings and were kept updated about the proceedings and decisions. They were given time for larger group consultations and open-ended meetings within their small select groups, which made them comfortable regarding horizontal as well as vertical flows of information. Notwithstanding these improvements, serious process-related errors were committed, which eventually destabilized the Conference.

One major *faux pas* was this circulation of a text by the Chair of the General Council, Ambassador Carlos Perez del Castillo, on his own responsibility. It was acknowledged that it was prepared in close collaboration with the Director General of the WTO. The intent was to make it the basis for negotiations during the Conference. This was a new, unusual and impromptu measure taken without any attempt to create a consensus among the participating members. The participants reacted adversely and saw it as an ill-conceived and controversial move. It immediately provoked exasperation among. them and created an air of confrontation in Cancún. Member delegations felt that by abandoning the old practice of preparing a text with square brackets, to indicate where disagreements existed, an agenda was being forced on them from the top.

The Castillo text became more controversial because while the accompanying letter from the Chair and the Director General stated that the Castillo text did not support any delegation's position on any of the issues under negotiation, it was perceived by the developing country delegations as privileging the proposals of some industrial economies, while marginalizing alternative proposals put forth by the developing economies. In particular, on agriculture the Castillo text incorporated many of the proposals from the EU–US compromise proposal, which was entirely unacceptable to the developing country members. The G-20 countries pointedly noticed that their counter-proposals did not find any place in the Castillo text. Similarly, on the Singapore issues it was perceived as leaning heavily toward the stand of the industrial countries and against the position of the developing countries. The strongest reaction against the Castillo text came from Brazil; its delegation threatened a walk-out if the text was used as the basis for the MTNs. Other EMEs and developing countries were also antagonistic toward it. Ignoring so much hostility, the text was used as a basis for negotiation. It was an ill-conceived, almost suicidal move.

The second major maladroit and equally controversial move was the appointment of five 'facilitators' to assist the Chairperson of the Conference, Mexican Foreign Minister Luis Ernesto Derbez. The objective was that they would assist the Chairperson in moving the negotiations forward and create consensus in five key negotiation areas, namely, agriculture, non-agricultural market access (NAMA), development, the Singapore issues, and other issues under negotiations. The five ambassadors chosen as facilitators were those from Canada, Guyana, Hong Kong SAR, Kenya and Singapore. This practice was followed during the GATT period and the developing economies were not averse to it at that time because their involvement and stakes in the Ministerial Conferences was of much lower order. It was also followed during the Doha Ministerial, when the 'friends of the chair' were appointed in a similar manner. However, reaction of the developing country members in Cancún was caustically averse to the appointment of the facilitators.

Notwithstanding the fact that geographical representation and developing country participation were taken into consideration in choosing the facilitators, the developing economies questioned the procedural proprieties of these appointments. The resentment of the developing country members originated from the fact that there were no rules, explicit or implicit, for selection of the facilitators. They were neither elected, nor was a consensus created about their selection. The developing country delegations questioned the stage at which they were chosen and the criteria for selection. There was an apparent lack of transparency in this matter. While *prima facie* their role as mediators appeared innocuous and small, in practice the facilitators wielded considerable power, particularly in the agenda-setting process. They decided whom to invite for meetings, the duration of meetings and finally whose views were reported in the text. Lack of transparency in the selection process created distrust among the delegations, in turn contaminating the negotiating environment.

A survey of the role played by the facilitators revealed that several developing countries were extremely dissatisfied by the way the facilitators went about calling and mediating in the meetings (Narlikar, 2005). It was reported that meetings were frequently terminated well ahead of time. Many were converted into bilateral consultations with the members. While such consultations have their value, they are no substitute for larger group meetings in multilateral negotiations, where agreements among a large number of members are created by deliberation and persuasion, contributing to harmonious proceedings. The excessive emphasis on bilateral consultations changed the nature of the ministerial forum and tipped the balance away from multilateralism. It made developing countries dig their heels deeper into hard-line positions, making compromises implausible.

The role of the Chairperson was also severely criticized by the participants. Derbez had aroused the ire of developing countries across regions and coalitions and lost their trust. His revised draft of the Castillo text, which was circulated on 13 September, was logically expected by the members to be a compromise text based on three days of energetic discussions and deliberations, and the formal responses to the Castillo draft. From the perspective of the developing economies, the revised draft made no attempt to compromise the diverse positions of member countries and country groups. It failed to address the concerns of the developing countries, some of whom assessed it as even more one-sided than the original Castillo draft. As if these deep-seated controversies were not enough, on the last day, instead of harnessing and supporting promises of feeble compromises, the Chairperson abruptly called the meeting to a close. The participants regarded this as the worst all the mistakes in the management of the Ministerial Conference at Cancún.

BEST THING ABOUT FAILURE

One learns nothing from success, but a lot from a failure. It is the best opportunity to identify errors, learn lessons and use them to achieve success. Several serious and avoidable errors were committed in Cancún, which contributed to failure. The first one was to insist on negotiating on the Singapore issues until the last morning of the last day of the conference. As noted above, an overwhelming majority of the WTO members eyed them with suspicion and considered them neither relevant or beneficial to them nor to the multilateral trade regime. The first three Singapore issues in no way gave an appearance of benefiting the developing country members of the WTO. Second, the EU position of linking agriculture and the Singapore issues in effect proved to be a stumbling block. Reforms of agriculture trade regime were long overdue and they were a crucial part of the DDA as well as a key to progress in the Doha Round. Linking them with the Singapore issues was 'counterproductive' (Hoekman, 2003). This linkage made many developing countries question whether MTNs are in their interest at all. In particular, negotiations on multilateral rules on trade and investment and trade and competition were considered issues that had little payoff for developing members of the WTO in terms of trade expansion and development.

Third, after decades of sitting on the sidelines the developing economies became active participants during the Uruguay Round, which was a healthy institutional development (Chapter 5). Their active participation went to strengthen and enrich the fabric of the multilateral trading system. Members of G-20 were able to form a negotiating coalition and to function – even though their individual positions differed. Frequently their negotiating positions did not always adhere to the demands of national constituencies, and they accommodated in order to keep the coalition together, which in turn displayed the maturity and far-sightedness of the members of G-20 as negotiators. Instead of letting the Fifth Ministerial fail, this coalition could aim at a Pareto superior outcome by presenting a negotiable alternative by agreeing to one Singapore issue, namely, trade facilitation, which was in every member's interest. A large number of developing members, if not all, needed improvement in their customs procedures and other trade infrastructure-related areas. Efficiency created by improvement in trade logistics would undoubtedly have benefited the developing countries.

Fourth, the negotiation modalities in Cancún did not require LDCs to reciprocate and further liberalize their trade regimes. Also, under SDT, other large developing economies were obliged to adopt only limited reciprocity. In order to harness reciprocity in the negotiations and impart dynamism to the MTNs, developing economies needed to change tack and make offers to the industrial economies in different areas so that the entire multilateral trade regime could benefit from trade liberalization. Successful traders like China and the other EMEs could go a step further and offer the OECD countries *quid pro quo* in market access negotiations in goods and services. In market access negotiations, both developing and industrial economies bargain in order to eliminate poor trade practices, which have salutary systemic implications. This line of thinking is eminently logical. However, what held these developing countries back was their experiences during the Uruguay Round. After the round, the developing countries were left feeling that they had naively overcommitted themselves (Chapter 2, pp. 38–40).

Fifth, it seems that during the post-Cancún period the old SDT concept needed to be revised and updated by making it more differentiated (Hoekman *et al.*, 2004). Exempting developing economies from reciprocity was no longer logical for a sub-group of developing economies like China and the EMEs. While LDCs face genuine difficulties in this area because of poor institutional capacity, other developing economies need to gradually advance toward progressively eschewing the privileges of SDT. Large and successful traders needed to take initiatives in this regard. Besides, developing economies are cognizant of the fact that not liberalizing their domestic trade regime has a boomerang effect on them, both individually and collectively. For starters, a short-term public policy objective should be to create domestic political constituency for such a change in the EMEs.

Sixth, Hoekman (2003) has redrawn attention toward 'the governance and procedures' of the WTO, which was intensely debated in the aftermath of the debacle in Seattle in 1999.[17] Large membership of the WTO has made consensus formation both 'a major strength and weakness of the WTO'. Although successful improvements have been made in the transparency of negotiations since the failure of the Green Room process in Seattle, transaction costs still remain exceedingly high. Cancún saw a move towards the formation of negotiating coalitions, which led to some ease in negotiations because only the 'principals' participated for their respective groups. The flip side of this coin was greater inflexibility and the heightened probability of a breakdown, particularly when negotiations are taking place against strict time deadlines.[18]

SUMMARY AND CONCLUSIONS

Failure of the Fifth Ministerial Conference of the WTO without any agreement had little element of surprise. This biennial conference was foredoomed. At the Cancún Ministerial Conference, divergence in the negotiating positions of developing and industrial economies existed on several significant issues and the gap could not be bridged until the beginning of the conference. Hopes for narrowing the gap in negotiating positions of the principal participants and groups among them were belied. The two principal areas of divergence in positions were agricultural trade reforms and the so-called Singapore issues. After learning from their participation in the Uruguay Round, the developing economies were fairly well prepared and integrated into negotiations on modalities and targets in Cancún. Their participation was of superior order compared to the past.

The origins of the failure in Cancún can be traced back to the Doha Ministerial Conference. Despite a veneer of harmony and optimism, several disagreements had existed in Doha and they were not resolved until the

Cancún Ministerial Conference. A vulnerable situation, resulting from differing views and negotiating positions on important issues, was worsened by highly inept conference management. Most analysts believed that one group of economies that stood to lose substantially from the failure in Cancún, and subsequently form the possible failure of the Doha Round, was the developing economies in general, particularly small and low-income developing countries. Frequent failures of this kind make the WTO look like a supranational body that is structurally flawed.

NOTES

1. Thus far five Ministerial Conferences of the World Trade Organization have taken place. They were held in: Singapore (9–13 December 1996), Geneva (18–20 May, 1998), Seattle (30 November to 3 December 1999, Doha (9–13 November 2001) and Cancún (10–14 September 2003).
2. The First Ministerial Conference of the WTO was held in Singapore in 1996. During this conference Ministers from WTO member-countries decided to set up three new working groups: (a) on trade and investment; (b) on competition policy; and (c) on transparency in government procurement. They also instructed the WTO Goods Council to look at possible ways of simplifying trade procedures, an issue sometimes known as 'trade facilitation'. Because the Singapore conference kicked off work in these four subjects, they have become known as the 'Singapore issues'.
3. At the time of writing, the G-20 has the following 21 members: Argentina, Bolivia, Brazil, Chile, China, Colombia, Costa Rica, Cuba, Ecuador, Egypt, Guatemala, India, Indonesia, Mexico, Nigeria, Pakistan, Paraguay, Peru, Philippines, South Africa, Thailand and Venezuela. The role of collegial leader of G-20 has been played by Brazil, China, India and South Africa.
4. This is an umbrella grouping of WTO member countries. The Group-of-Ninety includes Africa, Caribbean and Pacific (ACP), the Least Developed Countries and African Group (AG). This is the largest country group in the WTO system. In 2006, 64 of the G-90 countries had WTO membership.
5. Fifty countries are currently designated by the United Nations as the 'least developed countries'. Of these, 32 were members of the WTO in mid-2006. The list is reviewed every three years by the Economic and Social Council (ECOSOC). The criteria underlying the current list of LDCs are: (a) low income, as measured by the gross domestic product (GDP) per capita; (b) weak human resources, as measured by a composite index (Augmented Physical Quality of Life Index) based on indicators of life expectancy at birth, per capita calorie intake, combined primary and secondary school enrolment, and adult literacy; (c) a low level of economic diversification, as measured by a composite index (Economic Diversification Index) based on the share of manufacturing in GDP, the share of the labor force in industry, annual per capita commercial energy consumption, and UNCTAD's merchandise export concentration index.
6. The United States Trade Administration (USTA) signed eight bilateral trade agreements between September 2003 and May 2004.
7. See WTO (2001). Paragraph 2.
8. See Bacchetta and Bora (2003) for these statistics. Also refer to Lall (2000) for a detailed exposition on the changing structure of developing country exports over the last two decades.
9. See paragraph 45 of the Doha Ministerial Declaration, 14 November 2001.
10. They are referred to as the Singapore issues because they were raised for the first time by the industrial economies during the Singapore Ministerial Conference in 1996.

11. When the Cancún Ministerial Conference began, the Chairperson of the Ministerial Conference, Luis Ernesto Derbez, Foreign Minister of Mexico, had warned of the dangers of failure. He described the Cancún Conference as a 'once-in-a-generation opportunity', and that failure would mean loss of momentum and that negotiations would take 'a long time to recover'. Pascal Lamy, who was the EU's chief negotiator in Cancún. He had admonished the congregation at the outset to eschew 'the confrontational north–south ambiance of the 1970s and 1980s'.

12. See Hoekman (2003), who also provides a list of instances of creating such splits among the developing economies in the past.

13. The European development cooperation policy is run in conjunction with the 77 ACP countries and, following the Lomé Convention, is governed by the Cotonou Agreement.

14. Pascal Lamy did not inform the negotiating group about this decision until the last morning in Cancún. At that late hour hints were dropped that the EU could drop three Singapore issues, leaving only negotiations on trade facilitation on the table.

15. See, for instance Hoekman (2003) and Evenett (2003).

16. In the terminology of agricultural protection, the Green Box refers to domestic support, or subsidies, that does not distort trade and therefore it is permitted without limits. A Blue Box implies permitted support, or subsidies, linked to production. They are subject to production limits and therefore regarded as minimally trade-distorting.

17. See Das (2001) for this debate.

18. This section draws on the following two sources: Hoekman (2003) and Hoekman *et al.* (2003).

5. Enter the developing economies: transforming the landscape of the multilateral trade regime

Patience is power. Patience is skill. With time and patience a mulberry leaf becomes silk.

A Chinese Proverb

INTRODUCTION

Proactive participation of the developing economies in the multilateral trade regime came about belatedly, although they were a part of the GATT/WTO system since its inception (Chapter 2, pp. 34–40). Entry of the developing economies into the multilateral trade scenario has definitively and discernibly transformed the landscape of the multilateral trade regime. It has also swayed the pace, process, substance and spirit of the multilateral trade negotiations (MTNs). In the early stages, being neophytes, the developing economies were not able to perform in a satisfactory manner. Often they failed to achieve the objectives they were striving for. However, gradually they learned the ropes and began to understand the process and substance of the multilateral trade regime. Their performance in the multilateral trade arena has improved perceptibly.

This chapter is structured on the following lines. The next section focuses on how the developing economies initially remained passive and then cautiously entered the stage of multilateral trade before launching into active participation in it. The third section delves into the increased participation of the developing economies after the birth of the World Trade Organization (WTO). The difficulties faced by them due to lack of negotiation scholarship and *savoir-faire* is the subject of the fourth section. Although there were several coalitions among the developing economies, two were of greater significance. The birth and limited success of a small so-called Like-Minded Group (LMG) of developing countries on the multilateral trade scenario is the focus of the fifth section. Similarly, the sixth section examines the birth, activities and success that were achieved by the Group-of-Twenty (G-20) coalition. Notwithstanding the endeavors of the various groups of the developing economies, the Doha Round suffered from stagnation, which is examined in the seventh section. How it was salvaged and some negotiating momentum was generated is analyzed in the eighth section. The following section deals with the need for success in the Doha Round and what direct and indirect benefits the developing economies can reasonably hope to achieve. The final section provides a summary and conclusion.

TRADITION OF INERTIA AND PASSIVITY

It was noted earlier in Chapter 1 (pp. 15–17) that of the 23 founding countries of the General Agreement on Tariff and Trade (GATT), 12 were developed and 11 developing economies.[1] As the core trading economies of this era were the industrial economies, they overwhelmingly dominated multilateral trade as well as the multilateral trade regime. During the early decade of the GATT era, being small traders, the developing economies accepted the status of passive sideliners (Chapter 2, pp. 40–44). Their membership of the GATT system was almost notional and perfunctory. They saw the GATT as an unintrusive multilateral organization. During the early period, a minor leadership role for the developing economies in the GATT was played by Brazil and India. Both were regional economic powers in their own right, with diminutive international economic presence. Since the aborted negotiations for the International Trade Organization (ITO) in 1947, they were the small voice of the developing world in the GATT system.

Successive rounds of MTNs took place without the participation or contribution of developing economies. At the beginning of every round of MTNs the developing economies expressed vocal concern regarding the state of the multilateral trade regime, and then adopted an almost passive stance toward the proceedings and negotiations. However, during the 1960s and 1970s, the developing economies did make near unanimous calls for special and differential treatment (SDT) in the multilateral trading system. Yet their participation in the Kennedy Round (1964–7) was entirely marginal, while in the Tokyo Round (1973–9) it was limited merely to framework negotiations.

Their peripheral role and passivity during the GATT era was not irrational because, first, tariff negotiations in the post-War era were conducted on a reciprocal basis, which did not offer small trading developing economies any incentive to participate actively. As they were neither large import markets nor aggressive exporters, developing economies had little to offer and not much to ask for. Second, due to the most-favored nation (MFN) clause of the GATT, the non-participants would receive the resulting benefits of MTNs anyway. Third, most developing economies, particularly the large ones like Brazil, China, India and Mexico, did not regard trade as an engine of growth until

1980s. China had opted out of the GATT in 1950, while the other three were following the inward-oriented growth strategy of import-substituting industrialization (ISI) (see Chapter 3). Under this *mise-en-scène* the GATT system did not have much relevance or significance for them.

Shedding the Tradition and Switching the Growth Trajectory

China switched to its now famous 'open-door policy' in 1978, and during the decade of the 1980s many developing economies began to seriously re-evaluate the results of their ISI strategy. As discussed in the earlier chapters, the macroeconomic policy environment in developing economies began to transform.[2] They began, unilaterally as well as under the tutelage of the International Monetary Fund (IMF) and the World Bank, to liberalize their economies. The mindset of the policy-makers changed and they began to treat their external sector as an engine of growth and global integration. Serious macroeconomic reforms and policy changes were initiated with an objective of trade expansion and integration with the global economy. Although a clutch of Asian economies took the lead in this regard and turned in stellar trade performance year after year; this success became more widespread and a group called the emerging-market economies (EMEs)[3] began steadily to climb the high-growth trajectory and globalize (Chapter 2). This trend not only continued but accelerated.

In keeping with the novel macroeconomic policy stance adopted by them and the resulting improved trade performance, several developing economies not only entered the Uruguay Round (1986–94) of MTNs but also attempted meaningful participation. They submitted many proposals and took an active part in negotiating groups. This round of MTNs is regarded as the most ambitious under the aegis of the GATT; 123 contracting parties (CPs) of the GATT participated in it and it continued for eight years. The Uruguay Round was the veritable turning point in the status of the developing economies in the multilateral trade regime. Although progress was far from rapid and smooth, it spawned numerous beneficial results and substantively strengthened the structure of the multilateral trade regime. Its meritorious achievements included extension of the multilateral trade discipline to trade in services, agriculture and textiles and apparel, hitherto uncovered areas, and these are enumerated in Chapter 2 (pp. 40–45).

Initial Deficit in *Savoir-Faire*

The developing economies suffered from limitations such as small participating delegations and a knowledge gap regarding both the international trade regime and the negotiation process. During the early phase, supranational institutions like the IMF and the World Bank partly assisted them by way of some general research support. Notwithstanding the fact that they were, and continue to be, a diverse and disparate group, several large and middle-income developing economies – particularly the successful traders from Asia and Latin America – participated more actively in the Uruguay round than did the others. Together this sub-group of developing economies took several well-conceived stands during the course of the MTNs as well as in their respective negotiating groups.

The participation of the developing economies in the Uruguay Round of MTNs was the beginning of their learning process. In the preparatory phase, a Group-of-Ten (G-10) had come together, a first-ever coalition of the developing countries in the MTNs (Chapter 2, pp. 40–43).[4] For a novice in the multilateral trade system, the G-10 took some bold positions in the MTNs. For instance, against the endeavors of the Quad members, in particular the US, the G-10 tried to block the inclusion of trade in services in the GATT until some of the outstanding issues of this period, like standstill and rollback, were resolved. It did not consult other developing countries on the premise that the positions taken by the other developing countries were their own, while the position of the G-10 represented the position of the developing countries. The G-10 also tried to put forth its views on bloc-type arguments rather than make issue-specific cases for the positions that it was taking. Soon other developing economies came up with parallel, if differing, positions and G-10 became irrelevant. This discomfiting failure represented a lack of prescience and foresight. It became a valuable lesson for the developing economies.

Hindsight reveals that while the final results of the Uruguay Round agreements were fairly skewed and in many cases not in favor of the developing economies at all, by their energetic participation this country group did manage to make a mark on the proceedings. It was an educational experience for the developing economies *en masse* and prepared them for future participation in the multilateral trade regime as well as in the MTNs. During the Uruguay Round, and thereafter, developing economies suffered from a disconcerting knowledge gap regarding multilateral trade, which has increasingly grown into a technical subject matter. Developing economies, particularly the least developed countries (LDCs), needed substantial improvement in their comprehension of the multilateral trade issues as well as in their negotiation skills and strategies. Over the years they have become not only knowledge-based but also knowledge-intensive subjects. At present multilateral trade and negotiation process-related work is largely based on empirically grounded scholarship. Future orientation of the participating developing economies in the multilateral trade regime needs to be towards inculcating and acquiring this scholarship.

PARTICIPATION OF THE DEVELOPING ECONOMIES AFTER THE BIRTH OF THE WTO

The birth of the WTO saw a more active participation from the developing economies. More of them established or reinforced their missions in Geneva and participated in the Ministerial Conferences. The first two biennial WTO Ministerial Conferences in Singapore (1996)[5] and Geneva (1998) did not have large agendas or much to decide because they were held immediately in the aftermath of the Uruguay Round (1986–94), the most comprehensive round of MTNs under the aegis of the GATT. Therefore, they succeeded. However, the third one held in Seattle (1999) imploded ignominiously and the fifth one in Cancún (2003) collapsed among acrimonious disagreements and unqualified confusion (Das, 2003). The inconclusive end of the Fifth Ministerial, in Cancún, essentially precluded the prospects of the Doha Round ending by 1 January 2005, the originally scheduled completion date.

As opposed to them, the Fourth Ministerial Conference held in Doha, Qatar (2001), succeeded with a mandate for a new round of MTNs from the 146 WTO members. This Ministerial Conference had to succeed for several reasons. One of them was the 11 September 2001 terrorist attack in New York. At this point in time, the global community sorely needed a tangible symbol of success in cooperation and solidarity. Besides, a failure in Doha – on the heels of the debacle in Seattle – would have been a serious setback to the multilateral trade regime and put its systemic credibility under question. It could have resulted in long-lasting, if not permanent, damage to the multilateral trading system.

Flagging Enthusiasm for Participation

Many developing economies were less enthusiastic about a fresh round of MTNs in 2001 essentially because, as detailed in Chapter 2 (pp. 38–40), first, they were of the opinion that the Uruguay Round did not result in even modest gains for them. Second, they were having difficulties in implementing the recommendations of the Uruguay Round. Third, in the period following the Uruguay Round, realization dawned on an increasing number of developing economies that they had accepted far too many obligations and that the multilateral trade regime was evolving in an unfavorable manner for them. Fourth, implementation of many Uruguay Round agreements was also not being done in the originally perceived manner.

Developing economies had expected to gain from the dismantling of the Multi-Fiber Arrangement (MFA), but the quota relaxation process was heavily back-loaded and came into full effect only at the final stage, in early 2005. Agricultural liberalization initiated in the Uruguay Round ended quotas but replaced them with high tariffs and tariff-rate quotas (TRQs), without improving trading opportunities for the developing economies. The intellectual property agreements went too far and restricted developing countries' access to life-saving medicines, putting them beyond the reach of many. This problem was not resolved until the beginning of the Cancún Ministerial conference in September 2003 (Cline, 2005). During the pre-Doha Round period, the developing economies seemed to perceive collectively that the multilateral trade regime was not a level playing field.

It was obvious and understandable that until the Doha Round addressed the concerns of the developing economies and provided them with improved trading opportunities, they would remain cold and disinterested toward any round of MTNs, present or future. The skepticism of the developing economies was allayed by promises in the area of development by the mature industrial economies that were also the largest traders and occupied the highest positions in the WTO league table of exporters. During the Doha Round, economic growth and development objectives were made an intrinsic part of the MTNs for the first time. It was assigned a pro-development mandate, with integration of the developing economies into the multilateral trading system as one of its priority objectives. The WTO secretariat labeled it the 'Doha Development Agenda' or the DDA, the official title of the round. At the time of its launch, it was billed as more than merely another round of MTNs.

Improving the Preparations for MTNs

The preparatory period before the Third Ministerial Conference in Seattle in 1999 was a defining time point, when many developing economies formally expressed their opinions on trade, trade rules and negotiations-related issues in the multilateral fora. To that end, they presented dozens of formal proposals in an energetic manner. This amounted to a virtual explosion of formal participation by the developing economies in the multilateral trade system. It drew in many small or very small trading countries as well, which had been passive in the past. Some of them were not even CPs of the GATT.

Around this period, many developing economies, particularly the LDCs, increased their investment in training their trade officials with the help of the United Nations Conference on Trade and Development (UNCTAD) and the WTO. The developing economies are presently being proficiently assisted in this regard by new inter-governmental organizations like the Agency for International Trade Information and Cooperation (AITIC) and the South Center. The activities of the AITIC are exclusively and purposefully designed for the low-income developing economies, like the LCDs and the members of the African Group (AG). Large international Non-Governmental Organizations (NGOs) have become active in trade- and negotiation-related technical research. Some such NGOs have taken it upon themselves to prepare analytical proposals for the developing country delegations. To this end, they enlist the expensive expertise of reputed academics in the field, or former WTO officials.

While better prepared than ever in the past, the developing economies still cannot match the capabilities of the industrial economies in terms of research capabilities and resources deployed to the MTNs process. One indicator of this prowess is the sheer size of the delegations of the WTO member countries. In the Hong Kong Ministerial Conference, the EU had the largest delegation of 832 delegates, followed by the US (356) and Japan (229). In stark contrast to this 46 developing countries were represented by less than ten delegates. Combining research capabilities and pooling resources is evidently the best way out for the developing economies.

SCARCITY OF NEGOTIATION SCHOLARSHIP

Although a participation explosion was there for all to see, research-based empirically-grounded negotiation scholarship did not develop *pari passu* with the participation explosion of the developing economies. Despite noteworthy improvements, the serious gap in knowledge and analytical skills had persisted. MTNs can frequently be a complex meta-process. Empirically grounded negotiation scholarship of the negotiation process is a bottleneck for the industrial countries as well. The principal reason behind this general lack of knowledge is that practitioners who are part of the actual MTN process seldom write about it. Their reasons are lack of time, or little inclination to do so. Often they are not at liberty to publicize what they have learned about the MTN negotiation process and strategy. Those who are not part of MTNs find it impossible to dig deep into the actual negotiation process; they can often present a superficial broad-brush picture of reality.

Another academic method of acquiring knowledge about what precisely transpired in the MTNs is devising indirect methods to employee archival researches or by interviewing the actual participants, who are scattered all over the globe. The Geneva missions of the WTO members can be a rich source of information in this area. However, the high costs of such an operation are enough to stymie and discourage researchers. Besides, some scholars do not regard this process highly. They see it as not worth their while to undertake such a project because they believe that claims that cannot be supported by quantitative data are not worthy of academic study, and little quantitative data exists on negotiating strategies in the MTNs.

Rare Pearls of Wisdom

Knowledge and analyses needed as input in the MTN process and its outcomes are to be found with difficulty in research and publications primarily dedicated to areas other than to the negotiation process itself. Similarly, some empirical studies whose primary focus was different from MTNs compiled knowledge relating to the MTN processes. Studies on strategies of negotiation continue to be scarce. So are the facts and data regarding why different approaches and strategies produce different results.

Scholars like Bernard M. Hoekman, Michel M. Kostecki and John S. Odell, have made valiant endeavors to bridge this knowledge gap in recent years. The Geneva International Academic Network has also lately sponsored research in this area of knowledge. Case studies and game-theoretic models are being used to develop insights about the negotiation process during the MTNs.

LIKE-MINDED GROUP: SEEKING STRENGTH IN A SMALL ALLIANCE

The birth of the WTO did not change the fact that the largest traders were still the mature industrial economies and they wielded the maximum negotiating weight in the multilateral trading system, albeit the East Asian economies had started acquiring progressively higher places in the WTO league table of traders. The first Ministerial Conference of the WTO was held in 1996 in Singapore. In the lead up to the Singapore Ministerial, India initiated an attempt to bring together the developing countries into a WTO coalition. The success of this attempt was modest. First, only eight of them, namely, Cuba, Egypt, India, Indonesia, Malaysia, Pakistan, Tanzania and Uganda, came together to form what became known as the LMG of member countries. This coalition was motivated to come together essentially to oppose inclusion of the four Singapore issues, namely, (a) trade and investment, (b) competition policy, (c) transparency in government procurement and (d) trade facilitation, in the trade agenda. Additionally, the LMG was also adamantly opposed to inclusion of labor standards in the WTO. Its firm and oft-repeated opposition resulted in their obtaining a promise from the industrial countries against its inclusion in the WTO during the Singapore Ministerial Conference.

While the LMG was playing a proactively negative role in pressing for the exclusion of these issues in the WTO, after the Singapore Ministerial it also selected a positive role. The problems of the developing economies in relation to the implementation of the Uruguay Round recommendations were the most-talked about issue among the developing country delegations, therefore the

LMG adopted it as its first favorite issue to follow vigorously in the WTO arena. A second and related issue was capacity constraints faced by the LDCs which suffered from serious inadequacy in institutional development. The LMG decided to defend the cause of the developing economies during the preparatory phase of the Second Ministerial Conference in 1998, in Geneva. They insisted that until the imbalances of the Uruguay Round agreement were corrected, the idea of a new round of MTNs should not be broached. A large number of the developing country members were perturbed for this reason. Launching a new round of MTNs before resolving these challenging and contentious issues amounted to an invitation to chaos in the multilateral trading system. It was difficult to disagree with this LMG stance. The LMG put its entire weight behind this position.

The third post-Uruguay Round issue that attracted the LMG coalition was the alleged failure of the mature industrial economies to deliver on the promises made during the Uruguay Round. In addition, the mature industrial economies implemented several key agreements in such a manner it eroded their spirit and compromised their objectives. Fourth, LMG also began re-emphasizing the demand for SDT, which was muted during the Uruguay Round. The argument that they presented was that the SDT was of great significance to the LDCs, and would continue to be so in the foreseeable future.

Changing Status

Until this point the LMG was still operating as an informal and uninstitutionalized coalition of sideliners in the WTO system, not having much negotiating weight. When negotiations for launching a new round of MTNs in the Third Ministerial Conference in 1999 in Seattle began, the status of the LMG began to change. Membership of LMG expanded to include the Dominican Republic, Honduras and Zimbabwe. Some countries (Sri Lanka, Jamaica and Kenya) also began to attend meetings as observers. Gradually the LMG started convening weekly meetings, became institutionalized and also began taking consistent positions on the need for a launch of a Millennium Round of MTNs, which never occurred. While LMG neither sought nor had a formal status of a coalition within the WTO system, proposals it submitted could be recognized easily because the same set of countries signed them. What was noteworthy was that not all proposals were endorsed by all the members of LMG. Dissenting views among them, a legacy of the past, had continued to badger the developing economies.

At this point in time three more groups of developing economies were trying to form coalitions. They were the African Caribbean Pacific (ACP) Group, the LDC Group and the Small and Vulnerable Economies (SVE)

Group. The ACP and LDC were not new coalitions and had existed for some time. Memberships of these groups were far larger than that of the LMG. These initiatives were effective in information exchange and often in making joint proposals in the MTNs. There is no gainsaying the fact that they made their contributions to the Doha Round, but they were relatively less cohesive and effective than the LMG.

Dynamics of a Small Group

Only 14 developing economies out of 142 WTO members had come together, leaving the LMG as a small group in a large multilateral system. However, its strength lay in the fact that it succeeded in bringing together developing economies at different stages of economic growth. It included India and Malaysia on the one hand and Uganda and Tanzania on the other, both LDCs. Also, this small coalition comprised geographically dispersed countries from Asia, Africa, the Caribbean and Latin America. The geographical diversity and developing economies at different stages of growth lent legitimacy to the LMG. An immediate benefit of forming a coalition was that the members could share resources. It worked as follows. Almost every developing member country of the LMG enjoyed membership of other small sub-groups, which kept them abreast of parallel initiatives and negotiating positions. This knowledge was a valuable negotiating asset. It became instrumental in putting together a fresh negotiating position at the MTNs.

After championing the cause of developing economies in the implementation-related issues, the LMG picked up other development-related issues that were ignored during the GATT regime and negotiation process-related systemic concerns. The latter refers to the knowledge and analytical skills gap discussed on pp. 122–3. The LMG addressed this long-time weak spot of the developing members of the WTO. To be sure, the members of LMG themselves were no exceptions and suffered from this knowledge gap as well. As individual members they also had limited government resources for WTO negotiations. Therefore, LMG members took the initiative in proposing a division of labor for studying issues under negotiation and shared their knowledge for taking joint positions on individual issues.

Another noteworthy development that gradually took place before and during the Seattle Ministerial Conference and in the lead-up to the Doha Ministerial in 2001 was that the developing economies, in particular the LMG, gradually developed much needed technical expertise in the intricate trade issues. The technical quality of their analysis slowly improved. It was clearly visible in the proposals they made on a diverse set of WTO issues, which included Trade-Related Intellectual Property Rights (TRIPS), Trade-Related

Investment Measures (TRIMS), agriculture, integration of textiles and apparel, WTO rules and others.

The LMG also took a logical position on SDT under the emerging WTO regime because the industrial economies seemed to be changing its focus from what SDT was intended originally under the GATT regime. The LMG monitored the implementation of the Uruguay Round Agreement on Textiles and Clothing (ATC) and protested against the imbalance in its implementation, pointing to its lack of payoff until the final stage in its implementation. It called for a moratorium on antidumping actions by the importing countries until the end of 2004, when the ATC implementation was to be completed. They also chalked out a clear, detailed and precise framework of the demands of the developing countries in negotiations on agriculture. Similar developing country positions were prepared on TRIPS and TRIMS, particularly the demand that essential drugs must be exempted from patentability. The WTO rules and discipline, particularly anti-dumping (AD), anti-subsidy, safeguard and countervailing measures (SCM) and subsidies, were another area of focus of the LMG. They formulated tidy and precise positions for the developing economies on these issues. This was a fruitful learning phase for the LMG coalition.

Distributive Strategy Followed by the Like-Minded Group

Although none of them was a major trading economy, this small coalition of developing economies acted valiantly. What they attempted was far above and beyond their combined negotiating strength in the multilateral trade regime. Until the end of 2001, they earnestly and firmly adhered to their earlier position that no new issues, including the Singapore issues, could be brought into the fold of WTO system until the two post-Uruguay Round issues, and the imbalances created by them, were addressed and amended. Narlikar and Odell (2006) pointed out that the LMG made use of a 'distributive strategy' in MTNs. This strategy entails not negotiating an issue 'all at one time' but choosing one step at a time and accumulating a set of actions without considering them as a whole.

The LMG simultaneously took offensive and defensive stands and avoided having the image of a coalition of countries that simply blocked progress. In their demand for redressing the post-Uruguay Round issues and correcting the imbalance, in the implementation issues of both developing and industrial countries and in systemic issues LMG were offensive in negotiations. Conversely, in resisting the entry of new issues into WTO, including the Singapore issues, they were defensive. The LMG successively applied the distributive strategy by repeatedly criticizing the mature industrial economies for not keeping their end of the Uruguay Round agreements and giving little credit to developing economies for what they did. They did not ask for any new concessions from the industrial economies because they were cognizant of the high cost that the developing members will have to pay for them. Their 1999 demands in Seattle did not go beyond rationally and soundly redressing the Uruguay Round imbalances, if necessary renegotiating some of those agreements. The justification that the LMG offered for this demand was not the mutual or systemic benefit but 'legitimacy, correction of past injustice, and the exceptionality of the problems of the developing countries' (Narlikar and Odell, 2006). The LMG linked these demands to the high priority issues proposed by the Quad members. Such links are regarded as an important element of the distributive strategy.

Furthermore, in keeping with the distributive strategy, after tabling the proposals LMG never considered follow-up concessions. So much so that they neither prioritized their demands nor asked the Quad members for their priorities. Narlikar and Odell (2006) found that, 'All the demands seem to have been presented as an all-or-nothing package in which everything was a deal-breaker'. They did not formulate a collective fallback option, or a contingency plan for the eventuality of the Quad members responding by collective negotiating pressure of their own. It was obvious that as the largest trading economies the Quad members had a great deal of negotiating weight. This behavior pattern earned the LMG high marks for early maturity in the multilateral trade regime.

Death Knell for the LMG

The Quad members were not disposed to give in to the demands of the LMG. Given the disparity in negotiating weights, the Quad members could hold off to the demands of the LMG and allow an impasse to continue. An impasse normally has a high cost for the developing country members of the WTO because of their lack of alternatives – such as forming regional trade agreement (RTAs) and bilateral trade agreements (BTAs) (Das, 2004b). However, after the 2001 attack on the World Trade Center in New York, this option was regarded as having a high cost for the industrial country members as well. Therefore, during the Fourth Ministerial Conference in Doha, they began negotiating compromises with the developing countries or sub-groups among them, both inside and outside the LMG membership. This rang the death knell of the LMG.

The LMG did not, or could not, respond to these approaches, mostly carrots and sometimes sticks, from the Quad. The outcome was, first, division and finally fragmentation and cracking up of the LMG (Odell, 2003). Effective coalition forming among the developing economies went only so far. To be sure, its tangible outcome was unmistakably noticeable in the final Doha

Ministerial Communiqué (WTO, 2001a). Throughout the communiqué, there are numerous references to the developing economies and the SDT. One of the principal concerns of the LMG, implementation-related issues, found a place early in the communiqué, in paragraph 12. They were also discussed in enormous detail in another document, called the 'Decision on Implementation-Related Issues and Concerns'. Paragraphs 42 and 43 of the communiqué were completely devoted to the concerns of the developing economies, particularly those of the LDCs, although their phraseology takes the line of promises and good intentions. Paragraph 42 pays exclusive attention to SDT. Likewise, paragraph 35 clearly acknowledges the problems of the SVEs.

The achievements of the other groups, the ACP, the LDC and the SVE, were much paler than those of the LMG. They reflected their lack of energy and cohesion as well as strategic imagination. Judged in the backdrop of the historical inconsequentiality of the developing economies in the multilateral trade regime, the achievements of this developing-country coalition were worthy of commendation – small and fragile though it was. Although its successes had limits and it eventually disintegrated under pressure, it can still be regarded as the first ever effective and successful developing country coalition in the multilateral trade regime.

GENESIS OF THE GROUP-OF-TWENTY: AN IMPROMPTU REACTION

In the preparatory phase of the fifth WTO Ministerial Conference in Cancún, Mexico, during 2003, developing country members of the WTO became acutely aware of the EU and the US collusion on agriculture, non-agricultural market access (NAMA) and the other key issues to be taken up during the forthcoming conference. The combined negotiation weight of the two hegemonic trade powers indubitably inspired trepidation. Therefore, during the summer months, several anxiety-driven developing country coalitions sprung up. Prominent among them were, first, a Core Group of developing economies which was stringently opposed to the inclusion of the Singapore issues. The other three issue-specific groupings were the coalition on cotton, the coalition on Strategic Products (SP) and the coalition on Specific Safeguard Mechanism (SSM).

The origin of the G-20[6] can be traced back to June 2003, when Brazil, India and South Africa signed the Brasilia Declaration in Brasilia. Brazil was the catalyst, leader and organizer that made intensive efforts to bring together a progressive group of developing countries into a much needed coalition. The group derived its legitimacy from the fact that it has members from three continents, whose combined population is three-fourths of the global population. Furthermore, three large EMEs, namely Brazil, China and India were proactive members of the G-20.

The G-20 coalition was originally not planned as a strong collusive and collaborative group, but as an impromptu reaction of the developing economies to the joint EU–US compromise text on agriculture that was made public on 13 August 2003, it became a strong and mutually supportive group. With this there were qualitative improvements in the participation of the developing economies in the multilateral trade regime. The G-20 claimed to represent 69 percent of the world's farmers, which lent it both credibility and negotiating weight. It claimed to represent the farmers of the world. The other developing countries that had defensive and offensive interests in agriculture supported the G-20, when they realized that the EU and the US had taken a joint stand on agriculture. Differences in the positions of the developing economies began closing fast. The Cairns Group began working closely with the G-20. The two groups had three common members, namely, Argentina, Mexico and Thailand. Therefore, the final positions that emerged in Cancún were a clear division of opinions on North–South lines. In addition to taking a strong position on agriculture, the G-20 continued to take a strong stand on SDT issues at the Cancún Ministerial Conference.

Collusive Action on Dissenting Text

In response to the EU–US joint position, a dissenting text on agriculture was drafted by Brazil and India and publicized on 2 September 2003 (Chapter 4, pp. 107–9). It was signed by Argentina, Bolivia, Brazil, Chile, China, Colombia, Costa Rica, Cuba, Ecuador, El Salvador, Guatemala, India, Mexico, Pakistan, Paraguay, Peru, the Philippines, South Africa, Thailand and Venezuela. With China in the G-20 coalition, it consisted of a good number of emerging-market heavyweights and it could no longer be considered an insubstantial group in the MTNs. Egypt and Kenya joined the group late. Therefore, it is often confusingly referred to by various names, like G-20, G-20+, G-21 and also G-22.

In September 2003, Brazil, China, India and South Africa assumed the collegial leadership of the G-20 coalition (Chapter 4, pp. 107–9). It made its mark in the Fifth Ministerial Conference in Cancún and more so during the negotiations that culminated into the so-called July Package, or the July Framework Agreement in 2004. Since its creation, the G-20 endeavored to alter the landscape of international trade relations and the process of MTNs. Originally this group came together around the issue of trade in agriculture and was acknowledged as a new player on the MTNs stage. On both subsidies and market access it made new proposals. This proposal called for substantively higher levels of trade liberalization in agriculture than the EU-US paper had offered. The G-20 went beyond being a merely proposal blocking coalition. It began proactively participating in the MTNs with well-researched negotiating positions. It gained importance in the MTNs, provided momentum to the process and became a negotiating force in its own right. The G-20 members made conscious attempts to coordinate between different developing country coalitions and expressed their support for alliances like SP and SSM. Careful consultations and coordination with ACP, LDC and AG continued. These three groups coordinated their positions and formally became the Group-of-Ninety (G-90) on the last day of the Cancún Ministerial Conference.

New Player with Negotiating Weight

Narlikar and Tussie (2004) described the G-20 coalition as 'a new actor in negotiations. Its appearance was momentous, especially as it was the first coalition in which China played a leading and committed role since it became a member of the WTO.' The G-20 became a symbol of the diplomatic and negotiating capability of the EMEs, like Brazil, China, India and South Africa. The EMEs are emerging as a new group of players on the global economic stage. It was obvious that together the EMEs were not negotiating light-weights in MTNs and that a G-20 disagreement could become a serious threat to consensus formation. Although a greater part of the blame for the failure of the Cancún Ministerial went to the disagreement on the Singapore issues, even without it progress in Cancún was not possible because of unwillingness of the EU–US to improve their joint agricultural offer.

The G-20 had found the subsequent drafts unsatisfactory and had made this known. Negotiators and trade analysts believed that toward the end of the Conference, when the Quad members began to offer carrots and sticks to the individual EMEs, developing economies and sub-groups among them, the G-20 would go the LMG way. It did not come to pass. The coalition did not disintegrate and came out intact from the Fifth Ministerial Conference. Following the failure of the Cancún Ministerial, the G-20 convened two Ministerial Meetings, in Brasilia (December 2003) and São Paulo (June 2004), respectively. Interactions between its members also took place at the level of Heads of Delegation and Senior Officials in Geneva. The continued survival of the G-20 is a major achievement of the developing economies.

COMPLETE STAGNATION IN THE DOHA ROUND

While the launch of the MTNs was indeed a healthy and propitious development for the multilateral trade regime, progress in negotiations since its launch has been tardy in all the principal areas of negotiations. Mattoo (2006) described the Doha Round as 'a stagnant whole'; it is hard to take issue with this assessment. Both the replacement of the EU commission and a US presidential election were scheduled for November 2004, therefore, at that time it was assumed that the EU and the US would ignore vital multilateral issues, like the Doha process, and defer them for 2005. Of the two Ministerial Conferences since the launch, one failed miserably and the second barely avoided it (Chapters 4 and 6). Although there were some genuine problematic issues, instead of adopting flexibility, core trading nations and country groups became inflexibile and intransigent in negotiations. Consequently, since its launch the Doha Round has hit the doldrums.

A conspicuous trait of the recent rounds of MTNs was that the participating member countries tended to take a mercantilist approach. Adopting a mercantilist approach was borne of the desire of the members to improve their terms of trade through better access to the markets of other members. Therefore, typically the term 'proposal for liberalization' implied that that the other countries should liberalize their imports while the proposing country does next to nothing (Winters, 2005). The Doha Round has not been an exception to this mindset among negotiating delegations. This has made the negotiating process difficult and confusing because it is difficult to discern what is being realistically proposed and what is mere posturing.

Even at the end of 2006, the target of a successful culmination seemed more distant than ever. For all appearances, evolution was not being kind to the WTO. A silver lining in this cloud was that notwithstanding the standoff, member countries were proving to be resilient and the global economy had not drifted towards protectionism.

SALVAGING THE DOHA ROUND

The leading players and negotiating groups became concerned about the stalemate. Therefore, officially, the negotiations were not abandoned after much publicized failure to reach an agreement in Cancún on 14 September 2003. Members decided to continue them in Geneva. Negotiations to resuscitate the Doha Round began in earnest in October. The ambiance of criticism and recrimination gave way to grudging compromises and eagerness to break the stalemate. As noted on pp. 133–5, the maximum initiative was taken by the US in early 2004, albeit salvaging the Doha Round was a collaborative endeavor of both the developing and industrial economies. The four principal negotiating blocs, namely, the EU, the G-20, the G-90 and the US, began deliberations, albeit in camera. They began taking conciliatory stances and chipped away at their old Cancún positions.

Retreat from Intransigence

The initial focus of the four negotiating blocs continued to remain on the two core issues, namely, lowering agriculture subsidies and disciplining the tariff peaks and tariff escalation in NAMA. A willingness to learn from the failure of the past prevailed and the negotiating groups adopted much-needed flexibility and creativity in their positions this time. Conciliatory negotiating positions, clear and positive thinking, willingness to work together and the responsible action of the group leaders was instrumental in resolving an intractable impasse. The changes in the past positions and compromises that were on offer in mid-2004 vividly indicated a strengthening of political will to restart the stalled Doha process.

Much to the chagrin of the French, the EU made a fresh proposal in May 2004, which was quite different from the one made in August 2003.[7] This time export subsidies were not treated as a holy cow and their elimination was proposed. The developing economies welcomed it because export subsidies in the industrial economies do a great deal of damage to farmers in the developing economies. Also, it was the first ever confession by the EU that the subsidies were unfair and must be eliminated. If one takes a good look at it, this EU offer was not as dramatic as it appeared at first sight because export subsidies accounted for €3 billion ($3.6 billion). As opposed to this, the EU annually lavished €45 billion on supporting and subsidizing its protected farmers. Besides, this EU offer was conditional upon the Australian, Canadian and the US eliminating their own equivalents of export subsidies (*The Economist*, 2004a).

The EU also proposed that the G-90 economies be exempted from lowering of trade barriers, another conciliatory and accommodating gesture. According to this proposal, all the G-90 countries were to be offered greater access to the non-G-90 markets. Many countries in this sub-group had recorded a decline in their trade over the last two decades. The reaction of the developing economies to this proposal from the EU was clearly divided. One group of developing economies dismissed this EU proposal as divisive, while others regarded it as a noteworthy move toward a consensus. To break the impasse, the EU further modified its stand on the Singapore issues as well. The realization dawned that emphasizing them so much that they cause a complete collapse in the MTNs was a tactical error. The modified stand of the EU was that the Singapore issues be taken up one at a time and included in the DDA only after a consensus is arrived at among the members, not otherwise (*The Economist*, 2004a). However, the EU pressed for trade facilitation to be retained in the DDA, without making it a sticking point.

At this time the key MTN players on the global stage were demonstrating flexibility and far-sightedness. Ironically, as the July 2004 deadline approached, ironically some small, low-income, members of the ACP group took a recalcitrant and short-sighted stand. These small economies had small and disparate demands, which could stall the progress. The West African economies demanded that cotton subsidies in the industrial economies must be negotiated as a separate issue, outside the agricultural trade negotiations. Small economies of the ACP group that enjoyed preferential access to the markets in the industrial economies wanted to ensure that a successful Doha Round would not mean erosion of non-reciprocal preferences that they enjoyed (Chapter 3, pp. 85–6). In order not to lose their non-reciprocal preferences, they wished the round to fail. The sugar and banana exporters in this country group took an incongruous stand and reckoned that they were better off having preferential market access in a distorted global trading system. It would have been perverse and ironic if this sub-group of developing economies had succeeded in stalling the Doha Round, because the DDA was essentially designed to benefit the developing economies.

Positions were revised by the other negotiating blocs as well. The developing economies tended to create a great many tariffs and non-tariff barriers in intra-developing country trade (Chapter 3, pp. 69–72). Acknowledging this fact, in June 2004 UNCTAD took the initiative and organized a conference for the developing economies, with an objective of reducing mutual trade barriers and thereby strengthening their position in the Doha process. Brazil and China were the leaders guiding this initiative. Developing economies reacted in two ways. Some were averse to it because they saw it as a detracting force that could weaken the principal Doha process, while others believed that it would strengthen it and impart new momentum.

Formulating the July Framework Agreement

The Cancún failure led, first, to the members accepting that the dynamics of negotiations are overdue for a change and second, to consolidation in the position of the developing economies. This realization caused change in not only the process but also in substance of the MTNs (Clapp, 2006). Large trading economies began to plan and seek support from other members for the purpose of rescuing the Doha Round. As noted above (p. 132), in early 2004 the US took the initiative in re-launching the stalled negotiations. The US Trade Representative, Robert Zoellick, opened bilateral negotiations with key members of the G-20.

In March formal negotiations on agriculture restarted with the new Chair of the agricultural negotiation, Tim Groser of New Zealand, in place. A new deadline of July 2004 was set for coming to an agreement on a framework to produce modalities on all the three pillars (namely, export subsidies, domestic support and market access), while extra importance was given to market access. Another significant decision taken during the March meeting was regarding the negotiation process *per se*. To eschew the North–South confrontation that had emerged in the Cancún Ministerial Conference, the negation process shifted from various groups presenting texts to the Chair, who in turn prepared a compromise text for all members to agree on, to various members, coalitions and groups meeting together and consulting in small and large groups, and then preparing a text for the Chair. This approach was perceived as having greater transparency. Learning from the Cancún failure, the new Chair of the agricultural negotiations was completely averse to tabling a compromise draft on his own authority.

The WTO hosted a meeting of the General Council, the highest-level decision-making body in Geneva, to negotiate a broad framework agreement for the future MTNs in the last week of July 2004. The General Council chairman Shotaro Oshima prepared a draft agreement and hoped that it would be finalized before the 31 July deadline. Negotiations that took place during this stressful week were tense. Although after intense all-night negotiations a broad framework agreement was reached in principle, finer details were left for future negotiating sessions. The framework agreement in Geneva marked the end of talks about how to negotiate in the Doha Round. The most conspicuous achievement of the July Framework Agreement was a seven-page 'framework for establishing modalities in agriculture'. According to this document, the industrial economies were to eliminate all their export subsidies, although the target date has not been finalized.[8] Trade-distorting agricultural production subsidies were to be strictly limited. The G-20 countries succeeded in persuading the industrial economies to make deeper cuts in domestic farm production subsidies. Although the issue of cotton subsidy was not taken out of the general deliberations on agriculture, it was decided that the subsidy to the US cotton farmers would be dealt with 'ambitiously, expeditiously and specifically' (*The Economist*, 2004b). The July Framework Agreement was a long-awaited positive, propitious and promising step forward. It indeed energized the flagging Doha Round.[9]

A new formula was to be devised for tariff-slashing under the NAMA, which could cut the tariff 'spikes' the fastest.[10] This was one of the most contentious issues during the negotiations for the framework agreement. Debate on the type of formula to be adopted was long and agreement was not easy. The G-20 coalition was not prepared to accept the 'blended' formula endorsed by the EU and the US. They pointed out that this formula did not take into account the different tariff structures in the developing and industrial countries. If adopted, the EU and the US would retain high tariffs on many products because they have excessively high tariff peaks. As opposed to this, as the developing economies had a homogeneous tariff structure, their tariff cuts would be deeper than those of the industrial economies. The G-20 proposed a tiered approach, according to which the-higher-the-tariffs-the-steeper-the-cut, was to be accepted as the rule of thumb.

At this point it was obvious that the Doha Round was certain to continue beyond the originally scheduled deadline of January 2005, because there were whole swaths of issues where no progress had been made until that point. For instance, tariff reductions on industrial products and services needed a lot of time and negotiations. Three Singapore issues – trade and investment, competition policy and transparency in government procurement – were dropped from the Doha Agenda for the present at the behest of the developing economies. Negotiations on the fourth Singapore issue, namely trade facilitation, were continuing. It was also known that loopholes could emerge from what was negotiated and agreed during the July Framework Agreement. For instance, the US managed to exclude its 'counter cyclical' payments to farmers when world market prices are depressed. Also, the exemption given to low-income G-90 economies from the requirement of lowering tariffs was something of an ambiguity. To be sure, the G-90 governments considered it a coup because it could protect its nascent industrial sector for a longer period. However, consumers in these countries were required to pay higher amounts for a longer period. The Framework Agreement also left the door open for the rich countries to protect some 'sensitive' (or to be precise politically sensitive) products. Such loopholes would go a long way in diluting the achievement of the Doha Round.

New Negotiations Dynamics

During the preparatory phase of the July Framework Agreement members continuously met and deliberated on the outstanding issues on which consensus was proving to be elusive. When this process picked up momentum, a new negotiating group was born. This power circle was christened the Five Interested Parties (FIPs). It comprised the EU and the US as the key players, along with Brazil and India representing the G-20. Australia was belatedly included as the representative of the Cairns Group. The FIP played a thoroughly vital role in reinvigorating the negotiations. Agreement among these FIPs had helped resolve the impasse in the agricultural negotiations in July 2004. The FIPs worked together in an accommodating and mollifying manner, with their eyes clearly focused on the target of lifting the Doha Round from its morbid morass. Their mindset was positive and creative and they acted responsibly together. With ingenuity and dogged determination they were able to resolve an intractable gridlock.

The leader of G-20, Celo Amorim, the Foreign Minister of Brazil, emerged as a pivotal figure with Pascal Lamy and Rober Zoellick. The G-20 showed resolve where it was necessary to do so; it acted firmly and refused to move forward with trade negotiations until the EU, the US and Japan agreed to reduce their agricultural subsidies. The G-20 blamed farm subsidies in the developed countries for stimulating overproduction of agricultural products and driving world agricultural commodity prices below the cost of production, harming farmers in developing and least developed countries. It was difficult to challenge this premise. Even the G-90 played a constructive role, with Rwanda representing them as a leader.

The French earned the dubious distinction of being a curmudgeon. Taking a parochial and irresponsible and pathetically illogical stand, France sought the right to block the July Framework Agreement, claiming it was contrary to European interests. Their objections were brushed aside by the other EU economies, particularly Britain and Germany. A lot was riding on the success of the July Framework Agreement. Failure at this juncture would have meant the end of MTNs for an indefinite period and reducing the role of the WTO to an overvalued court for resolving multilateral trade disputes.

Putting the Doha Round Back on the Tracks

The July Framework Agreement, as the name indicated, provided a framework of specific commitments and the manner in which to achieve them in the subsequent negotiations. For further continuance of the negotiations on the lines indicated by the Agreement, the completion date of the Doha Round was moved to January 2006, although achievement of this deadline seemed highly unlikely at the time it was determined. Members knew that there would surely be more gridlocks and missed deadlines. In formulating the July Framework Agreement, the EU and the US acted sincerely, with an earnest intention to advance the MTNs. The G-20 achieved in Geneva what they failed to achieve in Cancún. The Doha Round was back on the track and 31 July 2004 was a self-imposed deadline for agreeing to a negotiating framework. The new positions of the members were far more realistic, and consequently an agreement on framework could be reached.

The July Framework Agreement was the most important event preceding the Hong Kong Ministerial, which provided a firm step forward and helped in jump-starting the Doha Round. The active and purposeful participation of the G-20 in these negotiations elevated their value as a negotiating group significantly in the WTO system. Although it was far from being a final agreement, the July Framework Agreement did succeed in setting key parameters for further negotiations in five key areas of MTNs, namely, agriculture, industrial tariffs, trade facilitation, development issues and services. It also identified the time and venue for the next biennial Ministerial Conference of the WTO, which was Hong Kong SAR, in mid-December 2005.

Agriculture had remained a highly contentious area of the negotiations since the Uruguay Round. In agriculture, the July Framework Agreement promised to deliver more farm trade liberalization than had taken place under the Uruguay Round Agreement on Agriculture (URAA). Substantial cuts in the trade-distorting agricultural support were agreed, and so was elimination of the trade-distorting agricultural export subsidies and significant market opening. The Framework Agreement also laid the basis for a solution of cotton subsidies within the framework of agricultural negotiations.

Another controversial and sensitive issue for the EU, the G-20 and the US was industrial tariffs. Agreement had eluded prolonged negotiations between the three. The Framework Agreement provided for a reduction of tariffs, according to a non-linear formula. This formula allowed deeper cuts for higher tariffs without *a priori* exclusions. It was also agreed to explore the possibility of excluding certain sectors of special interest to the developing economies from tariff reduction – the so-called sectoral initiatives. The agreement provided for making special rules for tariff slashing by the developing economies and giving them longer transition periods and flexibilities in tariff cuts. That is, the July Framework Agreement accepted the concept of 'policy space' for the developing economies. Although it provided general direction, it did not go into specifics regarding the tariff slashing modalities. The number of bands, the thresholds for defining the bands and the type of tariff reduction in each band were not specified in the agreement. The role of a tariff cap in a tiered formula with distinct treatment for sensitive products was also left for future evaluation (WTO, 2004). Thus, much in the 'tiered formula' approach still 'remain under negotiation' (Paragraph 30).

On services, the July Framework Agreement exhorted members to quicken the pace of the negotiations based on the old requests-and-offers methodology. It drew the time limit of May 2005 for the members to submit improved offers. The text provided guidelines for negotiations on trade facilitation. As regards the fourth Singapore issue, trade facilitation, eliminating red-tape at the border was to be given top priority, albeit the commitments of the developing countries were to be in accordance with their ability to implement them. Finally, regarding the development dimension, the agreement called for a strengthening of provisions on the SDT.

The July Framework Agreement succeeded in retaining an element of continuity since the launch of the Doha Round. It reiterated the importance of development as a cornerstone of the ongoing MTNs as well as stressing the pressing need for reform in agricultural trade. Its continual emphasis on these two vitally significant aspects of the Doha Round was noteworthy. The message that the July Framework Agreement communicated to the negotiating member countries was that notwithstanding disagreements and disappointments, the MTNs will stay the course. It affirmed to the members that the

WTO provides a workable forum for developing global trade policy for its erstwhile 147 member economies. The Doha Round was back on the rails, although it still had a long way to go to achieve the objectives set by the DDA. Despite the breakthrough, the Framework Agreement was nothing more than the start signal for the long-delayed marathon to come (de Jonquieres, 2004).

CAN THE DOHA ROUND OF MTNS BENEFIT THE DEVELOPING ECONOMIES?

There are realistic possibilities of valuable and gainful results for the developing economies, eventually leading to substantial welfare gains. It was well recognized in Doha that developing economies require improved access to technologies and markets – which means expansion in their trade – to underpin their growth endeavors. To be sure, world trade has grown and developing countries have not been excluded from it. Several developing countries that were classified as low-income economies in 1980 have successfully managed to raise their level of manufactured exports from 20 percent of their total exports to 80 percent. Many of them have entered the ranks of today's middle-income countries or the EMEs (Das, 2004a). Between 1980 and 2001, the share of developing economies in world trade increased by 20 percent, from 15 percent to 35 percent of the total. Expansion of exports in manufactures – not agriculture – accounted for bulk of this trade growth of the developing economies (WB, 2003).

Enhancing Competitiveness of the EMEs

One far-reaching consequence of the liberalization of tariff and non-tariff barriers (NTBs) by developing economies since the mid-1980s was an increase in their competitiveness in the global marketplace, leading to a large volume in their exports (Chapter 1, pp. 23–7). Some 25 EMEs have made impressive strides in exporting low- and medium-technology goods.[11] Others have succeeded in exporting high-technology products, particularly electronics goods, computer components, semiconductor, IC chips and various information technology (IT) related products. It has been pointed out in Chapter 1 (pp. 15–17) that in 2004 China overtook the US as the world's largest exporter of advanced-technology products such as laptop computers, information technology products, cellular phones and digital cameras. Exports of automobile parts from the low- and middle-income developing countries have accelerated with a rapid pace, at more than 22 percent per year (WB, 2003; Das, 2004a). Between 1981 and 2001, the growth rate of exports of this category of products from the developing economies was much higher than the global average export growth rate. Regional or global production networks, or production sharing, have also helped in raising export volumes of the EMEs. Integrated production networks, which are based on the principle of 'slicing of value chain',[12] tend to benefit the participating economies by allowing production to be broken into discrete stages. Each stage is performed in the country best suited for it. For instance, labor-intensive stages of production are undertaken in the labor-abundant countries, while capital- or knowledge-intensive stages occur in matured industrial economies. Production sharing can greatly expand the range of industrial activities that can be undertaken in a developing economy.[13]

The growth rate in export expansion of traditional low-technology goods, such as textiles and apparel, from the low-income developing economies was 14 percent per year over the 1981–2001 period. Export growth of other products accelerated with a faster rate. For instance, exports of electronics products grew at the rate of 21 percent per annum – fast enough to double in value every few years. This category of exports did not exist in 1980 in any developing economy. Not only market shares but also the range of markets of the developing economies increased considerably during this period. All the developing regions improved their competitiveness further during the 1990s and gained in market share at the expense of the industrial economies. This was not true for the 1980s.[14]

Disparity in Trade Expansion and Benefits

The disturbing aspect of this trade expansion was its uneven distribution among the developing economies. This entire expansion occurred due to the trade expansion of the middle-income developing economies. Conversely, the global share of 50 LDCs did not increase at all. In fact, in 43 countries in this sub-group, exports contracted over the 1981–2001 period (WB, 2003). At the present time, the multilateral trading system discriminates against the export products from the developing economies. Stern (2003) has identified 'pockets' of stringent protection in products in which developing economies have comparative advantage. For instance, Canada and the US still have tariff 'spikes' in textiles and apparel, while the EU and Japan have them in agriculture, food products and footwear. These pockets of tariffs have proved to be effective barriers to exports for a large number of low-income developing economies, particularly for those developing economies that are on the initial rungs of the technology ladder.

The global population of people in absolute poverty, who subsisted on $1.08 a day, was 1093 million in 2001 and those who subsisted on $2.25 a day was 2736 million (Chen and Ravallion, 2004).[15] About three-fourths of the world's poorest people live in rural areas, where agriculture is the mainstay of their economy. They cannot export their agricultural products to the OECD markets because the tariff barriers faced by them are ten times or more those on typical inter-OECD trade. In 2001, the agricultural subsidies and other support in the OECD economies amounted to $311 billion, which was 1.3 percent of the GDP of this country group. The level of support to the agriculture sector has not reduced much over the last decade and a half. The large magnitude of farm support – which led to large agricultural output in the OECD economies – tended to depress the international prices of agricultural products that low-income Group-of-Ninety (G-90) economies have been attempting to export (Stern, 2003).

Benefits from Liberalization in Agriculture

The whole array of agricultural subsidies in the EU and the US is an imperative issue for the developing economies because agriculture is typically a big part of their economies, but they have trouble competing with produce from rich countries because of those countries' export subsidies. Poor nations also find it hard to compete in the home markets of rich countries because of domestic subsidies. Together, the EU and the US support their farmers to the tune of $300 billion a year. Watkins (2003) emphasized the pernicious effect of subsidies on the farmers in the developing economies because they have to compete in the global and domestic markets against the surpluses of the EU and US, which are exported at prices that bear no relation with the costs of production. In addition, the developing country farmers cannot enter the industrial country markets because of some of the highest trade barriers in the multilateral trading system. Although governments in the industrial economies unmistakably support human development and poverty alleviation goals, their policies on agricultural continue to be at the heart of a system that is perpetuating poverty and uneven globalization.

Although in the URAA trade in agriculture was addressed squarely for the first time, it did not result in a good deal of trade liberalization. It was widely assumed that agricultural negotiations in the Doha Round would be where developing countries would make some of their largest gains. During the first two years, the key negotiations in agriculture were conducted between the EU and the US, or in large measure top-down. The two trade superpowers did this because, being members of the Quad, they were accustomed to conducting business in this manner. They assumed that any future agreement will have to be the product of an initial agreement among them. The Chair of the agricultural negotiations also functioned in a top-down fashion (Clapp, 2006). At this time, the WTO texts were prepared without consultation with the developing economies, which were once again marginalized and therefore frustrated.

While in the Cancún Ministerial Conference a number of industrial economies sought the use of WTO rules for promoting trade liberalization in financial services and foreign investment – areas in which they have comparative advantage – they systematically failed to apply the open-market principles to their agriculture sector in which many developing economies had comparative advantage. Double standards were as evident as the difference between rhetoric and actions. It was this negotiation dynamic that markedly frustrated the developing countries. They were disturbed in large part by the process as well as the substance with respect to agriculture negotiations. In the post-Cancún period, agriculture negotiations were less top-down and more consultative (Clapp, 2006). Initiatives by the G-20 not only contributed to this transformation but it also became a part of the core negotiating group on agriculture.

Rectifying Anomalies

In the majority of the important sectors in manufactured products, exports of developing economies face barriers in both industrial and developing economies' markets. The former impose five times higher tariffs on exports of manufactures from the developing economies than they do on exports of manufactures from other industrial economies. Tariffs and other NTBs imposed by other developing countries are even higher than those imposed by the industrial economies (World Bank, 2003). Protectionist measures in the developing economies generally take the form of non-*ad valorem* tariffs. Quantitative restrictions (QRs), specific tariffs and anti-dumping measures are presently endemic in the developing countries against exports from the other developing economies. On average, anti-dumping duties are ten times higher than tariffs in industrial economies, while they are five times higher than tariffs in the developing economies.

There is a pressing need to rectify such anomalies – absurdities, if you please – in the multilateral trading system during the Doha process. Although there has been some positive planning in this direction and schemes that grant tariff-free entry to exports from the poor G-90 countries have been devised, thus far they have had little impact. These schemes include the Everything-But-Arms (EBA) initiative by the EU and the Africa Growth Opportunity Act of the US. They exclude the poor countries and populations outside the narrow group of countries identified by each scheme. Agricultural support in sugar, cotton and rice has the maximum anti-development and trade-distorting impact in a large number of G-90 economies. Stern (2003) contended that, 'A successful round that removed all trade impediments would mean 300 million fewer people would live in dire poverty by 2015 – a decline of 13 percent. It is urgent to make progress in agriculture now, if the talks are to make sufficient progress.'

Another area in which the DDA can live up to its name is trade in services, a segment of world trade in which developing economies have increased their trade four-fold between 1991 and 2001. Their share of the global market in services increased from 14 percent to 18 percent over this period (World Bank, 2003). An increasing number of developing economies are carving out impressive niches in the global marketplace. Some of the conspicuous examples are: Barbados in data processing, China, India and the Philippines in computer software, supply chain management, business-process services (BPS) and South Africa in telecommunications. Negotiations in services progressed rather slowly during the Doha Round. Empirical studies have concluded that services liberalization could result in three to four times larger gains for the developing economies than those in the merchandise trade sector (World Bank, 2003). If the OECD economies take appropriate liberalization measures in this area and developing economies become more proactive in negotiations in the services, it might well help them in becoming competitive in several areas such as telecommunications, software, computer-enabled services, wholesaling and retailing, accounting, BPS and business and financial services.

SUMMARY AND CONCLUSIONS

During the early decade of the GATT era, being small traders, the developing economies accepted the status of passive sideliners. There were reasons for their passivity during the GATT era. However, during the decade of the 1980s, many developing economies began to seriously re-evaluate the results of their old strategy. The macroeconomic policy environment in developing economies began to transform and many of them adopted an outward-oriented macroeconomic stance. They tried to participate in the multilateral trade regime, although they faced an initial deficit in *savoir-faire*. The participation of the developing economies in the Uruguay Round of MTNs was the beginning of a learning process. The developing economies formed G-10, which was a novice in the multilateral trade system. Participation of the Developing Economies after the birth of the WTO increased. There were also qualitative improvements.

In 1996, during the Singapore Ministerial India initiated an attempt to bring together the developing countries into a WTO coalition called the LMG. The success of this attempt was modest. Initially it did not have much negotiating weight. When negotiations for launching a new round of MTNs in the Third Ministerial Conference in 1999 began in Seattle, the status of the LMG began to change and the membership of LMG expanded. The LMG did have some minor achievements to its credit.

Many developing economies were less enthusiastic about a fresh round of MTNs in 2001 essentially because they were of the opinion that the Uruguay Round had resulted in only modest gains for them. By this time the developing economies were able to prepare better for the MTNs. The preparatory period before the Third Ministerial Conference in Seattle in 1999 was a defining point, when many developing economies formally expressed their opinions on trade, trade rules and negotiations-related issues in the multilateral fora. To that end, they presented dozens of formal proposals in an energetic manner. Notwithstanding improvement in participation, the developing economies suffered from research-based empirically-grounded negotiation scholarship.

A G-20 was born in the preparatory phase of the Fifth WTO Ministerial Conference in Cancún, Mexico, during 2003. This was an impromptu reaction of the developing economies to the joint EU–US compromise text on agriculture that was made public on 13 August 2003, and the G-20 became a strong alliance. It emerged as a new actor in the MTNs. Its appearance was momentous, especially as it was the first coalition in which China played a leading and committed role since it became a member of the WTO. The G-20 became a symbol of the diplomatic and negotiating capability of the EMEs, such as Brazil, China, India and South Africa.

While the launch of a new round of MTNs was indeed a healthy and propitious development for the multilateral trade regime, progress in negotiations since its launch has been tardy in all the principal areas of negotiations. The negotiations had stagnated and the Fifth Ministerial Conference in 2003 failed. The leading players and negotiating groups became concerned about the stalemate. Therefore, members decided to continue negotiations in Geneva. Negotiations to resuscitate the Doha Round began in earnest in October. Salvaging the Doha Round was a collaborative endeavor of both the developing and industrial economies. It was the result of the four principal negotiating blocs, namely, the EU, the G-20, the G-90 and the US. The July Framework Agreement of 2004 provided a framework of specific commitments and the manner of how to achieve them in the subsequent negotiations.

There are realistic possibilities of valuable and gainful results from the Doha Round for the developing economies. It was well recognized in Doha that developing economies require improved access to technologies and markets – which means expansion in their trade – to underpin their growth endeavors. The expanding multilateral system has assisted in expanding the trade of the developing economies. However, a disturbing aspect of this trade expansion was its uneven distribution among the developing economies. A major part of expansion occurred due to the trade expansion of the middle-income developing economies. Conversely, the global share of 50 LDCs did not increase at all.

NOTES

1. When it came into effect in January 1948, the General Agreement on Tariffs and Trade had 23 signatories, namely, Australia, Belgium, Brazil, Burma, Canada, Ceylon, Chile, China, Cuba, Czechoslovakia, France, India, Lebanon, Luxembourg, the Netherlands, New Zealand, Norway, Pakistan, Southern Rhodesia, Syria, South Africa, the United Kingdom and the United States.
2. This was elaborated in Chapter 1 (pp. 19–21) and Chapter 2 (pp. 35–40).
3. The emerging market economy was a term coined by Antoine W. van Agtmael of the International Finance Corporation. It is loosely defined as a market economy with low-to-middle per capita income that participates globally by implementing reform programs. Such economies represent 20 percent of the world economy. Countries whose economies fall into this category vary from very big to very small. They are usually considered emerging because of their fast-clip growth rate and the reforms undertaken by them. Hence, even though China is deemed as one of the world's economic powerhouses, it is lumped into the EME category alongside much smaller economies with fewer resources, like Tunisia. Both China and Tunisia belong to this category because both have embarked on economic development and reform programs, and have begun to open up their markets and 'emerge' onto the global economic scene. EMEs are considered to be fast-growing economies. One key characteristic of the EME is an increase in both local and foreign investment, both portfolio and direct. A growth in investment in a country often indicates that the country has been able to build investors' confidence in the domestic economy. Moreover, foreign investment is a signal that the world has begun to take notice of the emerging market, and when international capital flows are directed toward an EME, the injection of foreign currency into the local economy adds volume to the country's stock market and long-term investment to the infrastructure.
4. The Group-of-Ten comprised Argentina, Brazil, Cuba, Egypt, India, Nigeria, Nicaragua, Tanzania, Peru and Yugoslavia.
5. The most important contribution of the Singapore Ministerial Conference was the addition of four 'new' issues to the agenda of the World Trade organization (WTO), which were subsequently christened the Singapore issues. They were (a) investment, (b) competition, (c) transparency in government procurement, and (d) trade facilitation.
6. At the time of writing, the G-20 has the following 21 members: Argentina, Bolivia, Brazil, Chile, China, Colombia, Costa Rica, Cuba, Ecuador, Egypt, Guatemala, India, Indonesia, Mexico, Nigeria, Pakistan, Paraguay, Peru, Philippines, South Africa, Thailand and Venezuela. The role of collegial leaders of G-20 has been played by Brazil, China, India and South Africa.
7. Jacques Chirac, the French president, declared that the draft framework was 'profoundly unbalanced'.
8. For precise details of the Agreement refer to WTO (2004).
9. See Das (2005) for a detailed discussion on the July Framework Agreement. Although known as the July Framework Agreement, it was reached in the wee hours of 1 August 2004.
10. Relatively high tariffs, usually on 'sensitive' products, amidst generally low tariff levels are known as tariff peaks. For industrial countries, tariffs of 15 percent or above are generally considered as high tariffs or spikes.
11. This category of exportables includes textiles and apparel, toys, sporting goods, iron and steel products, and engineering products like engines, pumps and other instruments.
12. Borrowing an expression from Paul Krugman.
13. See, for instance, Deardorff (2001) and Hummels *et al.* (2001) for interesting analyses of production networks and the newest trends in them.
14. Refer to WB (2003), in particular Chapter 2 and Chapter 6.
15. $1.08 a day is one of the two reference lines of poverty defined by the World Bank. The other reference line is $2.25 a day.

6. The Sixth Ministerial Conference: the lean Hong Kong harvest

Difficult things take a long time, impossible things take a little longer.

Unknown

INTRODUCTION

The sixth biennial Ministerial Conferences of the World Trade Organization (WTO) took place in the inspiring setting of the freest economy in the world, known for its buccaneering spirit of business and enterprise, between 13 and 18 December 2005. A total of 149 sovereign member countries of the WTO participated in it in Hong Kong SAR. The principal objective of this chapter is to shed light on the progress, or lack thereof, made during the sixth Ministerial Conference. While it successfully eschewed another Cancún-like disappointing failure, the Hong Kong Ministerial did not achieve much of substance. If success is defined as not failing, the Hong Kong Ministerial Conference could be judged a success.

This chapter begins with the two adverse rulings of the WTO dispute panel against the European Union and the United States in the second section, which influenced the thinking of these two hegemonic traders. There were some serious stumbling blocks in the multilateral trade negotiations (MTNs) which are discussed in the third section. A detailed fourth section delves into the sparse achievements of the Hong Kong Ministerial and their limited value for the multilateral trade regime. The fifth section deals with the lack of progress, in fact a small regression, in the negotiations in the services sector. However, one favorable feature of the Conference was skillful conference management, which has been discussed in the sixth section. A momentous consequence of this Conference was the old Quad receding into history and the emergence of a New Quad, which is the focus of the seventh section. The final section concludes.

PREPARATORY PHASE: A CASE OF TWO ADVERSE RULINGS

Negotiations on agriculture had continually managed to be the *bête noir* of the

Doha Round. Little progress in defining and arriving at the modalities was made during the preparatory phase of the Hong Kong Ministerial Conference. The term modality in WTO lexicon implies precise numerical formula, targets and timetable for implementation of agreed trade liberalization schedules. This lack of progress was closely associated with two rulings in agriculture handed down from the WTO dispute settlement panels in 2004–5, which had a bearing on the negotiations, particularly on the conduct, disposition and strategy of the EU and the US.

These two rulings emanated from complaints on agricultural subsidies. They inspired change in the conventional wisdom regarding multilateral trade relations between the members of the WTO. In the first case, Brazil initiated a dispute settlement procedure against the US about its practice of subsidizing its cotton producers. Brazil contended that what the US regarded as Green Box subsidies to its cotton producers actually depressed the global market prices, therefore, they were clearly trade-distorting subsidies and must be removed forthwith. The WTO's Dispute Settlement Mechanism (DSM) was put into motion, which ruled in favor of Brazil. The US appeal was turned down. In the second case, Australia, Brazil and Thailand initiated a dispute settlement procedure against the EU, which subsidized sugar beyond what the WTO rules allowed. The DSM concluded that the complaint was fair and ruled in favor of the complainants. The EU appealed and lost. Before the birth of the WTO, binding decisions on trade disputes were not possible. The GATT was a toothless institution. However, the new WTO dispute resolution process has changed that (Clapp, 2006). The rulings of the dispute panels have a real impact on the disputing members. It became evident that such litigations can be brought against the two hegemonic traders at any time in the future by any aggrieved WTO members. It would not matter whether the challenger is a large trader or a small one.

After the WTO rulings, the Group-of-Twenty (G-20) waited for the EU and the US to take stock of the new reality and take the initiative to table fresh offers on the three pillars of agricultural negotiations. These three pillars are: (a) market access; (b) export subsidies; and (c) domestic support. The EU did make a weak and delayed proposal. The reaction of the G-20 and the US was well-publicized disappointment. A revised proposal from the EU was not much better. To add to the complexities of the negotiations, the EU made it conditional and tied it to negotiations in non-agricultural market access (NAMA) and services. The G-20 and the US expressed their dismay at the new EU position. As time passed, it became evident to the WTO members that the forthcoming Ministerial Conference could not be able to accomplish much. Members might go through the motions of conducting a Ministerial Conference, but it would only be in name. An excellent opportunity for making progress and achieving the objectives of the Doha Development

Agenda (DDA) – to which the WTO members had shown repeated allegiance – was slipping by. A noteworthy fact was that the G-20 was perfectly active at this point and the Cairns Group of countries[1] had started working in closer collaboration with it, which augmented the negotiating weight of the G-20. They began giving joint press conferences and making press releases.

Defining Success as Lack of Failure

If success is defined as lack of failure, the sixth Ministerial Conference was a success. Candidly speaking, if it was not a failure, it did not achieve much of substance and cannot logically be regarded as a success either. Achievements of the Hong Kong Ministerial were less than what was expected in the lead-up to it, but more than what was expected at the time of its commencement, when expectations were recalibrated. On the eve of the Ministerial Conference expectations were so low among the negotiating members that any achievement short of a breakdown was going to be treated as a success. At the time of the launch of the Conference, it was apparent that the elusive modalities in agricultural and NAMA were not going to be agreed.

The Organisation for Economic Co-operation and Development (OECD) evaluated its outcome as 'weaker than (what) might appear at first sight' (Heydon, 2006). Disappointing as it was, the fact that the Hong Kong Ministerial did not collapse was its precious accomplishment. There was a generalized sense of relief among the WTO members that participated in this Ministerial Conference that a Cancún-like confrontation did not develop in Hong Kong. If the Ministerial Conference neither achieved much of substance nor energized the Doha Round negotiations in any notable manner, it did not leave the MTNs eviscerated either.

At the end of the Conference, Pascal Lamy, the Director-General of the WTO, optimistically assessed that the round was 'back on track' after a 'period of hibernation'. In his opinion the Hong Kong Ministerial Conference had 'rebalanced' the WTO agenda in favor of the developing economies as well as creating 'political energy' needed to make progress in the immediate future (*The Economist*, 2005). Optimistic assessments apart, the major trading economies and groups would need to expend substantially more political capital than they did if the Doha Round has to be successful, and honestly adhere to its mandate of being a development round.

Achieving a Low-Level Equilibrium

The July Framework Agreement of 2004 (WTO, 2004) was the vitally important event preceding the Hong Kong Ministerial (Chapter 5). While the intent conveyed by the July Framework Agreement was steadfastly that of moving forward toward the Doha Development Agenda (DDA) mandate, the reality after the Agreement turned out to be radically different. Stagnation in MTNs continued. In view of the disparity of negotiating positions among the large trading economies and country groups, major participants as well as trade economists had forewarned months before the Conference to keep expectations from the Hong Kong Ministerial low, rendering them easy to meet. Therefore, the Ministerial Conference commenced on a less sanguine note and kept its objectives so low that they could be achieved without much effort. The targeted low-level equilibrium was indeed achieved at Hong Kong. Few bold decisions were attempted. Many long-awaited decisions that were awaiting the Hong Kong Ministerial were put off for the future. Despite the tangles and complexities in the MTNs, success in Hong Kong was possible and could have been achieved by thoughtful, pragmatic and clairvoyant negotiations on the one hand and political will of the member governments on the other.

Most participating trade ministers were cognizant of the fact that another Cancún-like acrimonious breakdown in Hong Kong would have a high cost for the multilateral trade regime. For certain, it could potentially devastate the WTO as a multilateral trade negotiating forum. If one takes a constructive and charitable viewpoint of the Hong Kong Ministerial, the agreement reached in Hong Kong SAR can be seen as a minimal package, an incremental advancement, in the long-stalled MTNs. Modest advancement occurred toward bridging some of the differences between the EU, the G-20 and the US, the three country groups with substantive negotiating weights.

PRINCIPAL STUMBLING BLOCKS

Although there were a host of important areas under negotiation, the principal ones still were trade in agriculture, NAMA and services. The other important areas included special and differential treatment (SDT) of the developing economies, market access of the least developed countries (LDCs), trade facilitation and WTO rules in the areas of anti-dumping (AD), anti-subsidy and safeguard and countervailing measures (SCM). Of these, trade in agriculture was, and continued to be, the overwhelmingly dominant subject. It was also the most contentious issue, which had succeeded in adversely affecting negotiations in all the other important areas and casting a pall of stagnation over the Doha Round of MTNs. To be fair, it must be acknowledged that agriculture was not the only stumbling block in the Hong Kong Ministerial. The most important secondary issues included NAMA, services and development-related issues. The WTO rules were also an important, if controversial, issue under negotiation.

As elucidated above, little of value was achieved in any of these areas in Hong Kong. The harvest of decisions taken was meager because most of the politically difficult decisions were assiduously deferred for 2006. That negotiations on agriculture are as important as they are politically sensitive was evident in the Cancún Ministerial Conference also, where the developing economies, led by the G-20, had made it clear that further progress in the MTNs was not possible without industrial economies agreeing to lower their agricultural tariffs, domestic support and subsidies, and particularly to eliminate their subsidies on cotton.

New Geography of Negotiations

A new geography of MTNs vividly emerged at Hong Kong. The old power circle of the GATT era, the Quad group became progressively irrelevant and had retreated into history (pp. 157–9). The new power groups that emerged and functioned comprised the EU, G-20 and the US. Of these, the EU and the US were the two well-entrenched hegemonic powers in multilateral trade. However, the firm G-20 formation had ended the EU–US duopoly in the multilateral trade regime. This group of developing economies played a proactive and consequential role in Cancún as well as in Hong Kong. Their participation was constructive and salutary for both the WTO as a young supranational institution and for the MTNs. The most active G-20 members in Hong Kong were Brazil and India, which led the group. In the next ministerial conference, China, which is the third largest trader in the world and the largest emerging-market economy (EME),[2] can be assumed to play an equally active and evocative role in the MTNs, if not more.

To aggravate a disagreement-ridden situation, the G-20 was unwilling to negotiate any cuts in its own industrial tariffs until some progress was made in the agricultural negotiations in Hong Kong SAR. Disagreeing with this stand, the EU refused to change its position until the large EMEs (like Brazil, China, India and Mexico) liberalized their markets for industrial goods and services. A veritable catch-22 situation was created. The EU was not the only *demandeur* for EMEs' liberalizing their markets for industrial goods and services. Other industrial economies supported the EU in this regard.

What were the newest developments in the global economy that inspired such a pattern of demand in the MTNs? The novel development in this scenario was that China had emerged as a global trading power in manufactures followed by several East Asian economies, which were not as large as China in their export volume, yet were still significant. Brazil had emerged as an important trading economy in agriculture and agro-industrial products and India as an important trading economy in services. These were meaningful development for the MTNs, which further complicated issues. It is easy to see how a complex gridlock was created in the negotiations. The political will to take substantive steps to resolve this issues by way of compromises was conspicuous by its absence.

To a degree, the Hong Kong Ministerial Conference, like the Doha Round, had to endure the mercantilist mindset of the participants. The EU was censured most for its long-standing intransigence in negotiations on trade in agriculture, which had a far-reaching and damaging effect over the MTNs, depriving it of both progress and direction. Endless negotiations could not bridge the large gaps in the positions at Hong Kong. The US, the Cairns Group of 17 agricultural exporters and the EMEs, which are vocal members of the G-20, regarded the EU proposal on agriculture as hopelessly inadequate. The vociferous expression of their views in this regard soon created an overwrought and stressful negotiating environment. As an influential member of the EU, France could and did block any initiative of improvement in the EU position on agriculture, which added to the tensions and confusion. France had unsuccessfully tried to play the same role before the July Framework Agreement was reached in 2004. France earned the well-deserved reputation of being the reluctant liberalizer. It is nothing short of astonishing how the inflexibility of one country can hold up the entire trade negotiations process.[3]

HOW LEAN WAS THE LEAN HARVEST?

Was the outcome of Hong Kong Ministerial so dismal that it should be dismissed as another disappointing non-achiever in the series of such conferences? An honest answer will have to be in the negative. Not all that transpired in Hong Kong Ministerial Conference was trivial in value. Foremost, let us objectively evaluate and specify the minimal progress and marginal achievements in the lead-up to the Hong Kong Ministerial Conference and during the Conference, which could be treated as a small incremental advancement of the MTNs. After enumerating them, I shall focus on why the achievements can still be regarded as insubstantial.

Minimal Package

The minor achievements during the lead-up to the Ministerial Conference and in Hong Kong included a slight convergence in positions on agricultural policy among the members, although core modalities were not determined in this regard. As stated on pp. 148–9, agricultural negotiations are normally conducted under the so-called three pillars, namely, export subsidies, domestic support and market access. Limited progress in the form of a 'working hypothesis' was made under all the three pillars. Some semblance of agreement emerged in the working hypothesis on structuring four bands for tariff reductions in agricultural trade, with larger cuts for higher tariffs. In the July Framework Agreement of 2004, members had agreed to eliminate export subsidies on agricultural exports, albeit no deadline was agreed (Das, 2005b). The primary achievement, or deliverable, in Hong Kong was the last-minute agreement on a target period for the elimination of export subsidies; it was fixed at the end of 2013. A substantial part of subsidy elimination was agreed to be realized by the end of the first half of the elimination period, that is, by the end of 2009. The idea of year 2013 originated from the EU timetable for reform of the Common Agricultural Policy (CAP).

Second, the US pledged to end export subsidies to its cotton farmers. Cotton exports are of special interest to farmers in Benin, Burkina Faso, Mali, Chad and Senegal, referred to as the Cotton-4. Senegal was a latecomer to this group. All of them were low-income LDCs and had incessantly and stringently protested against the US subsidies for years. The US agreed to eliminate export subsidies in 2006.

Third, regarding the NAMA, the Hong Kong Ministerial declaration made small progress. In paragraph 12, the text provided for the application of the so-called Swiss formula, which for a given set of parameters cuts higher tariff rates proportionately more than the lower tariff rates. The Hong Kong declaration locked in the progress of the Framework Agreement of July 2004 and members agreed to reduce or eliminate tariff peaks, high tariffs and tariff escalation.

Fourth, of the 50 LDCs, 32 are members of the WTO. The development package agreed in Hong Kong included duty-free quota-free access (DFQF) for exports from LDCs by 2008. Also, a report on trade facilitation was finalized in the lead-up to the Hong Kong Ministerial, which claimed 'good progress' in all the trade facilitation-related areas covered under the DDA mandate. Immediately before the commencement of the Conference, members had agreed to amend the Trade-Related Aspects of Intellectual Property Rights (TRIPS) agreement. The modified TRIPS agreement allowed developing economies with insufficient manufacturing capacity to import generic versions of patented drugs for public health objectives.

Fifth, a small undertaking on 'aid for trade' was also a part of the Hong Kong Ministerial declaration (paragraph 57). Accepting the deliberations of finance and development ministers in various fora and the Development Committee of the International Monetary Fund (IMF) and the World Bank, an offer was made to assist small developing economies that lack the infrastructure for trade (WTO, 2005b). In the process of multilateral trade liberalization, this country group also loses out due to erosion of non-reciprocal preferences and increases in competition. The industrial economies offered this country group deals in the area of capacity building and debt relief. The three largest economies made large pledges in this regard. The EU and its member states announced that their spending on trade-related projects would reach €2 billion ($2.4 billion) a year by 2010. The US pledged that its aid would reach $2.7 billion a year by 2010. Japan took lead and committed $10 billion under a three-year program of Aid for Trade.

Sixth, a moratorium on tariffs on e-commerce was extended until the next Ministerial Conference.

Meager Real Value of the Inadequate Achievement

How valuable were these decisions on small reforms and liberalization measures and development assistance for LDCs? In trade in agriculture, the unofficial objective that was kept for the Hong Kong Ministerial was to come to an agreement on modalities. It was expected that those modalities will be used to calculate tariff cuts each member country makes on thousands of products, as well as cuts on a range of subsidies and supports. Before the Ministerial Conference began, it was expected that this would allow the full package of agreements in agriculture to be completed by the end of 2006. Contrary to expectations, the agreement that emerged was a rather superficial level, which did not advance the MTNs. The most substantive issue of setting negotiating modalities or core modalities was left unresolved in Hong Kong and postponed until 30 April 2006. A deadline for the submission of draft schedules was set at 31 July 2006. The list of unfinished business in agriculture was long. The most intractable issues of the relevant liberalization thresholds for the developing and industrial economies were also left undecided. Little of value was achieved in negotiation on agriculture.

The EU, which accounted for 90 percent of agricultural export subsidies, accepted 2013 as the deadline to end subsidies. This was a small step forward. However, nothing was decided on the large trade-distorting domestic farm support. The US, the developing economies – both the G-20 and the Group-of-Ninety (G-90) – and the Cairns Group had unsuccessfully tried to move this date to 2010, but the EU took a completely intransigent stand.[4] The MTNs had languished since 2001 because of an impasse over the politically sensitive agricultural issues. These issues were seriously impeding negotiations in the other areas of MTNs as well. Therefore, in the interest of progress in the MTNs, 2013 had to be reluctantly accepted by the other participants of the MTNs, which indeed is a gloomy tale.

What was more disappointing was that the two more difficult as well as significant areas of negotiations in agriculture, namely, market access, or tariffs on agricultural products, and trade-distorting domestic support payments were completely ignored and therefore failed to make any progress.

Any decision on them was also deferred for 30 April 2006. Market access was widely regarded as the most important pillar of agricultural negotiations. The Uruguay Round Agreement on Agriculture (URAA) set bound tariffs on farm products at levels much above the applied levels. Therefore, to drain the 'water' out of these tariff lines the Doha Round reform program needed to make deep slashes. In addition, triple-digit agricultural tariffs were the result of mismanaged 'tariffication' exercise of the Uruguay Round. This exercise had converted quantitative restrictions (QRs) into their tariff equivalents. This aberration needed to be rectified through agreement on caps for maximum tariffs, if possible in the range of 50–100 percent (Hufbauer and Schott, 2006). None of these issues could be taken up in the Hong Kong Ministerial. A huge gap existed in the offers of tariff cuts made by the EU and those proposed by the G-20 and the US. The EU had absolutely no intention of improving its offers.

Second, the demand of the Cotton-4 countries was finally met in the Hong Kong Ministerial. Once the final Doha Round agreement is reached and implementation of the recommendations begins, these countries would be provided DFQF access of their cotton exports. There will be no early harvest in the reduction of the cotton subsidy. Ironically, the US was obliged to repeal the subsidy because it was challenged by Brazil on this issue in the WTO dispute settlement panel (pp. 145–8). Due to the adverse ruling of the WTO dispute panel, the US Congress was expected to repeal the subsidy within days of this promise. Therefore, what happened in Hong Kong Ministerial cannot be considered an achievement of the MTNs.

Third, as regards core modalities in NAMA, not much of value was achieved because they were left undetermined. Although the Swiss formula was mentioned in the Hong Kong Ministerial declaration, no guidelines on coefficients were mentioned. These coefficients determine how deep the reduction in tariffs should be as well as the extent to which cuts should differ between developing and industrial economies. These important decisions on core modality were deferred for the future and were to be taken in April 2006. To all appearances this seemed an unrealistic target. It was obvious at the time of determining them that these deadlines will be ignored. This made the Hong Kong NAMA agreement insipid and of highly limited value. Mention of a higher coefficient for the industrial economies and a lower one for the developing economies in the agreement would have made the NAMA related declaration a little more consequential. The meaning of 'less than full reciprocity' for the developing countries was left unnegotiated, so were the development of sectoral initiatives and the treatment of preference erosion. A sagacious, positive and logical NAMA proposal came from the US, which was the elimination of all non-agricultural tariffs by 2015. It provided for a limited number of exceptions for the developing economies for a stipulated period as well as a longer implementation horizon. However, the probability of acceptance of this outcome was low.

Fourth, according to paragraph 47 of the Hong Kong Ministerial declaration, LDCs are to be provided DFQF market access for most – at least 97 percent of tariff lines – of their export products by 2008, or no later than the start of the implementation period of the Doha Round. This commitment is a modest augmentation of the status quo because the US allowed 83 percent of LDC trade DFQF in 2005. Besides, the 3 percent reservation would account for some 330 tariff lines, which covers the least competitive domestic production sectors in the industrial economies. For some LDCs this could mean effective deprivation of market access for their export products. It seems likely that ceramics, leather goods, sugar and textiles and clothing would be part of the list of products excluded from this concession to the LDCs. These are key export products of many LDCs. While 97 percent of the tariff lines do seem large and generous in terms of a trade liberalization measure, in reality it is not.

Fifth, while several issues in trade facilitation and negotiating modalities were agreed upon in the lead-up to the Hong Kong, this area is still regarded as unfinished business. The developing economies are still far from beginning legal drafting on the provisions of the agreement. They decided to wait until negotiations on technical assistance and capacity building make more progress (Heydon, 2006).

Sixth, the Doha Round did not make much progress since its launch in 2001. Negotiations in the three most important areas under negotiation (agriculture, NAMA and services) remained completely mired, yet the Hong Kong Ministerial declaration provided few guidelines on how to resolve the stand-offs in various areas of negotiations. Several new deadlines were announced for determining the modalities of trade liberalization in all three principal areas and submissions of schedules. In essence, April 2006 was made the new post-Hong Kong Ministerial target date for the MTNs to achieve what they should have achieved during the Ministerial, rendering April 2006 an exceedingly important month for the MTNs. By this date, negotiators were expected to agree on the core modalities in agricultural issues and NAMA. However, the Doha Round has had a perfect record of missing deadlines. Without fail it has missed every deadline in the past. When the self-imposed April 2006 deadline was determined, most negotiators tacitly understood that it was possible that the dubious record of missed deadlines will remain untarnished in the future (Hufbauer and Schott, 2006).

Seventh, negotiations on reforms of rules were given short shift. Clarification and reform of the trade remedies, which include anti-dumping (AD), anti-subsidy and safeguard and countervailing measures (SCM), and discipline on regional trading arrangements, were relegated to the background.

In Paragraph 28, the Hong Kong Ministerial declaration has merely one sentence on this subject, which said that negotiators 'recall the mandates in paragraphs 28 and 29 of the Doha Ministerial Declaration and reconfirm our commitment' (WTO, 2005b).

SERVICES IN THE HONG KONG MINISTERIAL

Liberalization of trade in services has had a history of stagnation since the inception of the GATS in 1995 (Chapter 2, pp. 61–4). The request-and-offer process of trade liberalization in services had proved to be slow and tedious and has not led to any progress in the services negotiations since its inception in 2000. The multilateral trade regime has been more or less devoid of evolution in this increasingly important area of trade. There was a pressing need for picking up the momentum in negotiations. Even at the end of 2006, issues of lack of progress in market access and in rule-making aspects were being debated. The deliberations regarding balancing rights and obligations in the services trade regime had not ended. Imagination and concerted efforts were required to design functional means of liberalizing of trade in all the four modes[5] of services trade, and members had to agree to them. However, services negotiations not only failed to make any progress in Hong Kong but they noticeably regressed.

The Doha Work Program addresses trade in services both in the main text as well as in its Annex C. The text of Annex C was presented to the Chair of the Council for Trade in Services (CTS), which operates under the guidance of the General Council and is responsible for supervising the functioning of the GATS. Until the last day of the Hong Kong Ministerial, the reference to services in the main text was 'bracketed', implying there was no consensus on it. The G-90 countries and the Association of South East Asian Nations (ASEAN) had put forth an alternative text for Annex C. Some developing countries went further and proposed to delete Annex C.

The main text of the Hong Kong Ministerial Declaration again drew attention to the overall objectives and the principles of negotiations in trade in services in paragraph 25 through paragraph 27. These were the existing principles in the GATS and the objectives of the Doha Declaration. The negotiating guidelines of the July Framework Agreement were also recalled. The importance of taking an appropriately flexible stand in negotiations, mentioned on several occasions earlier, was reiterated. Recognizing the economic situation of the LDCs, they were not expected to undertake any new commitments in services. The Hong Kong Ministerial Declaration presented absolutely nothing new in its text on trade in services.

Annex C added a fresh dimension regarding modal objectives, that is, proposed new ideas for trade liberalization based on each mode of services trade. It set out more details on plurilateral approaches for making progress in negotiations and commitments. It suggested that members to whom plurilateral requests were made were to consider them in accordance with paragraphs 2 and 4 of Article XIX and paragraph 11 of the Negotiating Guidelines, which provided flexibility to the developing economies. Annex C proposed specific timetable for submitting specific offers, plurilateral requests, and then a second round of revised offers to be submitted by July 2006. It determined that final draft schedule of commitments were to be submitted by the end of October 2006 (UNCTAD, 2006).

During the Hong Kong Ministerial, instead of making progress in negotiations in trade in services, it seemed that retrograde motion was made. The Hong Kong Ministerial declaration did not oblige members to enter into 'plurilateral' market access negotiations. Instead it simply made indicative guidelines which required that members 'shall consider such a request'.[6] The term plurilateral needs to be clarified here. It implies optional, that is, not binding on all members. The dysfunctional request-and-offer process of negotiations was not dropped. It was not even considered to devise a new more functional methodology. Led by South Africa, the G-90 pressured the conference to keep request-and-offer in as the principle negotiation process in the GATS. The concept of 'plurilateral' market access negotiations could possibly have resulted in progress, but the developing economies rejected it (Chapter 7, pp. 185–7). This created ideal conditions for further stalemate in this important area of MTNs.

There was a pressing need to change the tack. The Marrakesh Agreement, establishing the WTO, provides for a few plurilateral agreements in Annex 4. What was needed in Hong Kong was an earnest and concerted intensified request–offer process, augmented by action within plurilateral groups with shared sectoral interests, leading to multilateral commitments in the principal services sectors. It did not happen. The Hong Kong Ministerial declaration set the deadline for negotiations, requiring member countries to make offers to open their markets in financial services, telecommunications, computer and related services, distribution, and energy services. There was a need for some quantitative targets in this regard, which also never came about. On the whole the agreement in Hong Kong established little in trade in services, an important area of negotiations. Stalemate in services negotiations continued.

SKILLFUL CONFERENCE MANAGEMENT

One bright aspect was that procedurally the Hong Kong Ministerial performed far better than the preceding Ministerial Conference at Cancún. Negotiations followed a bottom-up approach, which implied that inputs came from the members rather than from above. It contributed to the success of widespread deliberations among the WTO members, collectively and in small groups. Transparency and inclusiveness was taken for granted. In unison, participating members expressed satisfaction about this method of negotiations. This was a lesson learned from the debacle of Seattle and Cancún Ministerial Conferences, where among other snags, efforts were made to dictate decisions from the top (Das, 2000). The bottom-up approach allowed the positions of all the delegations that had a plan and desire to be included, to be included.

The Hong Kong Ministerial Conference was chaired by John Tsang, who earned wide admiration for being a skillful and competent coordinator.[7] He appointed facilitators with a clear mandate to size up members' positions through the country group coordinators. The six facilitators were Kenya, Pakistan, Korea, Guyana, Chile and Norway, while the five country group coordinators were Mauritius (for G-90), Egypt (for the African Group), Brazil (for G-20), Indonesia (for G-33)[8] and Zambia (for the LDCs). Informal heads of delegation meetings were held at the end of every day to brief them of the developments and state of play. The bottom-up approach allowed topics with a growing degree of convergence to be elevated to the Chairman's Consultative Group (CCG). The CCG had 26 members and was christened the 'Green Room'. The Green Room meetings included the delegations of Argentina, Australia, Brazil, Canada, China, Costa Rica, Egypt, the EC, Ghana, Hong Kong, India, Indonesia, Jamaica, Japan, Malaysia, Mauritius, Mexico, New Zealand, Nigeria, Senegal, Singapore, South Africa, Switzerland, Thailand, the US and Zambia. The efficient management of the Conference was reflected in smooth information flows – both horizontal and vertical – an absence of snags and little resentment from the participating members.

EMERGENCE OF A NEW QUAD LEADERSHIP

Brazil, China, India and South Africa provided collegial leadership of the G-20 group during the Hong Kong Ministerial Conference. The G-20 also eagerly sought to find common cause with the G-90, in furthering the interests of the developing countries. During the lead-up to the Hong Kong Ministerial, and at Hong Kong, a good deal of negotiations and lobbying had taken place. The Brazilian and Indian delegations, the two new power brokers, had played the role of go-between the developing and industrial country members. These two delegations had played a highly constructive, something of a historic, role at the time of signing of the Marrakesh Agreement in 1994, which led to the creation of the WTO (Sutherland, 2004).[9]

A momentous development that took place in Hong Kong was that the Quad of the GATT era retreated into history because it had become completely irrelevant. In its place, Brazil, the EU, India and the US emerged as the most energetically negotiating WTO members, influencing both the process and substance of MTNs. They were informally christened the New Quad. Together they played a decisive role in setting the agenda for the Hong Kong Ministerial and providing initial direction to the MTNs. Their deepest concern was to avoid a Cancún-like ignominious failure and save the WTO system. In that, Brazil and India strove to seek acquiescence from the developing economies on a weak, minimal and unbalanced agreement, for which the *inter alia* lack of political will in the EU and the US was widely blamed. Delivering the consent of the developing member countries for such an agreement was the price Brazil and India paid for their membership of the New Quad. While the developing countries eventually agreed, their disgruntlement on several issues was evident.

Brazil and India gave the impression that they came to the Hong Kong Ministerial more or less predisposed to accept the EU's phase-out deadline for agricultural export subsidies, the Swiss formula for NAMA and to adopt the plurilateral approach in services negotiations. The question still open at Hong Kong was whether India would press the EU and the US for inclusion of more professional services into the GATS. However, the anxiety of the Indian delegation to steer clear of a Cancún-like controversy was so intense that they did not even broach the issue. Many developing countries considered this questionable behavior for a country having leadership ambitions.

In their joint leadership role, Brazil and India succeeded in getting the other developing member countries to assent on a minimalist covenant. This process entailed: (a) getting the LDCs to accept the proposal of DFQF into industrial country markets, which many of them felt was loop-hole ridden; (b) getting LDCs to accept the 'aid for trade' proposal which consisted partly of loans, albeit it was referred to as aid. It was regarded as 'a mere bauble', a trivial give-away, by a trade analyst (Halle, 2006); (c) cajoling the West African cotton producers to accept a proposal that gave the US one extra year to eliminate its export subsidies for cotton farmers; (d) coaxing the countries that were strongly opposed to plurilateral negotiations in services, namely, Indonesia, the Philippines, South Africa and Cuba, to accept them; and (e) neutralizing the opposition of the so-called NAMA-11 group of developing countries. This group expressed maximum dissatisfaction of the NAMA and wanted to link the demand of the EU and the US for rapid liberalization in industrial tariffs in the larger developing economies with rapid reduction in agricultural subsidies and tariffs. Paradoxically, both Brazil and India were members of the NAMA-11.

Did they play their leadership role in a sagacious manner? As one group of member countries had to finally bear an overwhelmingly larger burden of saving the Ministerial Conference than the other, an honest answer will have to be in the negative. This burden-sharing should have been even between the two groups of member countries. If their leadership succeeded in saving the Hong Kong Ministerial from a Cancún-like debacle, it palpably was at a high cost to the developing country members of the WTO, which has traditionally been a weak group of countries in the multilateral trade regime. Thus viewed, their leadership perceptibly produced unfair results.

SUMMARY AND CONCLUSIONS

This chapter sheds light on what transpired during the Hong Kong Ministerial Conference, its achievements and lack thereof. The negotiations on agriculture had been the *bête noire* of the Doha Round. They continued to be so in Hong Kong as well. If success is defined as lack of failure, the sixth Ministerial Conference was a success. Candidly speaking, if it was not a failure, it did not achieve much of substance and was not a success either.

Although there were a host of important areas under negotiation, the principal ones were trade in agriculture, NAMA, services, SDT of the developing economies, market access of the LDCs, trade facilitation and WTO rules in the areas of AD, anti-subsidy and SCM. Very little of value was achieved in any of these areas in Hong Kong. The harvest of decisions taken was meager because most of the politically difficult decisions were assiduously deferred for 2006. April 2006 was made a deadline for finalizing exceeding important modalities. Little progress on agreeing to core modalities could be made, although this had been the unofficial objective of the Hong Kong Ministerial Conference. Small decisions that could be taken had meager real value for the MTNs.

The liberalization of trade in services has had a history of stagnation. The request-and-offer process of trade liberalization in services has proved to be slow and tedious and has not led to any progress in the services negotiations since its inception in 2000. During the Hong Kong Ministerial, instead of making progress in negotiations in trade in services, it seems that some retrograde motion was made.

One bright aspect of the Hong Kong Ministerial Conference was that procedurally it performed far better than the preceding Ministerial Conference at Cancún. Negotiations followed a bottom-up approach, which implied that inputs came from the members rather than from above. It contributed to the success of widespread deliberations among the WTO members, collectively and in groups. Transparency and inclusiveness were taken for granted.

A momentous development that took place in Hong Kong was that the

Quad of the GATT era retreated into history because it had become completely irrelevant. In its place, Brazil, the EU, India and the US emerged as the most energetically negotiating WTO members, influencing both the process and substance of MTNs. They were informally christened the New Quad.

NOTES

1. The 18 members of the Cairns group are Argentina, Australia, Bolivia, Brazil, Canada, Chile, Colombia, Costa Rica, Guatemala, Indonesia, Malaysia, New Zealand, Pakistan, Paraguay, the Philippines, South Africa, Thailand and Uruguay.
2. The emerging market economy was a term coined by Antoine W. van Agtmael of the International Finance Corporation in 1981. It is loosely defined as a market economy with low-to-middle per capita income that participates globally by implementing reform programs. Such economies represent 20 percent of the world economy. Countries whose economies fall into this category vary from very big to very small. They are usually considered emerging because of their fast-clip growth rate and the reforms undertaken by them. Hence, even though China is deemed as one of the world's economic powerhouses, it is lumped into the EME category alongside much smaller economies with a great deal fewer resources, like Tunisia. Both China and Tunisia belong to this category because both have embarked on economic development and reform programs, and have begun to open up their markets and 'emerge' onto the global economic scene. EMEs are considered to be fast-growing economies. One key characteristic of the EME is an increase in both local and foreign investment, both portfolio and direct. A growth in investment in a country often indicates that the country has been able to build investors' confidence in the domestic economy. Moreover, foreign investment is a signal that the world has begun to take notice of the emerging market, and when international capital flows are directed toward an EME, the injection of foreign currency into the local economy adds volume to the country's stock market and long-term investment to the infrastructure.
3. With 3.5 percent of the French population on farms in 2005, the remaining 96.5 percent of the French population fails to see that the archaic agricultural policy of subsidies and tariffs not only made their food more expensive but deprived impoverished farmers in the developing economies of making an honest living. One answer is that the Common Agricultural Policy (CAP) of the EU has worked highly profitably for France. Even after recent reductions, French agriculture receives $9 billion annually through the CAP mechanism. France has traditionally been receiving the largest share of CAP spending. The recipient of these benefits is a powerful and unionized group, represented by the main French agricultural union, the FNSEA. In the recent past, this Union has become more aggressive because it does not want to be seen as weakening in the presence of a newly upcoming competing union called the Confederation Paysanne.
4. The Group-of-Ninety is a large group of diverse developing economies and includes the low-income developing economies such as the least-developed countries (LDCs), the African, Caribbean and Pacific (ACP) countries and the African Group (AG) countries.
5. The four modes of trade in services are as follows: (a) Mode-1 relates to cross border trade; (b) Mode-2 to consumption abroad; (c) Mode-3 to commercial presence; and (d) Mode-4 to presence of natural persons.
6. The need for a plurilateral methodology had arisen because 149 member countries were participating in the Hong Kong Ministerial. Therefore, the United States and other industrial economies argued that it would be difficult to make progress in the services agenda of the DDA if the negotiations were made only on the basis of individual offers and requests made on a bilateral basis. Instead, it was proposed that a plurilateral methodology, where groups of countries could negotiate general commitments on services, would be more effective. Such commitments could subsequently be extended to all GSTS member states on an 'MFN' basis.

7. He was the Secretary of Commerce, Industry and Technology of the Government of Hong Kong SAR.
8. The Group-of-Thirty-Three (G-33) is a group of countries interested in trade in agriculture. In 2006, it comprised 42 countries.
9. Peter Sutherland (2004), the Director General of the GATT at that point in time, paid rich compliments to the role played by these two delegations. They were not only skillful negotiators but also thorough in their tasks, hardly giving away anything. Sutherland called them the 'right constellation of negotiators' that fortuitously existed during that period.

7. The Doha Round: a disenchanting evolutionary process

> If we are facing in the right direction, all we need to do is to keep on walking.
>
> A Buddhist Proverb

INTRODUCTION

If one observes the developments and events of the preceding three decades, it is easy to comprehend how the evolutionary process of the multilateral trade regime has become progressively challenging. There is no gainsaying the fact that the Doha Round of multilateral trade negotiations (MTNs) has thus far proved to be egregiously problem-prone. Deep dissensions among members, distant negotiating positions on crucial issues and inordinate delays in coming to a rare agreement – if and when they did come to one – on the material issues of process and substance, have brought the Doha Round to a crisis point. The factors contributing to this unacceptable, if not melancholy, state of affairs go beyond the mercantilist mindset of the negotiators (pp. 164–7) from the principal trading economies and the country groups that wield significant negotiating weight in the multilateral trading system. Contretemps and mishaps continued even after the Hong Kong Ministerial Conference. The crucial deadline of 30 June was missed (Chapter 6; pp. 152–5) and mini-Ministerials of January 2006 and July 2006 failed to achieve anything, causing a great deal of gloom and disillusionment in the community of multilateral traders and trade policy mandarins. In this chapter we examine *inter alia* the causal factors behind the slow and sluggish progress in the Doha Round, both before and after the Hong Kong Ministerial Conference.

In July 2006, the MTNs were not in an acceptable state. What could possibly be achieved by their satisfactory culmination is not a mystery. We noted in Chapter 1 that the global community needed to adopt the policy objectives of economic growth and poverty alleviation by means of an ambitious program of multilateral trade policy reforms. To be sure, such a reform program would need to have an ambitious vision of coordinated global policy action at the highest political level, at the Group-of-Eight (G-8)[1] level (section 9), which comprises the strapping and most influential global economies. Growth, poverty alleviation, trade expansion and global economic integration are worthy policy objectives, calling for the attention of apex-level public policy professionals. The G-8 political leaders, in partnership with those from larger G-20 economies, needed to infuse fresh political capital in bringing the Doha Round negotiations back to its feet and moving.

The makeup of this chapter is as follows. The discussion in the next section begins with the need to promote and reinforce the multilateral trade regime, a global public good. The third section focuses on the principal reasons why the negotiations in Doha Round have been so slow and whether there were any other causal factors than the mercantilist mindset of the negotiators behind the sluggish progress. After the Hong Kong Ministerial Conference some efforts were made for the Doha Round to pick up momentum; their failure of these efforts is examined in the fourth section. It brought the round to a crisis point, an admission of which was made by the Director General of the World Trade Organization (WTO) (fifth section). The sixth section monitors the MTNs in the Doha Round and examines the state of play in the major areas of MTNs and plausible achievements in its key segments. The seventh section monitors the status of negotiations in trade in services. The eighth section attempts to assess the possible benefits from a properly completed Doha Round to the global economy as well as to the various groups of economies have been made. The ninth section discusses the initiative taken by the G-8 Summit held in St Petersburg in Russia in July 2006. The final section provides a summary of the chapter.

PROMOTING THE GLOBAL PUBLIC GOOD

Under the contemporary multilateral trade regime, multilateral trade expanded rapidly. In 1970 it was a paltry $314 billion. The corresponding figure for 1980 was $2.0 trillion, in 1990 it was $3.4 trillion and in 2000 $6.4 trillion.[2] The value of world merchandise exports rose by 13 percent in 2005, compared to 21 percent in 2004, but it exceeded the $10 trillion mark for the first time. The value of world exports of commercial services increased by 11 percent in 2005, compared to 19 percent in 2004. Its dollar value was $2.4 trillion in 2005. Together multilateral trade in goods and services amounted to $12.62 trillion in 2005. In the process of rapid expansion, since the birth of the General Agreement on Tariffs and Trade (GATT) in 1948, multilateral trade became a controversial issue for the global economy as well as for global economic governance. It also became a defining feature of national and global economic governance. The multilateral trade regime governing trade is a global public good (GPG), that is, using the concept in the positive sense, not in a normative sense. A GPG by definition has a universal intertemporal impact over a large number of countries, a large number of people and on several generations.

In terms of its costs and benefits the multilateral trade regime is a veritable GPG. This regime is a set of rules, codes, agreements, and institutions, which are fundamentally intended to facilitate and expand multilateral trade. As a GPG, the multilateral trade regime is essentially public in consumption, but the distribution of its net benefits is clearly skewed in favor of the mature industrial economies and some of the newly-industrialized economies (NIEs), giving rise to a great deal of understandable tension in the global trade fora and during the periodic MTNs.

In the post-Hong Kong Ministerial period, none of the major players has been willing to exert leadership in promoting this GPG. None of the members of the New Quad, including the two hegemonic trade powers, have been willing to take a leadership role. While the New Quad did provide leadership in the lead-up to the Hong Kong Ministerial conference, its eagerness to do so in the aftermath evaporated. The international community has been concerned and has continued the dialogue on this GPG.

WHAT IS BEYOND MERCANTILISM?

For the consistently tardy progress in Doha Round, the mercantilist mindset of the participants was blamed most frequently, almost in a routine manner. It is also regarded as the primary culprit for the lean harvest of the Hong Kong Ministerial (Chapter 6). It is time to put this accusation in a proper perspective and determine whether it has been an impetuous, unjust and excessive accusation. Does mercantilism have a strong grip over the minds of the negotiating trade ministers and delegations? Perhaps this is not the entire explanation for the lack of progress in the Doha Round.

Simplicity of Reciprocal Tariff Slashing

The earlier rounds of the MTNs, under the GATT regime, could be completed swiftly and on target, because they were relatively easy and negotiations were relatively simple. They essentially dealt with reciprocal tariff slashing on manufactured goods. Besides, they took place among the industrial economies, which were far less diverse in their economic structures and objectives. With increasing membership, the economic diversity of member economies went on increasing and the simplicity of reciprocal tariff slashing was lost forever. Present-day multilateral trade regime demonstrates an incredible range in asymmetry between players.

With the passage of time the multilateral trade regime matured, mutated and the agenda of MTNs went on becoming progressively larger, more multifaceted and consequently grew challenging to negotiate. The Uruguay Round exemplified this trend. Its agenda was exceedingly difficult in terms of the spread of issues and their complexity, and the Doha Round is no less so. The most problematical areas in the Doha Round are agriculture, non-agricultural market access (NAMA), services and the one Singapore issue that is still on the table, namely, trade facilitation. Such intricacy and complexity of the negotiating issues contributed to stupefaction and caused sluggish progress.

At the present stage of growth of the multilateral trade regime, many negotiating issues are far from simple. The sophistication and intricacy of the issues under negotiation have presently been exacerbated by, first, a much larger number of negotiating member economies than during the GATT era, with a large variation in the expectation of the multilateral trade regime. As noted in Chapter 1, this number is expected to increase further and touch 170 by 2010. Negotiations among a large number of participants also have the innate disadvantage of homeostasis and drift. Second, much enhanced economic diversity among the negotiating member economies contributes more than ever before to difficulties and delays in coming to agreements. Not only is the range of individual players in MTNs much larger than in the past, but new country groups like G-20, G-33 and G-90 have also emerged which throw their negotiating weight around in the MTNs. Third, during the GATT era, the Quad commanded hegemonic status and had a massive influence on the decision-making process as well as final results of MTNs. The GATT system worked through the Green Room negotiation process, with an active Quad.[3] This is no longer true. In groups, developing economies have also come to have negotiating weights. Leaders in these groups have been proactively seeking to secure developing countries' interests. This has changed the fabric and character of MTNs. The negotiation process has tended to become far more time-consuming and demanding than before.

Wide Diversity in Objectives

Due to diversity of objectives of the member countries, MTNs increasingly failed. Contrary to the GATT era many developing economies now have an important stake in international trade and therefore they participate proactively. Many of them try to contribute to and influence the decision-making process in the manner they consider is best for their domestic constituencies. For the first time, they have begun taking the attitude of 'What do we get out of the MTNs?' Each country seeks a trophy for domestic display out of the negotiations as a justification for concessions made to the trading partners. These new proclivities make negotiations taxing, testing and prolonged.

Frequent allegations of intransigence were made against the European Union, Japan and the United States, and of late it has been difficult to say that they are incorrect. However, that they have very little left to put on the negotiating table at the MTNs in terms of market access is ignored, except for those things that are very difficult for them to put on the negotiating table from the perspective of their domestic interests and considerations.

Domestic Polity Considerations

There are areas of domestic political, social and economic sensitivities, which incumbent governments often do not wish to disturb because of their high political costs. The industrial economies kept agriculture and textiles and apparel under stringent protection for decades. These two areas of trade have survived as protected areas for eight rounds of MTNs. To be sure, there can be little economic justification for not putting them on the negotiating table. If anything, it is poor economics not to do so, but because of domestic policy considera-tions and political sensitivity these large trading economies find it onerous to allow market access in these areas. It is not easy for trade ministers and negotiators to ignore domestic public opinions, legislatures and parliaments.

Opposition to outsourcing in general and business-process outsourcing (BPO) in particular in the industrial economies has the same roots, that is, domestic policy considerations and political reasons. Until the political leadership and populations in these countries are better educated on these issues and learn to recognize the benefits of free trade and payoff from the principle of comparative advantage, industrial economies will find it daunting to table these issues on the negotiating table. Market access in these areas will continue to be limited for the developing economies. Political will among the large WTO member countries could indeed surmount the difficulties and resolve stand-offs in the MTNs, but that has patently been in short supply. Sentiments that underlie the general lack of political will include the adverse reaction of domestic constituencies and the widespread anti-globalization in the industrial economies. Political leadership in the large industrial economies, which are also the large traders, frequently reflects the same sentiments.

To persuade the EU, Japan and the US to make market liberalization offers in these and other manufacturing sectors, the G-20 economies need to make attractive balancing offers when opening their markets. The emerging-market economies (EMEs) have not made it a secret that they are unwilling to steeply lower their trade barriers.

Active Role of NGOs

In addition, the active role played by non-governmental organizations (NGOs) oftentimes led MTNs to stand-offs. The large international NGOs, which are highly resourceful, significantly influenced the positions taken by the developing economies, particularly the least-developed countries (LDCs).[4] While the large NGOs have an impressive knowledge base and technical prowess in MTNs-related issues, there were occasions when their advice did not contribute to smooth progress in MTNs. A case in point is the services negotiations during the Doha Round, particularly during the Hong Kong Ministerial. By advising developing economies not to participate in plurilateral negotiations, NGOs did apparent disservice to the cause of developing country trade and the MTNs.

POST-HONG KONG DEVELOPMENTS

When the Hong Kong Ministerial Conference culminated without any noteworthy and meaningful achievements, the 149 participating members of the WTO promised to continue intense negotiations and converge their respective positions with the explicit objective to set down firm agreements in the most important and basic areas of MTNs by the end of April 2006. This decision was well publicized through the media, partly to put a positive spin on the lack of achievement in Hong Kong. For the same reason, the April 2006 deadline was self-imposed by the members, and it was vitally important to meet it (Chapter 6, pp. 152–5).

One small but encouraging development was that in April the EC signaled that it was willing to enhance its agriculture offer within the limits of its negotiating mandate, if the other industrial economies do the same. This initiative was considered wholesome and welcomed by the G-20 and Australia.

None of the members of the New Quad was willing to provide leadership during this difficult period. Members were aware that an immense task awaited them both in terms of achieving substance in negotiations and meeting the agreed deadlines. The two well known and widely acknowledged *bêtes noire* for the negotiators were agriculture and NAMA. The timeline for 2006 included the achievement of several important targets including: (a) establishing modalities in agriculture; (b) completing disciplines on export credit guarantees and insurance programs, reforming of state trading enterprises (in Australia, Canada and New Zealand) and US food aid and export credit systems; (c) eliminating all forms of export subsidies, together with agreed progressivity and parallelism; and (d) the NAMA modalities to be set. Efforts were needed to be stepped up to bridge divergences and outstanding issues were to be resolved, which required expending political capital. All this was to be achieved no later than 30 April.

Even during the post-Hong Kong period, agriculture and NAMA were regarded as the two most significant areas in which convergence of positions among the members and agreement was sorely needed. They were being regarded as the key to further progress in the MTNs. Services, trade facilitation, special and differential treatment (SDT), rules in the areas of anti-dumping (AD), and safeguarding, anti-subsidies and countervailing measures (SCM) were the other important and related areas in which members had to agree to a consensus position, or one that was close to it. Together these issues involved all the major traders and negotiating country groups, including the EU, the Group-of-Twenty (G-20), the LDCs and the US, and were regarded as the areas of critical significance at this stage of MTNs. These groups of members had significant negotiating weights and none could make a decisive move without the others. Initially during the post-Hong Kong period it was assumed that once modalities in agriculture and NAMA were settled by early summer 2006, the rest of the year could be devoted to trade in services, WTO rules and the other important issues. It was believed that this plan would help in completing the MTNs by the end of 2005, before the expiration of the US President's Trade Promotion Authority (TPA), or the so-called 'Fast Track' authority. This timeline proved to be overly optimistic and could not be realized.

The developing economies, including the LDCs, stand to gain from both increased market access in the industrial economies as well as expanded trade opportunities in the other developing economies. Also, it is widely acknowledged that trade-distorting domestic subsidies in many countries, particularly the industrial economies, have historically had an enormously deforming and deleterious influence over world trade in agricultural products. The Doha Round-induced reduction in domestic support will be of enormous benefit to world trade in agriculture, particularly for the developing country exporters. The Uruguay Round Agreement on Agriculture (URAA) made a significant contribution in this regard. Between 1995 and 2003, agricultural exports from the developing economies increased by 24 percent. By increasing their agricultural exports from $229 billion to $352 billion over the period under consideration, the developing economies succeeded in increasing their share of world exports from 40 percent to 42 percent. In agricultural trade, there are product-specific issues on board, namely, cotton, commodities, tropical products and those relating to preference erosion. Member countries have made proposals relating to these product-specific issues which were under negotiation and need to be settled.

The NAMA was another post-Hong Kong crucial issue for the members, particularly the G-20 and LDCs. A NAMA agreement will have a wide scope and be binding on tariff not only on industrial products but also on products like fisheries, jewelry, and so on, that is, on anything outside the URAA.

Market access both in the industrial economies and the other developing ones, is the principal area of negotiation. High tariffs, tariff peaks and tariff escalation still need to be addressed as much as non-tariff barriers (NTBs). The Uruguay Round of MTNs made a substantive contribution in this area. The developing member countries have an additional worry in this regard, namely, preservation of certain policy space. Many of them would like to protect their infant industries from the winds of intense global competition and maintain unbound duties in some sensitive sectors. The LDCs see NAMA negotiations as a means to enhance their DFQF access to industrial country markets.

Preference erosion, alluded to above, has continued to badger the LDCs. This group of small and low-income developing countries has been benefiting from preferential market access in many industrial country markets under various schemes of General System of Preferences (GSP). The GSP has played a role in making the LDC products competitive in industrial country markets. As the multilateral tariff rates are liberalized under the ongoing NAMA negotiations, the margin between a preferential tariff rate to which LDCs are entitled and the MFN tariffs will narrow, eroding the competitiveness of the their exports. LDCs have complained in the past that, due to stringent rules of origin (ROO) requirements under the GSP schemes, they could not utilize the GSP adequately. The rate of utilization in the EU was 54 percent and in Japan 53 percent. Compliance requirements erode that value of the GSP (Hoekman and Prowse, 2005). As the tariffs are liberalized further, the benefits enjoyed under the GSP schemes by the LDCs will significantly erode.

Deliberations in Mini-Ministerial in Davos

Cognizant of the modest achievements in Hong Kong SAR, trade ministers of 30 countries met in Davos, Switzerland, in late January 2006, in a mini-Ministerial.[5] This was a plurilateral meeting, which included trade ministers from Australia, Benin, Brazil, Costa Rica, Egypt, the EU, Ghana, Hong Kong SAR, India, Indonesia, Japan, Korea (Republic of), Malaysia, Mexico, New Zealand, Norway, Senegal, Switzerland and the US. The Director General of the WTO and Chairperson of the General Council were also among the participants. They commiserated on the lack of substantive achievement of the Hong Kong Ministerial Conference. Participants acknowledged that progress had to be made on all the outstanding issues, not on agriculture alone – although this has been a major problematic issue in the MTNs.

The participating ministers looked for practical measures to be taken so that deadline of April 2006 set in Hong Kong could be met. They also acknowledged that there is a critical need for political input at this point in time. Initiative was needed from the US on domestic agricultural support, from the EU on agricultural market access and from Brazil, China and India on services and NAMA. The key WTO members, particularly the members of the New Quad, were required to move in order to advance the Doha Development Agenda (DDA).

While deliberations took place on what and what not to do so that tangible progress can be made in the MTNs for negotiations to be brought to a close by the end of 2006, the mini-Ministerial did little to change negotiating dynamics. Negotiations on WTO reforms of trade rules were given short shrift in Hong Kong. Clarification and reform of the trade remedies, which include AD, anti-subsidy and SCM, and discipline on regional trading arrangements, were relegated to the background. In Paragraph 28, the Hong Kong Ministerial declaration has merely one sentence on this subject (WTO, 2005b). In Davos, mini-Ministerial trade rules were taken up for discussion and a new text was drafted. It did not advance deliberations further but proposed a similar timetable to advance negotiations as on agriculture and NAMA. However, despite good intentions and positive thinking, no material strategy could be devised for advancing the DDA. Anxious trade negotiators from Australia, Brazil, the EU, India, Japan and the US again met in a plurilateral consultative meeting in London for two days in mid-March 2006. This new group of countries is referred to as the Group-of-Six (G-6) and emerged as the most influential after the Hong Kong Ministerial.

Missed April Deadline

Since the beginning of 2006, intense negotiating activity took place at various levels across the whole spectrum of the MTNs. Many WTO members took the initiative in complementing the negotiations in Geneva so that tangible progress could be made at this crucial stage of the MTNs. To this end, seminars were organized in important world capitals and addressed by Pascal Lamy, the Director General of the WTO.

As further negotiations were linked to progress in two areas, agriculture and NAMA, it was logically – if optimistically – assumed that once material progress was made in these areas of MTNs, progress in the other related areas would follow and the Doha Round could be completed by the end of 2006. This resolve was laid down in paragraph 1 of the Hong Kong Ministerial Declaration (WTO, 2005b). The self-imposed 30 April deadline was missed without any achievement and the resolve of completing the Doha Round by the end of 2006 became an utterly unrealistic target.

Missing deadlines in any MTN is nothing extraordinary. Experience suggests that negotiators look at them as useful in principle but worth ignoring in practice. It happens so frequently that it is routinely accepted. History is an inadequate guide in this respect because past MTNs have dragged on for years before eventually completing, as it happened in the Uruguay Round. The Doha Round may not have this luxury. Missing the 30 April 2006 deadline was a meaningful loss because this deadline was very significant and happened at a time point when the Doha Round was at a decisive and crucial stage (Chapter 6; pp. 152–5). The first serious failure was that what was needed to be achieved in terms of modalities in the Hong Kong Ministerial was not achieved. Second, falling woefully short of tangible results in the Hong Kong Ministerial, it was decided that by 30 April the negotiating members would reach agreements on the outstanding issues. Modalities (meaning thereby the numerical formulas, targets and timetable for implementation of trade liberalization for the member countries) were to be belatedly agreed so that members could start real progress in terms of trade liberalization by changing their policy structure.

Reneging on Promises: Disillusioning Evolutionary Process

Not reaching an agreement on modalities by the self-imposed deadline of 30 April by the members was seen as an enormous collective mistake of the members, if not the multilateral trading system. 'Back loading the three key areas of agricultural domestic support and market access in agriculture and industrial products was something of a recipe for failure.' Rapid progress in these three areas held the key to 'unlock the many other issues which also needed to fall into place to conclude this Round' (Lamy, 2006b).

Agriculture negotiations have lagged, evidently because the EU and the US would not reduce their subsidies and import barriers. The trade liberalization proposals they tabled are weak by any standard. Some analysts believe that the developing economies have grown justly wary of the seriousness of the offers (Hufbauer and Schott, 2006). Their anxiety is that the key areas of reform in agriculture may be excluded or subject to long deferment. They even anticipate possibilities of the Doha Round concluding without meaningful progress in agriculture. On their part, the developing economies that are *demandeur* in this area of agriculture, do not wish to lower their barriers in agricultural trade, largely due to pressures from the domestic farm lobbies. Ill at ease, the G-20 group of countries responded by hesitating in tabling meaningful liberalization offers in manufactures and services. This is how a negotiating gridlock has come into being.

An agreement on modalities on the three issues named above would not have led to the successful culmination the Doha Round. However, it would have helped in resolving the impasse in the MTNs and certainly moved them forward and prepared the ground for the successful culmination of the Doha Round. The agenda could have been advanced after such an agreement toward trade liberalization in services, the WTO rules in the areas of AD, anti-subsidy and SCM, bilateral trade agreements, trade facilitation, Trade Related Intellectual Property Rights (TRIPS), dispute settlement and aid for trade. Agreement on modalities had not reached a take-off point even after 30 April, the missed deadline. The negotiating texts were being prepared for the agreement on modalities so that the Trade Ministers of the member countries could make their decisions. If the revised target date to conclude the Doha Round is to be end of 2006, this measure needed to be completed without further delay. A show of strong political will is needed from the negotiating member countries and their trade ministers.

Disarray in the Geneva Mini-Ministerial

Another desultory mini-Ministerial was called by the WTO in Geneva on 29 June through 2 July 2006, with the objective of negotiating on modalities in agriculture and NAMA. The mini-Ministerial was marked by apathy, in which trade ministers arrived late and left early. The EU and the G-20 were coaxing the US to make a stronger offer on cutting trade-distorting domestic farm subsidies, which had continued to rise to the highest level ever. There was some speculation about the US working on new positions in this area. However, in one meeting after another, delegations waited for the US to table its improved offers – particularly on agricultural domestic support – which never came through. Neither during the G-6 meeting nor during the Trade Negotiations Committee (TNC) was the renewed US offer, which went beyond the 2005 agricultural proposal, tabled. The G-20 countries did not wish to make fresh offers until the EU and the US improved their commitments in agriculture.

The EU showed some willingness to improve its offer but insisted that the developing economies open their market for industrial products by adopting a coefficient of 15 in the Swiss Formula. The reaction of the G-20 was that this was a Development Round, concerning market liberalization of the industrial countries for the developing country products, not the other way round. The mini-Ministerial broke down, with members requesting Pascal Lamy to step up consultations with the governments to identify possible compromises.

PROSPECTS OF FAILURE CLOSING IN

As set out in Chapter 2 (pp. 44–5), there was a surfeit of evidence of the commitments of members to the objectives of the DDA. These were reflected in a series of official pronouncements. Their good intentions, appropriate thinking, positive mindset and correct values could not be more evident. Ironically, with the passage of time it became obvious that those expressions of positive and virtuous intentions were completely misleading. There was a large distance between what was being said and what was being achieved in terms of tangible agreements and core modalities. Although the New Quad had come into being, the MTNs suffered acutely from a lack of imaginative and responsible leadership. Settling on the core modalities was not an impossibility, but when the sticking points called for creativity and flexibility, important trading economies, and the members of the New Quad – particularly the two trade superpowers that have the largest negotiating weight – responded with apathy.

In July 2006, the languishing Doha Round seemed ripe for a failure. On 1 July, when Pascal Lamy stated, 'We are now in a crisis', no one disagreed.[6] Efforts continued to bridge the gaps and conclude the MTNs before the end of 2006, in time for the Bush Administration's expiration of the TPA. During the Hong Kong Ministerial Conference a Chairman's Consultative Group (CCG) was set up. The CCG had 26 members and was christened the 'Green Room' (Chapter 6). On 1 July, after a smaller Green Room meeting of trade ministers, Pascal Lamy was asked to commence intensive and wide-ranging consultations with an objective to facilitate the establishment of modalities in agriculture and NAMA, and report the result of these consultations to the TNC.

Accusation of Let-down

The failure of the Geneva mini-Ministerial portended to two possibilities. First, that the three leading actors in the MTNs, that is, the EU, the G-20 and the US, saw no need to reach to reach an agreement and assumed that the Doha Round, like its predecessors, is likely to drag on for years. They assumed that history will repeat itself and something will eventually evolve by simply holding off. Second, these authors of any possible deal assumed that it does not matter if the Doha Round fails.

The US was held culpable for the failure of the mini-Ministerial in Geneva by demanding too much from the EC and the G-20, while offering too little. It blamed the proposal from the other two for having a 'black box' of loopholes which would allow them to minimize tariff reductions (*The Economist*, 2006b). In agriculture, the US wanted the EU to slash tariffs by an average of 66 percent, while the EU offered to slash them by 39 percent. The G-20 wanted a 54 percent cut from the EU and the US, and proposed that the developing countries would cut them by two-thirds as much. As usual, there would be a lot of exceptions to the general rule, weakening these proposals.

Possible Way Out of the Stagnation

The essence of a deal that could spur MTNs needed parallel progress in, first, the US improving its offer to make deeper cuts in domestic farm support; second, the EU improving its commitment to agricultural market access, and third, the EMEs (in particular Brazil, China, India and Mexico) offering more on industrial tariff cuts. While plenty of text was there on the table, the numerical measures on these three vitally important issues on which the three sides agreed were missing. The three sides tabled inadequate proposals, reflected in weak numbers, that the other two sides promptly rejected.

Whenever countries feel that multilateral negotiations are likely to fail, or not go far, one immediate reaction is that a large number of regional trade agreements (RTAs) or bilateral trade agreements (BTAs) start springing up – despite their unarguable economic inferiority. This happens as a manifestation of weakening faith in multilateralism. In the first half of 2006, a good number of RTAs and BTAs were inspired by what was transpiring in the Doha Round and what happened first in Cancún and then in Hong Kong. Economies that were forming RTAs and BTAs were aware of their unarguable economic inferiority.

The ten-member Association of South East Asian Nations (ASEAN)[7] began negotiations for a free trade area (FTA) with India in mid-June 2006. ASEAN's negotiations with the EU and the Republic of Korea for an FTA were scheduled for the latter half of 2006. Thailand's negotiations for an FTA with the US were in progress in 2006 and were due to start soon after with Malaysia. The US has signed over ten BTAs in the recent past. Those with Colombia, Peru and Vietnam were signed. US BTA negotiations with countries in Latin America (Ecuador and Panama), Asia (Korea, Malaysia and Thailand) and the Middle East (Oman) were in progress in 2006. US endeavors to create a hemisphere-wide Free Trade Area of the Americas (FTAA) are virtually dead, largely owing to sharp differences over US farm subsidies. They have been supplanted by BTAs in Latin America.

Such RTAs, BTAs and FTAs can be made more swiftly than MTNs because, first, only a small number of countries participate in the negotiations, and second, these participating countries can choose to keep their sensitive areas of trade out by mutual consent. Paradoxically, these are often precisely the goods and services in which trade liberalization could be most beneficial. For instance, Korea tries to keep trade in rice out of all such agreements. When the Korean negotiators tried to negotiate an FTA with Thailand and tried to keep out trade in rice, Thailand balked because it is the largest exporter of rice in the world. In its negotiations with ASEAN, India had a list of 1400 'sensitive' goods, which it wanted to keep out of the negotiations. It was made to whittle this list down to 850 goods by ASEAN.

Members concurred in general that the US proposal for cutting agricultural subsidies was less attractive than it sounds. It promised to halve them and proposed the new ceiling at $23 billion. This is much lower than the corresponding EU figure, but more than what the US actually spent. In 2005, the US spent $19.7 billion. In this background of incongruity and disagreement, Pascal Lamy's so-called 20/20/20 proposal appeared eminently level-headed and sagacious. According to this proposed deal, the US needs to cut its subsidy ceiling to below $20 billion, the EU needs to accept the agricultural tariff cuts proposed by the G-20 and on their part the G-20 need to cap their industrial tariffs at 20 percent. This is a compromise formula. It would lower tariff barriers by less than what the US proposed, but prevent agricultural subsidies from rising. It has the benefit of bring about some liberalization in both the troublesome sectors of trade: agricultural and industrial.

STATE OF PLAY IN THE NEGOTIATIONS

In this section, I shall focus on the status of negotiations in the principal areas of the MTNs and see what, if anything, has been achieved. We shall start with agriculture.

Quagmire around Agriculture

Although agriculture and agro-industrial products contribute merely 4 percent to global GDP and approximately 9 percent to merchandise trade, it was and continues to be the linchpin in the on-going MTNs. Since the birth of the present multilateral trade regime, manufacturing tariffs have declined by nine-tenths to less than 4 percent. Conversely, protection in agricultural trade has intensified. Average applied tariffs on agricultural products are five times the tariffs on manufactures, while average bound tariffs are ten times the bound tariffs. This sector presently has the highest trade barriers. Modeling results show that agricultural product markets continued to remain the most costly of all goods market distortions in world trade (Anderson, 2004). Trade barriers are high both in the developing and industrial economies. If the developing economies are to be constructively engaged in MTNs, they need to be convinced that they will receive sufficient benefits from agricultural trade reforms to warrant the inevitable cost of negotiations and adjustments.

Although a declining sector of the global economy, agriculture still employs a large proportion – 54 percent – of the work force in the developing economies. This sector of multilateral trade has enormous significance of the developing economies. Not freeing trade in agriculture from barriers works fundamentally against the interest of the developing economies. Also, it cannot be ignored that the majority of the poor in the developing economies live in rural areas. It is widely acknowledged that poverty is overwhelmingly a rural phenomenon in the developing economies. Therefore, if the final outcome of the Doha Round of MTNs is to be pro-poor and if the first Millennium Development Goal (MDG) is to be achieved, trade in agriculture needs to be an area of exclusive attention during the MTNs. Liberalization of agricultural trade would gradually change market shares of countries and country groups and eventually reflect the comparative advantage of countries and country-groups in multilateral trade.

Although theoretically agriculture was within the ambit of the GATT-1947, some exceptions were allowed in the 1950s under pressure from the US, the largest trading economy. Besides, the articles of agreements of the GATT-1947 had loopholes, which were freely exploited by the contracting parties (CPs). Consequently, agriculture became the most distorted area of multilateral trade. Industrial economies – in particular the EU, Japan and the US – increasingly subsidized their farm sector and agricultural trade and erected ever-rising trade barriers. Consequently trade in agriculture was virtually outside the ambit of the GATT system. It was not easy to bring it under the multilateral trade regime like other merchandise trade.

During the Uruguay Round (1986–94) this issue was squarely tackled. After enormous and long drawn-out efforts, the URAA was instrumental in drawing agricultural trade within the sphere of the multilateral trade regime. These efforts not only contributed to slowing down the negotiations in the Uruguay Round but also prolonged them. The URAA imposed new disciplines on trade in agricultural products. The new rules were implemented between 1995 and 2000. Under the URAA industrial economies committed to: (a) reducing domestic support to agriculture; (b) reducing export subsidies; and (c) improving access to their markets. These were referred to as the 'three pillars' of the agreement. As progressive liberalization of agricultural trade was a long-term process, the WTO members committed to continue negotiations on it under the so-called 'built-in agenda' of the Uruguay Round. This was the mandate of the Marrakesh Agreement of April 1994. Accordingly, the agricultural negotiations began in January 2000.

Since the URAA agricultural trade has continued to grow, but ironically more slowly than in the pre-URAA period and more slowly than non-agricultural trade (OECD, 2005a). While trade in agriculture came within the domain of the multilateral regulations, the URAA failed to deliver significant multilateral liberalization in agricultural trade (Messerlin, 2002). Developing economies complained that on the whole the URAA did not work as intended and that they did not get a fair deal. Evidence supported their gripe that tariff cuts made by the developing economies were significantly deeper than what was agreed to by the industrial economies (Finger and Winters, 2002). In addition, they had to commit to costly commitments that were embodied in the Sanitary and Phytosanitary (SPS) agreement and TRIPS agreements. Some of the requirements for the developing economies under the SPS agreements are more stringent than those for the industrial economies. Given this background of malcontent, higher market access commitments were sought by the developing economies in the Doha Round from the industrial economies.

As expected, the Doha Round began with high expectations of reforms in agricultural trade, but members did not agree on the first draft on modalities which was presented in February 2003. The Cairns Group found the draft unambitious, conversely the EU, Japan, Norway and Switzerland found it not only overly ambitious but also unbalanced in terms of the three pillars of negotiations. Among many disagreements and contretemps in the Fifth Ministerial Conference, held in Cancún, was the sectoral initiative taken by the Cotton-4 opposing cotton subsidies in the industrial economies because they depressed cotton revenues in the West African countries by $250 million per year. The demand of the Cotton-4 countries was met in the Hong Kong Ministerial.

Before the Cancún Ministerial, the EU and the US agreed on a broad framework for negotiating agricultural trade liberalization and presented a joint EU–US framework paper on agricultural negotiations, which paid little attention to the concerns of the developing economies and was found weak by them. It was followed by a counter-proposal by the G-20. The second framework paper by the G-20 was more ambitious than the joint EU–US framework paper, particularly in the areas of export subsidies and domestic farm support. There were significant differences in the two framework papers and deep disagreements regarding how to proceed. A veritable negotiations log-jam was created.

After intense negotiations, an elaborate 'Framework for Establishing Modalities in Agriculture' was prepared and made into an Annex of the July Framework Agreement of 2004. This Annex was the most significant part of the Framework Agreement and was structured around the well-known three pillars. Members had decided upon a framework to eliminate all forms of export subsidies as well as render better discipline on export credit and exporting state trading enterprises. Regarding the trade-distorting farm subsidies, it was agreed in the Framework Agreement that the new discipline will include deeper cuts in farm subsidies in countries that have the highest levels of subsidies. 'Progressive tariff reductions' was also a part of the July Framework Agreement. However, the timeframe of implementation was left without mention.

The industrial economies dominated the global trade in agriculture when the Doha Round was launched, as they did at the time of the Hong Kong Ministerial. While developing economies' exporters have more market access opportunities in agriculture than in textiles and clothing, even at the time of the Hong Kong Ministerial their exports faced high tariffs in the industrial economies. While average tariff rates faced by agricultural exports from the developing economies are 15.6 percent in the industrial economies, they are 9.3 percent for textiles and apparel exports and 2.5 percent for the other manufactures (Anderson and Martin, 2006).[8] Producer support estimates (PSE) for the OECD economies were almost the same in 2001–3 as in 1986–8, hovering around \$240 billion annually (Anderson and Martin, 2006).[9] Agricultural tariffs are high in the developing economies as well, therefore, this sector *a fortiori* deserved special attention in the ongoing Doha Round negotiations.

In various negotiations during 2005, the industrial economies made it obvious that they prefer the Uruguay Round tariff reduction formula, which was linear, lenient and cut only the average tariff rates. They found the non-linear Swiss formula unappealing because it cuts higher tariff rates more than the lower ones. Three months before the Hong Kong Ministerial Conference, the US had made a proposal for deep cuts in both tariffs and subsidies, but the EU made a weak counter-proposal that would have resulted in little additional market access to what is currently available. Differences in positions were wide and agreement on trade in agriculture was not reached in the Hong Kong Ministerial, but some progress was made in the year and a half since the Cancún Ministerial, which led to a narrowing of differences. However, negotiations were nowhere near deciding on modalities. Therefore, a new schedule was agreed in Hong Kong for continuing negotiations in 2006 and for resolving the unfinished agenda by the end of the year.

The situation in mid-2006 was that the members agreed in the Hong Kong Ministerial to eliminate agricultural subsidies by 2013 (Chapter 6). Negotiators agreed to a broad framework for cuts on trade-distorting domestic farm support and export subsidies. The EU has committed to reducing trade-distorting domestic farm support most, followed by the US, Japan and others. The EU has agreed to cut domestic support by 70 percent by 2013 and eliminate export subsidies. On agricultural market access, a broad agreement was reached on a system of tariff bands, which allows the deepest cut to the highest tariffs. The EU offered to cut its highest agricultural tariffs by 60 percent as well as cut its average agricultural tariffs in half, to 12 percent. The current average farm tariffs in the US are 12 percent. Trade-distorting domestic farm support has been highest in the US, and has had a rising trend. Therefore, members have been asking the US to make larger commitments to slash them. The current US offer leaves the level of US domestic farm support higher than in 2001, to which the other WTO members strongly disagree.

Non-Agricultural Market Access

While launching the Doha Round, it was agreed to negotiate to reduce or eliminate tariffs on industrial or primary products. Tariff peaks, high tariffs and tariff escalation were to be the special focus of this segment of negotiations. For the industrial economies, tariff rates higher than 15 percent are regarded as tariff peaks. They protect sensitive products from competition. Rising rates of tariff with an increase in value-added in a product are known as tariff escalation. The negotiations are also seeking to eliminate the incidence of non-tariff barriers (NTBs) which are created by import licensing, quotas and other forms of quantitative restrictions.

In general NAMA negotiations have lagged behind agricultural negotiations. The first deadline for determining modalities for reduction or elimination of tariffs and NTBs was May 2003, which passed eventlessly. Subsequent deadlines were also missed. However, in the July Framework Agreement of 2004 members had agreed to adopt a broad non-linear tariff reduction formula so that higher tariffs could be reduced more than lower tariffs. Agreement on modalities still remained elusive. The July Framework Agreement clarified that tariff reductions should be computed from bound rates, not the applied rates of tariffs. In case of unbound tariff lines, it was decided that reduction would be carried out from twice the currently applied rates.

The NAMA Negotiations Group, under the chairmanship of Ambassador Stefan Johannesson of Iceland, continued its work during 2005 in Geneva. Although the major negotiators were eager to finalize them, they waited for any meaningful movement in negotiations on agriculture and stopped short. NAMA was being held a hostage to agriculture. Most delegations – particularly the EU – wanted to reveal their NAMA cards only after the level of commitment in agriculture was revealed by the major trading economies. Although no agreement was reached, there was some 'broad acceptance' and convergence around modalities favored by the developing economies. Finalization of NAMA would have meant meaningful consequences for the developing economies. The issues that continued to be contentious were the nature of tariff-reduction formula, treatment of unbound tariffs, the flexibility issue for the developing economies, whether to adopt a sectoral approach to accelerated tariff elimination and the NTBs.

Before the Hong Kong Ministerial, negotiators concentrated on technical issues like tariff reduction formulas, further modalities on the unbound tariff lines and to conversion of specific duties into advalorem duties. Negotiations focused on two variations of the Swiss formula, the first one was the simple Swiss formula, which was proposed by Switzerland during the Tokyo Round of MTNs (1973–9). The key element of this formula is a number which is negotiated and plugged into the formula. It is known as coefficient A, given in the formula below:

$Z = AX/(A+X)$

where
X = initial tariff rate
A = coefficient and maximum final tariff rate
Z = resulting lower tariff rate at the end of period

This also determines the maximum final tariff rate. The developing country members pushed for it because it would slash higher tariffs more than the lower ones. The second was the version suggested by Argentina, Brazil and India, which was based on tariff averages. This proposal came under attack from the other developing economies because it was not regarded as equitable. It rewarded countries with high tariffs, while punishing those with low ones. Between March and September 2005, several member countries submitted their versions of the Swiss formula individually and collectively. These proposals included one by the US for a Swiss formula with two coefficients, for developed and industrial economies. The EU submitted a Swiss formula with a single coefficient, but the developing economies could earn credits by not making use of flexibilities. Norway proposed a Swiss formula with two coefficients as well as credits for the eligible developing economies. Chile, Colombia and Mexico proposed different sets of options. No agreement was reached regarding which version should be finally applied. For each version of the Swiss formula, there were a small number of supporting members.

Despite its significance in the MTNs and continuing negotiations, there was virtually no forward movement in NAMA in Hong Kong. The most important decisions were deferred for 2006, and NAMA was included in that list. The developing economies made it evident that in the area of NAMA they intend making smaller tariff cuts than industrial economies want them to because they wish to protect their infant industries. Similarly, LDCs do not expect to make any cuts in their non-agricultural tariffs at all. As opposed to this, the industrial economies made it obvious that while they would like the developing economies to apply the Swiss formula in NAMA, they themselves would not like to use it in their agricultural tariff cuts because it will cut their higher tariffs at deeper rates.

Development Dimension

The Doha Round was billed the development round and it was intended that it will help them expand trade, with an expectation that it would spur growth, which in turn would alleviate poverty in the developing economies. As stated in Chapter 1 (pp. 25–6), by synthesizing the results of household surveys one can conclude that a 1 percent increase in real per capita income reduces the incidence of poverty by 2 percent.[10] Elasticity of poverty with respect to growth was found to be lower in absolute terms in the developing economies where the degree of income inequality was lower, and higher where income inequality was higher.

Given this concern for growth and poverty alleviation, Doha Round negotiations in all the important areas could be reasonably expected to be pro-development, but the MTNs so far have not transpired in this manner. Two specific developing country-related issues for the Doha Round are: compulsory licensing of medicines and patent protection and review of the age-old SDT. The issue of balancing of patent protection on the one hand and compulsory licensing of life-saving medicines on the other falls in the domain of the TRIPS agreement. The 2002 TRIPS Council proposal allowed countries that lacked manufacturing capacity to produce life-saving drugs and issue compulsory licenses for imports of medicines. The US was the only member that saw possibilities of exploitation of compulsory licenses, while other members approved of it. A concern that the pharmaceutical industry expressed was that of diversion of medicines to another country. This apprehension was resolved by an agreement to mark the medicines produced under license so that their inappropriate movement can be tracked. In August 2003, members reached an agreement. An interim waiver of the TRIPS Agreement allowed a member country to export pharmaceutical products made under compulsory license to the LDCs and some other member countries (Das, 2005b). The US accepted this decision provisionally, that is, under the condition that this decision should be used to protect public health and not for promoting industrial or commercial objectives.

Reaffirming the SDT for the developing economies, the Doha Declaration had expressed an interest in reviewing it 'with a view to strengthening them and making them more precise, effective and operational' (see Chapter 3, pp. 82–4). A work program on SDT was approved by the ministers, who also tasked the WTO Committee on Trade and Development (CTD) to examine additional ways in which SDT provision can be made more effective and to report to the General Council with clear recommendations for a decision by June 2002. However, soon a wide gulf emerged on the SDT issues between the developing and industrial economies. While the developing economies wanted to negotiate changes on SDT provisions, keep proposals in the CTD and keep short deadlines for completing negotiations, industrial economies preferred to study SDT provisions, send only selected proposals to the negotiating committee, and leave deadlines open. Developing countries began complaining that the industrial economies were not negotiating in good faith and the industrial economies countered the charge by saying that the developing countries were putting forward unreasonable proposals. By the Cancún Ministerial, developing economies had offered 85 proposals on SDT issues, and the industrial economies had agreed to only a handful of them.

Negotiations on SDT continued during 2005, and the developing economies insisted on less than full reciprocity in liberalization commitments, but the industrial countries questioned the definitions, meanings and implications of such proposals. On their part, the industrial countries demanded aggressive reduction of bound and applied tariffs in the developing economies. No common ground could be reached. Even during the Hong Kong Ministerial, despite repeated calls, members were unable to agree on proposals for enhanced SDT provisions.

Aid for Trade

Promises of substantive amounts of finances have been made under the broad Aid for Trade initiative. There is some concern about motivation behind it. It could certainly be compensation of the perception of loss on the part of the most disadvantaged WTO members. Small economies and the LDCs could gain much from this initiative. As set out in the preceding chapter, strategic decisions about Aid for Trade will be made by the international financial institutions (IFIs), notably the International Monetary Fund (IMF) and the World Bank (Chapter 6, pp. 150–52). Small country delegations need to watch the decision-making process carefully and ensure that they maximize the potential of this initiative to their own trade benefits. At present there are many uncertainties and ambiguities regarding this initiative. The unknown variables are how much additional finance will come through Aid for Trade, how these pledges fit the wider Monterrey Consensus of 2002 on Financing for Development (Chapter 1), who will be the potential recipients and what will be the disbursement channels (AITIC, 2006).

One cannot escape the fact that this initiative has been intended for those small developing economies and LDCs that are the weakest players in the multilateral trading system and are not going to gain immediately from the Doha Round negotiations. Some of them may even face short-term losses due to preference erosion. This sub-set of developing economies should take the Aid for Trade initiative most seriously. They need to astutely and pragmatically utilize this opportunity for pressing ahead with their development objectives.

Some thinking, planning and action related to Aid for Trade had taken place during 2005, well before the Hong Kong Ministerial. During the G-8 meeting in Gleneagles, Scotland, in July 2005 and the G-7 Finance Ministers' meeting in London in December 2005 the decision was taken to increase the volume of official development assistance (ODA). The G-7 meeting expressed the intention to increase Aid for Trade to $4 billion a year. Subsequently, the two IFIs were charged with drawing out a proposal for additional assistance to low-income developing countries so that their capacity to trade may be strengthened as well as their ability to compete in more open world markets being enhanced. The IFIs responded to this call and presented a position paper to the Development Committee of the IMF and the World Bank at their Spring 2006 meeting (IMF/WB, 2006).

Reforming the Rulebook

The multilateral trade regime includes several mechanisms through which a country can suspend the market access it has previously granted. Anti-dumping duties, anti-subsidy rules and SCM come under this category of measures. Together they are known as the trade remedies, or discretionary protection, or administered protection measures. Before the Uruguay Round these measures could only be applied on the MFN basis, that is, they had to be applied to all countries and not in a selective manner. They were also subject to such conditions as notification to the GATT Secretariat and consultation with the principal suppliers.

When the Doha Round was launched, there was mounting concern among the members regarding excessive use of AD and SCM. There were some concerns among the members regarding discipline in the RTA also. The articles of agreement that address AD and SCM are ambiguous, perhaps by design. The developing economies' perception is that the industrial economies, particularly the US, abused the AD and SCM measures and appled them for protectionist purposes. Therefore, one of the explicit objectives of the Doha Declaration was to clarify and improve discipline under the WTO agreements on AD and SCM. A coalition of developing and industrial countries' members emerged calling itself the 'Friends of Anti-dumping', which strongly supported improvement in the AD and SCM regulations.[11] The EU joined this group largely because it had been a frequent target of AD and SCM measures and complained of differences among the member economies in interpreting and applying the WTO rules in their domestic trade remedy procedures. The US initially opposed any fresh negotiations on AD and SCM, but relented when it saw that a new round would not take off without some concession in this area. The US tried to keep these negotiations outside the MTNs, but many members expressed preference for making them part of the MTNs. However, the US negotiators were able to include language in the Doha declaration that limited radical change in the related articles of agreement.

As the US and other industrial economies were accused by developing economies of using the AD action as disguised protection, the US was initially on the defensive. However, circumstances changed in this regard and the developing economies began using AD and SCM action themselves. China and India have used AD and SCM action actively in the recent past. This irked the US and the industrial economies, which began pressing for thoroughly re-examining rules and disciplining the implementation of AD and SCM agreements. After agreeing to re-examine and reform the AD and SCM agreements, the US committed to push an 'offensive agenda' on trade remedies in order to address the increasing 'misuse' of trade remedy measures.[12]

By August 2003, members had identified key provisions in the area of WTO rules that they sought to address in the MTNs. Most of the proposals on improving the trade remedies envisaged making them more specific and applying restrictions on the AD and SCM agreements in terms of definitions and procedures. Many of the suggested changes were highly technical in nature, involving calculations of dumping margins, determining injury and granting relief. These proposals were submitted formally to the WTO Negotiating Group on Rules (NGR).[13] After the Cancún Ministerial more elaborate proposals were submitted to the NGR in this area. While the Chairperson of the NGR undertook an extensive series of consultations, both bilateral and plurilateral, there was little progress in decision-making because members took different positions, which were not even close. As these were controversial issues, active negotiations did not take place on trade remedies in 2005. During the Hong Kong Ministerial negotiations on trade remedies were relegated to the back seat. In the Ministerial declaration they were dismissed in one sweeping sentence, which was no more than repetition of previous negotiating mandate on this subject. The likely route that the MTNs take on trade remedies will be to focus on suggested changes and proposals for which there seems to be a broad support among the members.

It seems probable that members will begin negotiating on agreements related to rules once the Doha Round nears its culmination point. At this point, differing viewpoints will be put forward and this sensitive issue will grow increasingly more contentious. The reason for this increase in sensitivity is that some members have a clear preference for clarification of rules and curtailing AD and SCM action. They have been clear about preventing the abuse under the AD and SCM action, and have therefore taken strong positions. As opposed to this other members are likely to see a negotiating tactic in it. That is, they may choose to use this area of negotiations for putting their own sensitive issues on the table. A third possibility is that some developing country members may seek to rein in the US and industrial country members in terms of the AD and SCM action on the one hand and to allow the developing economies its flexible use as a safeguard tool on the other.

STATUS OF NEGOTIATIONS IN TRADE IN SERVICES

The proportion of trade in the global economy has gone on expanding. This applies not only to the industrial economies but also to the high- and middle-income developing economies. Trade in services has expanded at a more rapid pace over the preceding two decades than that in merchandise. Its growth rate is expected to remain high in the foreseeable future (Chapter 2, pp. 61–2).

Long Standing Stagnation

The services commitments that were made during the Uruguay Round did not result in significant trade liberalization effects. With the exception of two sectors, namely, telecommunications and financial services, where negotiations had continued after the Uruguay Round had ended, commitments made in the other sectors were limited to binding existing regimes in a limited number of sectors. Trade in services began to be covered by the General Agreement on Trade in Services (GATS) since its inception in January 1995.[14] Negotiations in this area proved to be difficult and progressed slowly. Commitments under the GATS remained shallow and modest (Chapter 2, p. 64). This observation applies to all the four modes of services, and particularly in the areas of foreign direct investment and temporary movement of labor, what is referred to in WTO parlance as 'presence of natural persons', or movement of natural services suppliers under Mode-4.

Two Essential Objectives

Negotiations in trade in services lagged seriously behind in the Doha Round also. Two imperious Doha Round objectives in services negotiations are: first, to reform the current GATS rules, and second, to liberalize the services markets of the GATS member countries so that foreign competition in the services markets may take hold. Negotiations on services had begun well before the launch of the Doha Round because like agriculture they came under a part of the 'built-in-agenda' of the Uruguay Round. Although they were launched in January 2000, meaningful progress in the services negotiations was exceedingly slow, if it happened at all. Missing deadlines on decisions became a common and oft-repeated malaise.

The inertia in negotiations had three principal causes. First, services negotiations suffered from the general inertia of the Doha Round. Second, lack of progress in agriculture became a necessary condition for progress in services, although it was not a sufficient condition. The EU linked its market access in agriculture to its demand for concessions in services by the G-20 countries. Third, trade in services is a difficult area of negotiations at the best of times. To come to an outcome that is consistent with the development objective of the Doha Round negotiators needed 'extraordinary intellectual, technical and political efforts' which so far have not come about (Mattoo,

2006). In addition, there were intra-sector stand-offs. For instance, developing country demand for Mode-4 (that is, the movement of natural service provider) was pitted against the expectations of the industrial countries on Mode-3 (that is, commercial presence).

The common method for liberalizing trade in services under the GATS is the request-and-offer process noted in Chapter 2, which has proved to be slow and tedious. A negative perception about this process has been gradually emerging and strengthening. It failed to produce expected and desirable results in the recent past. From the perspective of negotiations in services, the Cancún Ministerial was not a disaster because there were no major disagreements and hold ups. Participating trade ministers recognized what little progress was made and agreed to further intensify the negotiations. As agriculture and NAMA dominated the Doha Round negotiations, services received much less attention from the members, and consequently they lagged. This important sector of multilateral trade was treated as almost marginal in the Hong Kong Ministerial.

The confidence level among participants in negotiations was low. The causal factor was that the old request-and-offer method was being followed in negotiations. The progress was made in terms of a large number of confidential, albeit ambitious, requests that both developing and industrial country members made to each other for market access, but the response in terms of offers of market access was exceedingly weak.

By July 2005, revised offers of market access were made, leading to some improvement in offers. A total of 62 offers were tabled by this point, which came from 62 percent of the GATS members. LDCs are exempt from tabling offers because of their development needs considerations. But also, sizable number of developing economies, including Ecuador, Nigeria, South Africa and Venezuela, refrained from tabling offers. The small number of offers tabled masked even smaller projected reforms. The overall quality of both initial and revised offers was disappointing. Based on the state of offers in July, little additional market liberalization could be expected for the services suppliers. Negotiations had stagnated, as the request-and-offer process was failing to perform. A need to develop complementary negotiating tools was sorely felt by the GATS negotiators.

As stated in the preceding chapter, there was some retrograde movement in services negotiations in Hong Kong because the developing economies were reluctant to enter into plurilateral market access negotiations. As alluded to in Chapter 6 (pp. 155–6), the Marrakesh Agreement provides for a few plurilateral agreements in its Annex 4. This is a permitted deviation from the most-favored-nations (MFN) principle. Most decisions in this area of MTNs were put off during the Hong Kong Ministerial for 2006, with seemingly unrealistic deadlines. The present state of negotiations in services is a low-level equilibrium, where members expect little from each other in terms of request-and-offer. That is, the pre-Hong Kong Ministerial inertia persisted and the adopted process of liberalization, that is, the request-and-offer process, suffered from an acute lack of energy and forward motion.

To energize negotiations and further liberalize multilateral trade in this important sector, members need to identify ambitious and desirable goals that are feasible in the present *mise en scène*. To start a self-propelling cycle of mutually beneficial liberalization Mattoo (2006) suggested the following four steps. First, the languid request-and-offer process should be complemented with a collective approach to negotiations where groups of members should collectively build opinion for achieving clearly specified goals. Second, a significant number of members should lock in the current openness in a wide range of trade in services. Third, a significant number of members need to eliminate barriers to foreign participation in those service sectors in which there is little reason to defer liberalization. Fourth, if a good number of members promote greater freedom for temporary presence of service providers to fulfill specific services contracts, it may be the beginning of a new and innovative trend in multilateral trade. If a critical mass of member economies agrees to undertake these measures, there would surely be advancement in market liberalization in trade in services in the foreseeable future.

Services Suppliers under Mode-4

Even without the knowledge of various estimates that have been made, it is a widely acknowledged fact that many developing economies have a lot to gain from liberalization of trade in services under Mode-4. India and several large Latin American economies took a great deal of initiative in these negotiations in the Doha Round. Position papers presented by them were detailed, well-reached and thoughtful. However, the movement of natural services providers has been one of the most contentious issues in the GATS negotiations for a long time. In this important area of services negotiations complete disagreement among the members continued to exist down to the Hong Kong Ministerial, and thereafter. The positions of the developing and industrial economies were irreconcilable.

Mode-4 covers the following four categories of services personnel: (a) service sales persons; (b) intra-corporate personnel like business executives, managers, and specialists; (c) business visitors like personnel engaged in establishing a foreign office and subsidiary; and (d) independent contract suppliers like doctors and architects. Workers under Mode-4 are not granted access to the local labor market, which is eminently logical. Those who come under this category must either be employed by a foreign firm with commercial presence where the service is being provided or under a contract for the provision of a specific service. If this service provider is not providing the contracted service, she will have to return to the country of origin. Her right to stay is completely dependent on the employment.

An individual country decides how many workers, occupations and sectors to commit under Mode-4. The developing countries have argued that the present level of commitments is highly limited. It includes only the upper end of the skilled professionals, like physicians, surgeons, company executives, professors, and so on. Some developing economies proposed inclusion of medium- and even low-skilled workers, like school teachers, nurses and health technicians, domestic and construction workers, because many of them have a strong comparative advantage in these categories of laborers. Under the MFN principle, such a program can turn into a global guest worker program in the industrial economies, which could have a large effect on the domestic labor markets. Industrial economies have a general distaste for permanent migration that may take place under the shroud of Mode-4.

Since the developing economies proposed expansion of commitments under Mode-4 to cover medium- and low-skilled workers, the negotiations under the DDA on this issue have come to a halt. The industrial economies have been reluctant to cede control of immigration to the WTO. In the post-11 September world, they all justly wanted to be extra cautious regarding the security issue intertwined with the movement of natural services suppliers under Mode-4. This is a valid concern. By the Hong Kong Ministerial, the Mode-4 issue had taken the proportion of a potential deal-breaker for the developing economies, particularly the LDCs.

ART OF THE POSSIBLE

The opportunity that the Doha Round offers to the global economy, particularly the trading economies, is that of multilateral, non-preferential, legally-binding partial liberalization. It can positively contribute to the achievement of the first MDG of halving the income-poverty in the global economy by 2015. A successful Doha Round can go a long way in building up the next stage of the multilateral trade regime, particularly in redressing anomalies of the past and integrating the emerging-market and other developing economies into the global economy. If achieved, this would be a meaningful achievement that would strengthen the fabric of the multilateral trade regime as well as the global economy. A reasonably successful Hong Kong Ministerial could also have contributed to welfare gains for the global economy, and its different regions and sub-regions. Estimates of gains from partial reforms promised under the Doha Round *inter alia* were made by Anderson *et al.* (2006) and Anderson and Martin (2006). The principal conclusions of these two empirical studies, which utilized a newly released database on protection and the latest version of the World Banks Linkage model, are as follows:

- If one were to take under consideration merely the static benefits, the potential gains from liberalization of trade under the Doha Round are large. In addition, there will be dynamic gains stemming from increased scale economies and competition, which is enormously value-creating.
- While the developing economies' share of the global GDP is 20 percent, their gains from trade liberalization under the Doha Round will be 30 percent of the total. This would lead to 0.8 percent rise in welfare in the developing economies, compared to 0.6 percent rise in the welfare in the industrial economies.
- Complete liberalization of merchandise trade would result in 45 percent of the global welfare gains going to developing economies. Their welfare could increase as much as 1.2 percent compared to an increase of 0.6 percent rise for the industrial economies.
- The proportion of welfare gains going to the developing economies is higher than those to the industrial economies because their tariff barriers are higher. Trade policy reforms would lead to higher efficiency gains in the developing economies. Also, their agricultural and textile exports face much higher tariffs in the industrial economies' markets than do exports from the industrial economies.
- Reforms and liberalization by the developing economies in their own economies will be as meaningful in terms of economic benefits as those in the industrial economies. By delaying reforms in their own economies, the developing economies will fail to realize the full potential gains from the Doha Round. Deferring reforms will slow the macroeconomic evolution process in the developing economies.
- Trade in agricultural and agro-industrial products, that began during the Uruguay Round, is the newest frontier of trade liberalization. This sector still suffers the stigma of the highest bound tariffs and largest subsidies, and needs sizable cuts in both.
- Trade liberalization in agriculture is of crucial importance, although the importance of agriculture in the global GDP has been on a decline. Trade liberalization measures in agriculture will have far-reaching implications for the developing economies as well as the global economy. Approximately two-thirds of the total gains from the Doha Round are likely to come from liberalization in this sector, compared to almost a quarter from textiles and apparel and a tenth from other merchandise trade liberalization.

Thus viewed, there are substantive gains from liberalization of merchandise trade in the Doha Round of MTNs, particularly that in agricultural trade. The on-going MTNs are likely to culminate in partial trade reforms of the multilateral trade regime. The old assessment of global gains from partial trade reforms was $400 billion in 2015, which was computed with the help of the World Bank's LINKAGE model (World Bank, 2004). Revised estimates of global gains have been scaled down to $290 billion in 2015 (van der Mensbrugghe, 2004). There were three reasons for this difference in the two estimates. First, a new Global Trade Analysis Project (GTAP) dataset was used to compute the second estimates, which had a different base year from the earlier computations. The benchmark of the earlier estimates was 1997, while that for the revised one was 2001. The new dataset also incorporated the trade policy reforms undertaken between 1997 and 2001. It also reflected the non-reciprocal tariff preferences, which the previous data set did not incorporate. Second, the new dataset successfully reflected the transformations that came about in the global economy, particularly the changing value of the dollar *vis-à-vis* other major currencies after 1997 and the rising importance of several Asian economies as traders of global significance. Third, the new benchmark also included major global economies developments like China's WTO accession and liberalization commitments, implementation of the Uruguay Round commitments, of which dismantling of the multifiber arrangement (MFA) was an important part, and the expansion of EU from 15 to 25 members that took place in May 2004. Together these developments have had an appreciable impact the multilateral trade regime, multilateral trade and the global economy. The value of welfare gains stemming from them was estimated to be $70 billion to the global economy in 2015. As they were incorporated into the new baseline, they cannot be expected to make a renewed contribution to the estimates of welfare gains from the ongoing round of MTNs.

Using a global model, Anderson *et al.* (2005) estimated the potential consequences of a successful Doha Round agreement. According to their estimates, it could annually generate income gains for the global economy between $95 billion and $126 billion. While making these estimates, it was assumed that no exemptions were being made for sensitive and special agricultural products. Agriculture trade liberalization was found to have the largest impact. Reforms in this one sector will be responsible for 60 percent of the total gains from merchandise trade liberalizations. On the whole, larger income gains were estimated to go to the industrial economies because they were assumed to undertake more aggressive trade reforms in the Doha Round. As the developing economies suffer from a large binding overhang, and negotiations are based on bound tariffs, not applied tariffs, the reforms undertaken by them will have only a minor impact in terms of genuine liberalization of the trade regime.[15] Given this scenario, the industrial economies would achieve between 40 percent and 45 percent of what they could under full merchandise trade reforms. Similarly, the developing economies will achieve approximately 20 percent of what could be achieved under full merchandise trade reforms. Adding these gains, total global welfare gains that are likely to be achieved come to one-third of those from freeing global merchandise trade totally.

Developing economies have more to gain from full elimination of merchandise trade barriers. As trade reforms engender positive externalities in the form of improved productivity in the economy, the gains to developing economies could increase up to $200 billion in 2015 (Anderson *et al.*, 2005). The state of MTNs at the time of the Hong Kong Ministerial Conference clearly indicated that liberalization measures adopted in agriculture and manufactures can be realistically expected to be modest, albeit improvements in agricultural market access in the industrial economies is well within the realm of possibility. Empirical evidence is available to show that trade liberalization contributes to poverty alleviation.[16] Also, estimates of the impact of trade liberalization under the DDA on poverty had a positive result. This was essentially due to the fact that the existing pattern of global protection favors skilled labor and capital relative to unskilled workers. Therefore, the reduction or elimination of barriers in merchandise trade would lift unskilled wages, the primary source of income for many of the world's poor. In real terms this wage increase was found to be modest.

Hertel and Winters (2006) show that the poorest in the developing economies can potentially benefit most from the liberalization endeavors during the Doha Round of MTNs. However, that was found to be conditional. For the poor to benefit, the liberalization targets 'under the DDA have to be ambitious if the round is to have a measurable impact'. Only deep tariff cuts would have a poverty-friendly impact. Even then the 'near-term poverty impacts are likely to be mixed' (Hertel and Winters, 2005). If the developing economies decide not to take reform measures, the estimated impact on poverty would decline markedly. Notwithstanding this pessimism, the long-term impact of the DDA on poverty reduction is more definite and pronounced.

A case study of China, which has not only recorded unprecedented economic growth but also become the third largest trader in a short time span of two decades, revealed that MTNs do support poverty alleviation endeavors.[17] Using a household-disaggregated applied general equilibrium model to estimate the impact of trade liberalization under the Doha Round on poverty in China, Zhai and Hertel (2005) found that multilateral trade reforms did support poverty alleviation. They concluded that the largest impact of the Doha Round liberalization was on rural-poor households in China. This was the result of rising prices of farm products. A large majority of China's poor are to be found in the rural areas and therefore stand to benefit from this trend.

Urban poverty was observed to decline, but only in two of the three urban household groups considered for this study. Higher food prices in these two groups were offset by rising factor earnings resulting from sharply accelerating Chinese exports growth. The third group of urban-poor households did not show the positive impact of trade liberalization because it was heavily dependent on the transfer payments.

COMMITMENT BY THE G-8

The looming possibility of failure of the Doha Round worried political leadership in the leading industrial nations. To infuse political momentum to the moribund Doha Round, five G-20 members (Brazil, India, China, Mexico and South Africa) were invited to the St Petersburg G-8 summit of 15–17 July 2006. The objective was to avert the hiatus of several years and come to an agreement in the principal areas of multilateral trade. The stalled Doha Round was the subject of intense and exhaustive discussion on the second day of the Summit. All the participants agreed that flexibility was badly needed to come to a decision regarding the core modalities. The G-8 communiqué called for 'a concerted effort to conclude the negotiations of the WTO's DDA and to fulfill the development objective of the Round'.[18]

Together the participants set a deadline of mid-August to settle the outstanding issues and decide on the core modalities. Once again the French briefly resisted the new deadline. Jacques Chirac argued that the EU's stance on trade policy was not an issue for the G-8 countries to decide, but he relented due to lack of support from the other G-8 members. The sense of resolve at St Petersburg could translate into a long-awaited breakthrough in the Doha Round. Sensing that advancement might occur, the G-6 countries (Australia, Brazil, the EU, India, Japan and the US) became active in Geneva in putting together the framework of an agreement on core modalities that could be acceptable to the 149 members of the WTO.

SUSPENSION OF THE DOHA ROUND: PYRRHIC VICTORY FOR THE PROTECTIONISTS?

Potential compromise offers were informally made in a 14-hour long G-6 meeting in Geneva. Pascal Lamy, the Director General of the WTO, tried to bring the members to concur on or around the compromise formula he had proposed. However, they failed to bridge the differences in positions on modalities on agricultural subsidies and industrial tariffs. The large trading economies evidently preferred a collapse to a compromised, if somewhat diluted, final outcome of the Doha Round. The gavel was slammed on 24 July and the Doha Round was formally suspended, leading to a veritable crisis of some magnitude in the life of the WTO. This collapse epitomized defeat of the common good by special-interest politics and therefore was 'senseless and short-sighted' (*The Economist*, 2006c).

The immediate and normal result was furious recrimination and blamesmanship between members. Candidly critical of the US stance, the EU, India and Japan put the blame for collapse at the door of the US. Most trade delegations were disappointed at the US not coming up with any new proposal on domestic farm subsidies in Geneva, as did the other G-6 members. The US response was that no such new offer was necessary because the EU and the EMEs, particularly India, failed to table meaningful improvements on agricultural market access. The US was also critical of the exceptions of farm tariff cuts sought by the EU and the EMEs, arguing that they were looking for loopholes to avoid legitimate trade liberalization. Judged fairly, not the US alone could not be blamed for the demise of the Doha Round, many other participants were also culpable. From the point of view of a trade economist, trade-distorting subsidies should not have been there in the first place. It was paradoxical that the US was demanding a *quid pro quo* of extensive market-opening measures for the removal of trade-distorting subsidies. Such a stipulation was something approaching an absurdity. Furthermore, the stand taken by the US was tantamount to spurning the July Framework Agreement of 2004.

However, for three principal reasons, the US deserved to receive a disproportionate amount of blame for the demise of the Doha Round. First, the compromise package that Pascal Lamy was advancing after the G-8 Summit would have brought real, albeit modest, reductions in agricultural tariffs and subsidies in the industrial countries as well as industrial tariffs in the EMEs. To an extent, it would also have led to liberalization of trade in services. However, the US took a hard line and insisted that it was not in favor of a modest kind of Doha Round agreement. If an agreement of appropriate magnitude was not reached, the US had made it known that it would not settle for a weak final outcome. Second, the US was perceived as being overly responsive to the demands of its domestic politics by the other trade delegations and insensitive to multilateral needs. During the negotiations It had frequently demanded maximum concessions, making it impossible for the MTNs to progress at an even pace. It was evident that the political clout of the US farm lobbies was enormous. It outweighed any promise to take suitable and effective measures for alleviating global poverty (Switzer, 2006). Undeniably political leadership cannot ignore the demands of the domestic constituencies, but there was an imperious need to balance it with multilateral obligations and the need to be a good global citizen. Third, in the recent period, the commitments of the US in the MTNs and its deeds have remained far apart. Rhetoric was seldom backed by action. In the recent past, the US has been turning away from its traditional commitment to multilateralism. The US signed nine of its total 12 FTAs between 2001 and 2006. An additional six FTAs were awaiting approval in the Congress. When the Doha Round was suspended, 11 more were at various stages of negotiations.

Finger-pointing apart, reforms that the EU was expected to agree to by the G-6 member countries were difficult but attainable, considering the past agricultural policies in the EU. Likewise, slashing of farm subsidies by the US was politically difficult, more so in the background of the November mid-term elections, but absolutely possible. All that was needed was the political commitment to right the long-term wrongs. The demise of the Doha Round evidenced political unwillingness of the member countries to face the protectionist lobbies, particularly farmers, in their own countries. Complacently ignoring the need to right the agricultural subsidy structure was wrong for the US for an additional reason. The US farm bill is to be reauthorized in 2007. The Doha Round was an ideal opportunity – and instrument – for the US to start eliminating farm subsidies. Failure of the Doha Round effectively eliminated an opportunity of overhauling the US farm subsidy program and structure. The loss of this opportunity has made the US government vulnerable to litigation at the Dispute Settlement Panel of the WTO. The WTO found the US cotton subsidies illegal in 2004; rice and soybean subsidies may well be the next to be declared illegal under WTO rules.

By letting the Doha Round collapse after prolonged stagnation, the industrial economies also exposed themselves to another allegation. The Doha Round was conceived as the first ever Development Round and the intentions of the members were to rebalance the multilateral trade regime. That the development objective of this round is highly valuable has been noted since the beginning, at the time of the launch, down to the G-8 Communiqué in July 2006. Accordingly, since the launch of the Doha Round industrial economies promised support for the DDA, which was expected to help the developing economies, particularly the small and low-income ones, through brisk trade expansion. It was also believed that the Doha Round would help achieve the MDGs, particularly the first one of halving the global income-poverty by 2015. Goodwill and commitment to these noble objectives were expressed repeatedly in various Ministerial Declarations in enthusiastic and effusive terms. Demise of the Doha Round was an obvious loss of credibility for the rich countries in this regard. It became a testimony of the insincerity of political leadership at the highest level.

Breakdowns in MTNs are not unknown. In December 1990, the Uruguay Round had caved in because of insoluble differences between the EU and the US on agricultural subsidies. It was resuscitated by the erstwhile

Director-General of the GATT, who came up with the unusual plan of preparing a draft compromise agreement and presenting it to the CPs as the basis for a future agreement. He succeeded. The Uruguay Round was completed after failing because eventually all CPs were willing to make compromises and accommodations, albeit it took much longer than originally planned. Could the Doha Round be a repetition of history? An optimist always has enough to go on.

Suspension of the Doha Round cannot be seen as Pyrrhic victory for the protectionists lobbies and forces. It was not followed by calls for increasing protectionism and the ocean of world trade remained placed at the sad news of the demise of the Doha Round. During the contemporary period, multilateral trade has been growing at a higher rate than the global GDP growth rate. Although a major setback, this failure represents an inability to advance the multilateral trade regime, not a retrograde movement in it. The probability of the multilateral trade regime falling apart in the short-term is virtually nonexistent, however, with the passage of time this failure will decisively show its pernicious effect and cast a debilitating shadow over the multilateral trade regime. This medium- and long-term incapacitating influence over the multilateral trading system cannot and need not be doubted.

SUMMARY AND CONCLUSIONS

Since its birth in 1948, multilateral trade and trade regime – which are a fully-fledged global public good – became a controversial issue in the global economy as well as for the global economic governance. For the tardy progress in the on-going Doha Round, the mercantilist mindset of participants has been blamed most frequently. However, there are other causal factors like a large number of diverse members of the WTO with varying objectives, the increasing complexity of the issues, domestic political and economic sensitivities, a clear lack of political energy committed to the MTNs and the activities of the NGOs.

After the completion of the Hong Kong Ministerial Conference without any noteworthy and meaningful achievements, member countries continued intense negotiations. Deliberations continued in the mini-Ministerial in Davos, yet the crucial April deadline for settling down on modalities was missed. It was yet another major setback to the accident-prone MTNs. The Geneva mini-Ministerial also ended in complete disarray. Prospects for a collapse of the Doha Round loomed large and real. That the 'crisis' is close at hand began to be acknowledged in the highest circles.

This chapter provides a clear picture of the state of play in the current round of MTNs, both in the areas of merchandise and services trade. It provides detailed analysis of the long-standing stagnation in the MTNs. The evolution of the multilateral trade regime has been a disenchanting process. The Doha Round offers an enormous opportunity to the trading economies as well as the global economy. It can positively contribute to the achievement of the first MDG of halving income-poverty in the global economy. A successful Doha Round can go a long way in the building up the next stage of multilateral trade regime, particularly in redressing anomalies of the past and integrating the emerging-market and other developing economies into the global economy. If achieved, this would be a meaningful achievement that would strengthen the fabric of the multilateral trade regime as well as the global economy. Recent empirical studies, which were based on newly released database on trade and protection and used the latest version of the World Bank's Linkage model, concluded that there are significant welfare implications to a successful completion of the Doha Round for both the developing and industrial economies. The political commitment of the global community to its success should have been larger than it has so far been. The Doha Round was officially suspended on 24 July, 2006.

NOTES

1. The Russian Federation is not a member of the WTO as yet. To that end, negotiations are in progress. Therefore it is correct to say that the G-7 countries had some contribution to make in this regard.

2. The source of these statistical data is the *Monthly Bulletin of Statistics,* New York, United Nations, for 1997 and 2000.

3. During the life and time of the GATT, the Green Room process worked well and facilitated consultations among the Contracting Parties (CPs). This process got its name from an actual green room that existed next to the Director General's room in the GATT headquarters, at 154 rue de Lausanne, Geneva, where the most important meetings took place. The GATT period is known for its businesslike diplomacy and negotiating effectiveness. The flip side of this coin was that a lot of relatively smaller traders had to play the role of the second fiddle. Since the birth of the WTO this legacy of the GATT came in for a lot of criticism and was painted in villainous colors. An increasing number of WTO members were eager to contribute to the decision-making process. Accession of many sovereign countries in quick succession slowed down the decision-making process. Participation in the Green Room process was decided on the basis of the issue, and only the most active delegations were invited to participate. As for the question which CPs were typically included for consultations other than the members of the Quad, the answer is Australia, New Zealand, Norway, Switzerland, sometimes one or two transition economies and some developing economies.

4. Several large international NGOs are known to have larger budgetary resources than the WTO.

5. Joseph Deiss, Swiss Minister of Economic Affairs, took the initiative to organize this mini-Ministerial during 27 and 28 January 2006. The Swiss Government hosted the mini-Ministerial.

6. Pascal Lamy's statement was quoted in the economic and financial press worldwide, including in the *Bridges Weekly Trade News Digest,* Vol. 10, Special, 3 July 2006, page 1. This statement was quoted in an article entitled, 'WTO Talks in "Crisis" as High-Level

Meeting Fails'.

7. ASEAN stands for the Association for Southeast Asian Nations. It was established on 8 August 1967 in Bangkok by the five original member countries, namely, Indonesia, Malaysia, the Philippines, Singapore and Thailand. The ten present ASEAN members are Brunei Darussalam, Cambodia, Indonesia, Lao PDR, Malaysia, Myanmar, the Philippines, Singapore, Thailand and Vietnam.

8. OECD (2005b) buttresses this point using producer support statistics for the 1986–2004 period.

9. The Producer Support Estimate (PSE) is defined as the annual monetary value of gross transfer from consumers and taxpayers to agricultural producers, measured at the farm gate level, arising from policy measures that support agriculture, regardless of their nature, objectives or impact on the farm production or income.

10. See Bigsten and Levin (2001), Cline (2004) and Dollar and Kraay (2001).

11. The membership of this group comprised, the European Union, Brazil, Chile, China, Colombia, Costa Rica, Hong Kong SAR, India, Israel, Japan, Republic of Korea, Mexico, Norway, Singapore, Switzerland, Thailand and Turkey.

12. A statement by Robert B. Zoellick who was cited in the following press release: 'USTR Zoelick Says World Has Chosen path of Hope, Openness, Development and Growth' Office of the United States Trade Representative. Press release, 14 November 2001.

13. See World Trade Organization (2003), *Compilation of Issues and Proposals Identified by Participants in the Negotiating Group on Rules,* 22 August, TN/RL/W/143, Geneva.

14. All WTO Members are at the same time members of the GATS and, to varying degrees, have assumed commitments in individual service sectors.

15. The term 'binding overhand' needs to be explained. A country may decide to apply a tariff rate of 20 percent on the import of a good, but it may keep the bound tariff at 50 percent. The WTO rules allow this country to raise its tariff rate to 50 percent if it so decides. The difference between the bound tariffs and applied tariffs is known as the 'binding overhang'.

16. See, for instance Dollar and Kraay (2004), Winters (2004) and Winters, *et al.* (2004).

17. For a detailed account of China's emergence as an economic power and trade juggernaut see Das (2006).

18. See the G-8 Joint Statement on Trade on the Internet at http://en.g8russia.ru/docs/16-print.html.

Bibliography

Acemoglu, D. and F. Zilibotti (2001), 'Productivity Differences', *Quarterly Journal of Economics*, **116**(3), 563–606.

Adlung, R. and M. Roy (2005), 'Turning hills into mountains', current commitments under the GATS, World Trade Organization Economic Research and Statistics Division, working paper ERSD-2005-01, March, Geneva.

Agency for International Trade Information and Cooperation (AITIC) (2006), 'Aid for Trade: a moving target', at accessed www.acici.org/aitic/documents/notes/note38_eng.htm.

Alexandraki, K. and H. P. Lankes, (2004), 'The impact of preference erosion on middle-income developing countries', International Monetary Fund working paper no. WP/04/169, September, Washington, DC.

Anderson. K. (2004), 'Trade liberalization, agriculture and poverty in low-income countries' in B. Guha-Khasnobis (ed.), *The WTO, Developing Countries and the Doha Development Agenda*, Houndmills: Palgrave Macmillan, pp. 37–61.

Anderson, K. and W. J. Martin (2006), 'Agriculture, trade reform and the Doha agenda', in Anderson, K. and W. J. Martin (eds), *Agricultural Trade Reform and the Doha Agenda*, London and Washington, DC: Palgrave Macmillan and World Bank, pp. 3–35.

Anderson, K., W. J. Martin and D. van der Mensbrugghe (2005), 'Global impact of the Doha scenario on poverty', mimeo, Washington DC: World Bank.

Anderson, K., W. J. Martin and D. van der Mensbrugghe (2006), 'Market and welfare implications of the Doha Round scenario', in K. Anderson and W. Martin (eds), *Agricultural Trade Reform and the Doha Development Agenda*, London and Washington, DC: Palgrave Macmillan and World Bank, pp. 333–99.

Anderson, K. and E. Valenzuela (2006), 'The World Trade Organization's Doha Cotton Initiative: a tale of two issues', World Bank, Policy Research working paper WPS 3918, May, Washington, DC.

Bacchetta, M. and B. Bora (2003), 'Industrial tariff liberalization and the Doha development agenda', WTO working paper.

Balassa, B (1971), *The Structure of Protection in Developing Countries*, Baltimore, MD: The Johns Hopkins University Press.

Berg, A. and A. O. Krueger (2003), '*Trade, growth and poverty: selective survey*', International Monetary Fund working paper WP/03/30, February, Washington, DC.

Bernard, A. and B. Jensen, (1999), 'Exporting and Productivity', National Bureau of Economic Research working paper no. 7135, Cambridge, MA.

Bigsten, A. and J. Levin (2001), *Growth, Income Distribution and Poverty: A Review*, May, Helsinki: World Institute for Development Economic Research (WIDER).

Bolaky, B. and C. Freund (2004), 'Trade, regulations and growth', World Bank Policy Research Working Paper 3255. March, Washington, DC.

Bourguignon, F (1999), 'Absolute poverty, relative deprivation and social exclusion', paper presented at the workshop World Development Report, organized by the

Deutsche Stiftung fur Internationale Entwicklung, 2–3 February, Berlin.

Bourguignon, F. and C. Morrisson (2002), 'Inequality among world's citizens: 1820–1992', *The American Economic Review*, **92**(4), 727–44.

Brenton, P. (2003), 'Integrating the Least Developed Countries into the World Trading System', *Journal of World Trade*, **37**(3), 623–46.

Brenton, P. and M. Manchin (2002), 'Making the EU trade agreements work', *The World Economy*, **25**(1), 22–40.

Brown, D. K., A. V Deardorff and R. M. Stern (2003), 'Multilateral, regional and bilateral trade policy options for the United States and Japan', *The World Economy*, **26**(6), 803–28.

Chen, S. and M. Ravallion (2004), 'How have the world's poorest fared since the early 1980s?', World Bank, accessed 20 April at www.worldbank.org/ research/povmonitor/MartinPapers/How_have_the_poorest_fared_since_the_early _1980s.pdf.

Choudhri, E., H. Faruque and S. Tokarick (2006), 'Trade liberalization, macroeconomic adjustment, and welfare: unifying trade and macro models', paper presented at the trade conference organized by International Monetary Fund Research Department, 13 April, Washington, DC.

Clapp, J. (2006), 'Developing countries and the WTO agriculture negotiations', Center for International Governance Innovation working paper no. 6, March, Waterloo, ON, Canada.

Cline, W. R. (2005), 'Doha and Development', *Foreign Affairs*, **84**(7), 44–51.

Cline, W. R. (2004), *Trade Policy and Global Poverty*, Washington, DC: Institute for International Economics.

Collier, P. and D. Dollar (2002), *Globalization, Growth and Poverty*, New York: Oxford University Press for World Bank.

Das, Dilip K. (2000), 'Debacle at Seattle: the way the cookie crumbled', *Journal of World Trade*, **34**(5), 181–201.

Das, Dilip K. (2001), *Global Trading System at the Crossroads*, London and New York: Routledge.

Das, Dilip K. (2003), 'The Doha Round of Multilateral Trade Negotiations: causal issues behind failure in Cancún'. Harvard University Center for International Development, Cambridge, MA, accessed at www.cid.harvard.edu/ cidtrade/site/new.html, 15 October.

Das, Dilip K. (2004a), *Financial Globalization and the Emerging Market Economies*, London and New York: Routledge.

Das, Dilip K. (2004b), *Regionalism in Global Trade*, Cheltenham and Northampton, MA: Edward Elgar Publishing.

Das, Dilip K. (2005a), *Asian Economy and Finance: A Post-Crisis Perspective*, New York: Springer Publications.

Das, Dilip K. (2005b), *The Doha Round of Multilateral Trade Negotiations: Arduous Issues and Strategic Responses*, Houndmill: Palgrave Macmillan.

Das, Dilip K. (2006a), 'The Doha Round of Multilateral Trade Negotiations and trade in agriculture', *Journal of World Trade*, **40**(2), 259–90.

Das, Dilip K. (2006b), *China and India: A Tale of Two Economies*, London and New York: Routledge.

Deardorff, A. (2001), 'International provision of trade services, trade and fragmentation,' *Review of International Economics*, **9**(2), 233–48.

Deardorff, A. V. and R. M. Stern (2003), 'Enhancing the benefits for developing countries in the Doha development agenda negotiations', University of Michigan

Ford School of Public Policy discussion paper no. 498, 13 August, Ann Arbor, MI.

de Jonquières, G. (2004), 'Real trade negotiations still lie ahead', *The Financial Times*, 1 August.

Diakosavvas, D. (2004), 'The Uruguay Round Agreement on Agriculture in practice: how open are OECD markets?', in M. D. Ingco and L. A. Winters (eds), *Agriculture and the New Trade Agenda*, Cambridge, UK: Cambridge University Press, pp. 400–32.

Dollar, D. (1992), 'Outward-oriented developing economies really do grow more rapidly: evidence from 95 LDCs, 1976–85', *Economic Development and Cultural Change*, **40**(3), 523–44.

Dollar, D. and A. Kraay (2001), 'Growth is good for the poor', World Bank, Policy research working paper no. 2587, April, Washington DC.

Dollar, D. and A. Kraay (2002), 'Institutions, trade and growth', *Journal of Monetary Economics*, **50**(1), 133–62.

Dollar, D. and A. Kraay (2004), 'Trade, growth and poverty', *The Economic Journal*, **114**(493), F22–F49.

The Economist (2003), 'The WTO under fire,' 18 September, accessed at www.economist.com./PrinterFriendly.cfm?Story_ID=2071855.

The Economist (2004a), 'Trade: from Cancún to can-do', 15 May, pp. 72–3.

The Economist (2004b), 'Progress at last, but still a long way to go', 2 August, accessed at www.economist.com/agenda/PrinterFriendly.cfm?Story_ID=2983066.

The Economist (2005), 'Hard truths,' 24 December, pp. 97–8.

The Economist (2006a), 'Coming of age', 21 January, pp. 10–11.

The Economist (2006b), 'World trade: under attack', 8 July, pp. 65–6.

Edwards, S. (1998), 'Openness, productivity, and growth: what do we really know?', *Economic Journal*, **108**(2), 383–98.

Ehlermann, C. D. and L. Ehring (2005), 'Are WTO decision-making procedures adequate for making, revising and implementing worldwide and plurilateral rules?', in E. U. Petersmann (ed.), *Developing Countries in the Doha Round*, Florence, Italy: European University Institute, pp. 91–118.

European Commission (EC) (2004), 'The Doha Development Agenda after Cancún', 25 September, Brussels.

Evenett, S. J. (2003), 'The failure of the WTO ministerial meeting in Cancun', *CESifo Forum*, **4**(3), 11–27.

Finger, J. M. and P. Schuler (2002), 'Implementation of WTO commitments: The development challenge', in P. English, B. M. Hoekman and A. Mattoo (eds), *Development, Trade and the WTO: A Handbook*, Washington, DC: World Bank.

Finger, J. M. and L. A. Winters (2002), 'Reciprocity in the WTO', in B. Hoekman, A. Mattoo and P. English (eds), *Development, Trade and the WTO: A Handbook*, Washington, DC: World Bank.

Francois, J. and W. Martin (2003), 'Formula approaches for market access negotiations', *The World Economy*, **26**(1), 1–26.

Frankel, J. A. and D. Romer (1999), 'Does trade cause growth?', *American Economic Review*, **89**(3), 379–99.

Fugazza, M. and D. Vanzetti (2004), 'A South–South survival strategy: the potential for trade among developing countries', paper presented at the European Trade Study Group, Sixth Annual Conference, 9–11 September, Nottingham, UK.

General Agreement on Tariffs and Trade (GATT), (1994), *The Results of the Uruguay Round of Multilateral Trade Negotiations: The Legal Text*, Geneva: GATT.

Gereffi, J. and O. Memedovic (2003), *The Global Apparel Value Chain: What*

Prospects for Upgrading the Developing Economies?, Vienna: United Nations Industrial Development Organization.

Giles, J. A. and C. L. Williams (2000), 'Export-led growth: a survey of the empirical literature and some non-causality results', *Journal of International Trade & Economic Development*, **9**(3), 261–337.

Grossman, G. M. and E. Helpman (1991), *Innovation and Growth in the Global Economy*, Cambridge, MA: MIT Press.

Grossman, G. M. and A. O. Sykes (2005), 'A preference for development: the law and economics of GSP', *World Trade Review*, **4**(1), 55–79.

Halle, M (2006), 'Is Let's Make a Deal now dead at the WTO?', 6 January, in *IISD Commentary*, Geneva: International Institute of Sustainable Development.

Harrison, A. (1996), 'Openness and growth: a time-series, cross-country analysis for developing countries', *Journal of Developing Economies*, **48**(3), 419–47.

Hart, M. and W. Dymond (2003), 'Special and differential treatment and the Doha Development Round, *Journal of World Trade*, **37**(2), 395–415.

Haveman, J. D. and H. J. Shatz (2003), 'Developed country trade barriers and the least developed countries: the economic result of freeing trade', United Nations University World Institute of Development Economic Research, discussion paper no. 2003/46, June, Helsinki, Finland.

Hertel, T. W. and R. Keeney (2006), 'What is at stake: the relative importance of import barriers, export subsidies and domestic support', in K. Anderson and W. Martin (eds), *Agricultural Trade Reform and the Doha Development Agenda*, London and Washington, DC: Palgrave Macmillan and World Bank, pp. 37–62.

Hertel, T. W. and L. A. Winters (2005), 'Poverty impacts of a WTO agreement: synthesis and overview', in T. W. Hertel and L. A. Winters (eds), *Putting Development Back into the Doha Agenda: Poverty Impact of a WTO Agreement*, Washington, DC: World Bank, pp. 3–28.

Hertel, T. W. and L. A. Winters (2006), *Poverty and the WTO: Impacts of the Doha Development Agenda*, London and Washington: Palgrave Macmillanand World Bank.

Hertel, T. W., M. Ivanic, P. V. Preckel and J. A. L. Cranfield (2004), 'The earning effects of multilateral trade liberalization: implications for poverty', *The World Bank Economic Review*, **18**(2), 205–36.

Heydon, K. (2006), 'After the WTO Hong Kong Ministerial Meeting: what is at stake?', Organisation for Economic Co-operation and Development Trade Policy working paper no. 27, Paris.

Hoda, A. and M. Verma (2004), 'Market access negotiations on non-agricultural products', Indian Council for Research on International Economic Relations, working paper no. 132, May, New Delhi.

Hoekman, B. M. (2003), 'Cancún: crisis or catharsis', paper presented at the joint roundtable of the Brookings Institution and George Washington University, 20 September, Washington, DC.

Hoekman, B. M. (2004), 'Developing countries and the WTO Doha Round: market access, rules and differential treatment', in B. Guha-Khasnobis (ed.), *The WTO, Developing Countries and the Doha Development Agenda*, Houndmill, Palgrave Macmillan, pp. 10–33.

Hoekman, B. M. (2005a), 'Operationalizing the concept of policy space in the WTO', in E. U. Petersmann (ed.), *Developing Countries in the Doha Round*, Florence, Italy: European University Institute, pp. 163–84.

Hoekman, B. M. (2005b), 'Making the WTO More Supportive of Development',

Finance and Development, (March), 14–18.

Hoekman, B. M. and S. Prowse (2005), 'Policy response to preference erosion: from trade as aid to Aid for Trade', background paper prepared for the project of the Department for International Development on the Global Trade Architecture and Development, 15 May, London, UK.

Hoekman, B. M., C. Michalopoulos and M. Olarreaga (2003a), 'Differential and more favorable treatment, reciprocity and fuller participation of developing economies', mimeo, Washington, DC: World Bank.

Hoekman. B. M., C. Michalopoulos, L. A. Winters, M. Pangetsu, K. Saggi and J. Tybout (2003b), 'Special and differential treatment for developing countries: objectives, instruments, and options for the WTO', Geneva: mimeo, World Trade Organization.

Hoekman, B. M., C. Michalopoulos and L. A. Winters (2003c), 'More favorable and differential treatment of developing countries: a new approach in the WTO', World Bank Policy Research working paper no. 3107, Washington, DC.

Hoekman, B. M., C. Michalopoulos, L. A. (Winters), (2004), 'Special and differential treatment of developing countries in the WTO: moving forward After Cancún', *The World Economy,* **27**(4), 481–506.

Hoekman, B. M., F. Ng and M. Olarreaga (2002), 'Eliminating excessive tariffs on exports of least developed countries,' *World Bank Economic Review,* **16**(1), 1–21.

Hufbauer, G. C. and J. J. Schott (2006), 'The Doha Round after Hong Kong', in *Policy Brief in International Economics,* no. PB06-2, February, Washington, DC: Institute for International Economics.

Hufbauer, G. C., E. Wada and T. Warren (2002), *The Benefits of Price Convergence: Speculative Calculations,* policy analysis in international economics, no. 65, Washington, DC: Institute for International Economics.

Hummels, D., J. Ishii and K. M. Yi (2001), 'The nature and growth of vertical specialization in world trade', *Journal of International Economics,* **54**(1), 75–96.

Inama, S. (2003), 'Trade preferences and the WTO negotiations on market access', mimeo, Geneva: United Nations Conference on Trade and Development.

Ingco, M. D. and J. D. Nash (2004), 'What's at stake? Developing country interest in the Doha Development Round', in M. D. Ingco and J. D. Nash (eds), *Agriculture and the WTO,* Washington, DC: World Bank, pp. 1–23.

International Monetary Fund (IMF) (2002), *World Economic Outlook: Trade and Finance,* September, Washington, DC.

International Monetary Fund (IMF) (2003), *World Economic Outlook,* April, Washington, DC: IMF.

International Monetary Fund (IMF) (2006), 'Integrating poor countries into the world trading system', economic issues series no. 37, Washington, DC.

International Monetary Fund/World Bank (IMF/WB) (2006), *Aid for Trade: Competitiveness and Adjustment,* Washington DC: IMF, World Bank, 12 April.

International Monetary Fund/World Bank (IMF/WB) (2002), 'Market access for developing country exports: selected issues', Washington DC, accessed 26 September at www.imf.org/external/np/pdr/ma/2002eng/092602/htm.

Krueger, A. O. (1978), *Liberalization Attempts and Consequences,* Cambridge, UK: Ballinger Publications.

Laird, S., D. Vanzetti and S. F. de Coroba (2006), 'Smoke and mirrors: making sense of the WTO industrial tariff negotiations', United Nations Conference on Trade and Development Trade Analysis Branch, study series no. 30, New York and Geneva.

Lall, S. 2000. 'The technological structure of developing country manufactured exports', Oxford University, Queen Elizabeth House working paper series no. QEHWPS No. 44, Oxford.

Lamy, P., (2003), 'Can the Doha Development Agenda live up to its name?', accessed 10 September at http://europa.eu.int/comm/commissioners/lamy/ speeches_articles/spla188_en.html.

Lamy, P. (2006a), 'The perspectives of the multilateral trading system', address delivered at a Development Round Table, 31 January, Lima, Peru.

Lamy, P. (2006b), 'The WTO and the Doha Round: the way forward', address delivered at the Indian Council for Research on International Economic Relations, 6 April, New Delhi, India.

Little, I., T. Scitovsky and M. Scott (1970), *Industry and Trade in Some Developing Countries: A Comparative Study*, Oxford: Oxford University Press.

Low, P. and R. Piermartini (2005), 'Multilateral solutions to the erosion of non-reciprocal preferences in NAMA', World Trade Organization, Economic Research and Statistical Division, working paper ERDS 2005-05, Geneva.

Lucas, R. E. (1988), 'On the mechanism of economic development', *Journal of Monetary Economics*, **22**(1) 3–42.

Lucke, M. and D. Spinanger, (2004), 'Liberalizing international trade in services: challenges and opportunities', Institut Für Weltwirtschaft Kiel, discussion paper no. 412, July, Kiel, Germany.

Martin, W. and L. A. Winters (1996), *The Uruguay Round and the Developing Countries*, Cambridge, UK: Cambridge University Press.

Mattoo, A. (2006), 'Services in a development round: proposals for overcoming inertia', in R. Newfarmer (ed.), *Trade, Doha and Development: A Window into the Issues*, Washington, DC: World Bank.

Mattoo, A. and A. Subramanian, (2003), 'What would a development-friendly WTO architecture really look like?', IMF working paper WP/03/153, August, Washington, DC.

Mattoo, A. and A. Subramanian (2004), 'The WTO and the poorest countries: the stark reality', International Monetary Fund working paper no. IMF/WP/81, May, Washington, DC.

McCulloch, N., L. A. Winters and X. Cirera (2001), *Trade Liberalization and Poverty: A Handbook*, London: Center for Economic Policy Research.

Messerlin, P. A. (2002), 'Agriculture in the Doha Agenda', paper presented at the World Bank Roundtable on Policy Research in Preparation for the 5th Ministerial Conference in Cancún, Cairo, 20–21 May.

Messerlin, P. (2003), 'Making the Doha Development Round work for the poorest countries', in P. Griffith (ed.), *Rethinking Fair Trade*, London: Foreign Policy Center, pp. 22–38.

Miller, S. (2003), 'WTO seeks to jumpstart talks, but finding that consensus is difficult', *The Wall Street Journal*, 25 July, p.16.

Narlikar, A. (2001), 'WTO decision-making and developing countries', South Center trade working paper no. 11, Geneva.

Narlikar, A. (2005), 'WTO institutional reforms: a role for G-20 leaders?', paper presented at a conference on The Agricultural Subsidies and the WTO organized by the Center for International Governance Innovation, 8–9 June, Waterloo, ON, Canada.

Narlikar, A. (2006), 'Fairness in international trade negotiations: developing countries in the GATT and the WTO,' *The World Economy*, **29**(8), 1005–29.

Narlikar, A. and J. S. Odell (2006), 'The strict distributive strategy for a bargaining coalition: the Like-Minded Group in the World Trade Organization', in J. S. Odell (ed.), *Negotiating Trade: Developing Countries in the WTO and NAFTA*, Cambridge: Cambridge University Press, pp. 115–44.

Narlikar, A. and D. Tussie (2004), 'The G-20 at the Cancún Ministerial: developing countries and their evolving coalitions in the WTO', *The World Economy*, **27**(7), 947–66.

Odell, J. S. (2003), 'Making and breaking impasse in international regimes: the WTO, Seattle and Doha', accessed at www.odell.usc.edu.

Office of the United States Trade Representative (2001), 'USTR Zoelick says world has chosen path of hope, openness, development and growth', press release, 14 November.

Organisation for Economic Co-operation and Development (OECD) (2005a), 'Tackling Trade in Agriculture', policy brief, November, Paris.

Organisation for Economic Co-operation and Development (OECD) (2005b), 'Agricultural Policies in the OECD Countries', October, Paris.

Oyejide, T. A. (2002), 'Special and Differential Treatment', in B. Hoekman (ed.), *Development, Trade and the WTO*, Washington, DC: World Bank.

Ozden, C. and M. Reinhardt (2003), 'AGOA and apparel: who captures the tariff rent in the presence of preferential market access?', *The World Economy*, **28**(1), 63–77.

Panitchpakdi, S. (2003), 'Cancún: the real losers are the poor', accessed 18 September at www.wto.org/english/news_e/news03_e/news_sp_18sep03_e.html.

Parsley, D. C. and S. J. Wei (2001), 'Limiting currency volatility to stimulate goods market integration: a price-based approach', National Bureau of Economic Research working paper no. 8468, Cambridge, MA.

Reimer, J. J. (2002), 'Estimating the poverty impact of trade liberalization', World Bank Policy Research working paper no. 2790, Washington, DC.

Rodriguez, F. and D. Rodrik (2001), 'Trade policy and economic growth: a skeptic's guide to the cross-country evidence', in B. Bernanke and K. Rogoff (eds), *NBER Macroeconomic Annual*, Cambridge, MA: MIT Press, pp. 110–43.

Rodrik, D. (2001), *The Global Governance of Trade as if Development Really Mattered*, New York: United Nations Development Program.

Rodrik, D. (2002), 'Feasible globalization', National Bureau of Economic Research working paper no. W9129, Cambridge, MA.

Rogers, J. H. (2001), 'Price level convergence, relative prices, and inflation in Europe', Board of Governors of the Federal Reserve System International Finance discussion paper no. 699, Washington, DC.

Romer, P. M. (1986), 'Increasing returns and long-run growth', *Journal of Political Economy*, **94**, 1002–37.

Sachs, J. D. and A. Warner (1995), 'Economic reform and the process of global integration'. *Brooking Papers on Economic Activity*, (1), 1–118.

Sala-i-Martin, X (2002), 'The world distribution of income (estimated from individual country distribution)', National Bureau of Economic Research working paper 8933, May, Cambridge, MA.

Schiff, M. and L. A. Winters (2003), *Regional Integration and Development*, Oxford, UK, Oxford University Press.

Schott, J. J. (2004), 'Reviving the Doha Round', paper presented at the International Workshop on The Transatlantic Relations and the Relaunching of the WTO Round after Cancun at Instituto Affari Internazionali, 14 May, Rome.

Spinanger, D. (2003), 'Beyond eternity: what will happen when textiles and clothing quotas are eliminated', United Nations Conference on Trade and Development research paper No. 30, Geneva.

Stern, N. (2003), 'Trade, aid and results: can we make a difference', paper presented at the Annual Bank Conference on Development Economics – Europe, 15–16 May, Paris.

Stern, R. M. (2000), 'Developing country interests in the forthcoming WTO negotiations', University of Michigan discussion paper no. 456, 16 February, Ann Arbor, MI.

Stevens, C. (2002), 'The Future of SDT for developing countries in the WTO', Institute for Development Studies working paper no. 163, May, Sussex.

Stiglitz, J. E. (1999a), 'Two principles for the next round: or how to bring developing countries in from the cold', mimeo, 21 September, Washington, DC.

Stiglitz, J. E. (1999b), 'Addressing developing countries' priorities and needs in the millennium round', speech delivered at the Harvard University Center for Business and Government, 29 November, Cambridge, MA.

Stiglitz, J. E. and A. Charlton (2005), *The Development Round of Trade Negotiations: In the Aftermath of Cancún*, London: Commonwealth Secretariat.

Subramanian, A. and S. J. Wei (2005), 'The WTO promotes trade, strongly but unevenly', Center for Economic Policy Research discussion paper no. 5122, July, London.

Sutherland, P. (2004), 'An interview with Peter Sutherland', published in the Open Democracy: Free Thinking for the World accessed 12 January at www. opendemocracy.net/content/articles/PDF/1674.pdf.

Switzer, P. (2006), 'Bilateral deals mock Doha', *The Australian*, 21 July, p. 6.

Tang, M. K. and S. J. Wei (2006), 'Is bitter medicine good for you? The economic consequences of WTO/GATT accession', paper presented at the Trade Conference organized by Research Department, International Monetary Fund, on 13 April, Washington, DC.

Tangermann, S. (2005), 'How to forge a compromise in the agriculture negotiations', in E. U. Petersmann (ed.), *Developing Countries in the Doha Round*, Florence, Italy: European University Institute, pp. 121–60.

United Nations Conference on Trade and Development (UNCTAD) (2004), 'Assuring development gains from the international trading system and trade negotiations: implications of ACT termination', Geneva, 30 September.

United Nations Conference on Trade and Development (UNCTAD) (2006), 'Trade in services and development implications', Geneva, 16 January.

van der Mensbrugghe, D. (2004), 'Linkage technical reference document: version 6.0', World Bank. accessed at siteresources.worldbank.org/ INTPROSPECTS/Resources/334934-1100792545130/LinkageTechNote.pdf.

Wacziarg, R. and K. H. Welch (2003), 'Trade liberalization and growth: new evidence', National Bureau of Economic Research working paper no. 10152, Cambridge, MA.

Watkins, K. (2003), 'Northern agricultural policies and world poverty: will the Doha Round make a difference?, paper presented at the Annual Bank Conference on Development Economics, 15–16 May, Washington DC.

Whally, J. (1985), *Trade Liberalization and Major World Trading Areas*, Cambridge, MA: MIT Press.

Winters, L. A. (2000a), 'Should concern about the poor stop trade liberalization?', paper presented at the Annual Bank Conference on Development Economics (ABCDE) in Europe 2000, Development Thinking at the Millennium, 26–28 June.

Winters, L. A. (2000b), 'Trade, trade policy and poverty: what are the links?' Center for Economic Policy Research discussion paper 2382, London.

Winters, A. L. (2003), 'Doha and the world poverty targets', in B. Pleskovic and N. Stern (eds), *New Reform Agenda: Proceedings of the Annual World Bank Conference on Development Economics 2002/2003*, Oxford: Oxford University Press, pp. 91–121.

Winters, L. A. (2004), 'Trade liberalization and economic performance: an overview', *Economic Journal*, **114**(1), F4–F21.

Winters, L. A. (2005), 'Developing country proposals for the liberalization of movements of natural service suppliers', in *Developing Countries in the Doha Round*, Florence, Italy: European University Institute, pp. 271–90.

Winters, L. A., N. McCulloch and A. McKay (2004), 'Trade liberalization and poverty: the empirical evidence', **114**(1), pp. F72–115.

Winters, L. A., T. L. Wolmsley, Z. K. Wang and R. Grynberg (2002), 'Negotiating the Liberalization of the Temporary Movement of the Natural Persons', University of Sussex, *Economics Discussion Paper*, **87**(4), pp. 22–42.

WITS/TRAINS (2004), *Database on International Trade and Tariffs*, Geneva and Washington DC: UNCTAD and World Bank.

Wolf, M. (2003), 'The abominable no-men', *Financial Times*, 23 September.

Wolfe, R. (2004), 'Crossing the river by feeling the stones: where the WTO is going after Seattle, Doha and Cancún', *Review of International Political Economy*, **11**(3), 574–96.

World Bank (WB) (2002), *Global Economic Prospects and the Developing Economies: Investing to Unlock Opportunity*, Washington, DC: World Bank.

World Bank (WB) (2003a), *Global Economic Prospects and the Developing Economies*, Washington, DC: World Bank.

World Bank (WB) (2003b), *Global Economic Prospects 2004*, Washington, DC: World Bank.

World Bank (WB) (2004a), *Global Economic Prospects and the Developing Economies*, Washington, DC: World Bank.

World Bank (WB) (2004b), *Global Economic Prospects: Realizing the Development Promise of the Doha Agenda*, Washington, DC: World Bank.

World Bank (WB) (2006), *Global Monitoring Report*, Washington, DC: World Bank.

World Trade Organization (WTO) (2001a), 'Doha Ministerial declaration', Geneva, 14 November.

World Trade Organization (WTO) (2001b), *Market Access: Unfinished Business*, Geneva: WTO.

World Trade Organization (WTO) (2003a), *World Trade Report 2003*, Geneva: WTO.

World Trade Organization (WTO) (2003b), 'Compilation of issues and proposals identified by participants in the Negotiating Group on Rules', TN/RL/W/143, Negotiating Group on Rules, Geneva, 22 August.

World Trade Organization (WTO) (2004a), 'Decision adopted by the General Council in August', WT/L/579, Geneva, 1 August.

World Trade Organization (WTO) (2004b), 'Text of the "July Package": The General Council's Post-Cancún Decisions', 1 August.

World Trade Organization (WTO) (2005a), 'The Future of the WTO: Addressing Institutional Challenges in the New Millennium', Geneva, 17 January.

World Trade Organization (WTO) (2005b), 'Ministerial Declaration: Adapted on 18 December 2005', Geneva, 22 December.

World Trade Organization (WTO) (2005c), 'Developmental aspects of the Doha Round of Negotiations', Geneva, 25 November.

Zhai, F. and T. W. Hertel (2005), 'Impact of the Doha Development Agenda on China', in T. W. Hertel and L. A. Winters (eds), *Putting Development Back into the Doha Agenda: Poverty Impact of a WTO Agreement*, Washington, DC: World Bank, pp. 210–42.

Index